Homage to the
Spanish Exiles

Homage to the Spanish Exiles
Voices from the Spanish Civil War

Nancy Macdonald

INSIGHT BOOKS
HUMAN SCIENCES PRESS, INC.
72 FIFTH AVENUE
NEW YORK, N.Y. 10011-8004

This book is dedicated to
Carmen Aldecoa
Pedro and Pepita Duran
and
Virginia Chamberlain

Copyright © 1987 by Human Sciences Press, Inc.
72 Fifth Avenue, New York, New York 10011
An Insight Book

Printed in the United States of America
0 987654321

Library of Congress Cataloging-in-Publication Data

Macdonald, Nancy.
　　Homage to the Spanish exiles.

　　Bibliography: p.
　　Includes index.
　　1. Spain—History—Civil War, 1936–1939—Refugees.
2. Spain—History—Civil War, 1936–1939—Civilian
relief—France. 3. Spanish Refugee Aid (Organization)
I. Title.
DP269.8.R3M33　　　　946.081　　　　86-10541
ISBN 0-89885-325-7

"They had a tremendous eager vitality, a kind of spiritual generosity and always a reserve, a beautiful inner dignity."

John Sommerfield, *Volunteer in Spain*

"What we are out for is to live the way men ought to live, right now and here; or else to damn well die."

André Malraux, *Man's Hope*

"Little you were, a little Andalusian peasant, with soft slightly prominent eyes, one of the poor and humble. This book is dedicated to you. What good does it do you? You could not read it even if you were still alive. That is why they shot you, because you had the impudence to wish to learn to read. You and a few million like you, who seized your old firearms to defend the new order, which might perhaps some day have taught you to read."

Arthur Koestler, *Dialogue with Death*

Contents

7

Acknowledgements

First of all I want to thank all those refugees who told me their stories back in 1967 and 1968, and who lived through with me, on tape, memories of their difficult and often grim lives. My sons, Michael and Nick, encouraged me to write and remember my life, and so did Seymour Krim and Louis Stein. Without Isadore From, I would never have produced this book. Robert Cummings, Odette Ester, and Antonio Trabal supplied me with information and Crispin Larangeira admired the tapes and thought them film-able. Lisa Commager, Beatrice Grabbe, Juan and Rocio Linz, read, commented, and suggested changes. Olaf Domnauer helped with the SRA translations for many years. Amparo and Eugenio Granell, Teresa Palacios, and Chloe Vulliamy helped me with the taped translations from the Spanish. (Translations from the French, and the editing of the tapes, were done by me.) May Dikeman, who copy edited painlessly, made many good suggestions.

Carmen Aldecoa, my Spanish mentor, moved in and out of my work and my life, as did Carel Sternberg and Hanne Benzion. My friend, Virginia Chamberlain, travelled with me and took part in the many visits I made in France, Belgium, England, Switzerland and Germany. My appreciation to the Dwight Macdonald Archives at Yale University and to Black Flag Press, SIMIAN Series. And special thanks to my grandson, Ethan, who typed and typed and typed, carefully and tirelessly. Finally, a note of appreciation to Norma Fox, Editor-in-Chief, and the fine staff at Human Sciences Press who have made this book a reality.

List of Acronyms for Spanish political parties, as used in the text

AIT	International Worker's Association
CEDA	Confederación Española de Derechos Autonomas (Spanish Confederation of Autonomous Rightists)
CNT	Confederación Nacional del Trabajo (National Confederation of Labor)
Esquerra	Catalan Autonomist Party
Euskadi	Basque Autonomous Party
FAI	Federación Anarquista Iberica (Spanish Anarchist Federation)
IC	Communist International
Izquierda Republicana	Left Republicans
Izquierda Republicana de Cataluñia	Left Republicans of Catalonia
PCE	Partido Communista Español (Spanish Communist Party)
Phalange	Spanish Fascist Party
POUM	Partido Obrero de Unificación Marxista (Unified Marxist Workers Party)
PSOE	Partido Socialista Obrero Español (Spanish Socialist Workers Party)
PSUC	Partido Socialista Unificado de Cataluñia (United Socialist Party of Catalonia)
Requetes	Carlist military organization
SIM	Servicio de Inteligencia Militar (Republican secret police)

| Tercio | Spanish foreign legion |
| UGT | Union General de Trabajadores (General Union of Workers) |

Note: All Spaniards have two last names. For example, for Antonio Gomez Baños—Gomez is his father's father's name and is always used. Baños is his mother's father's name and is sometimes used. A married woman may use her maiden name like Faustina Garcia de Castro (Castro is her husband's name). Or she may call herself Amelia Alvarez (née Faya): here Faya is her father's father's name and Alvarez is her husband's first last name.

Foreword

The Legion of the Forgotten

This book about Spanish Refugee Aid (SRA) is dedicated to the real heroes and heroines of modern times, who have been victims of both Communist and Fascist totalitarianism. These are the political refugees of the Spanish Civil War, whom I have come to know through SRA. In 1953, with the help of American friends, I founded this committee to raise money and distribute it to the thousands of needy among the 120,000 exiles then living in France. For 32 years I have been in touch with about 5,500 families and 13,000 individuals. As Director of SRA I went to France 18 times, where I met and listened to them. I tape-recorded their histories, read about their lives, corresponded with them, and tried to help solve some of their problems. I have come to admire enormously their courage and generosity, their dignity and devotion to the cause of freedom for Spain.

Luisa V. is one of these. Before the death of Franco she said to me: "I would have to be dragged through the streets by my hair before I would go to the Spanish Fascist consulate." Juan C. is another. "*You* are my family," he told me and the staff at our Foyer Pablo Casals in Montaubon. José Antonio M., a teacher, who spent 6 years in Franco's prisons, spoke this vow: "I am a political refugee and will not return to Spain until freedom comes and I can live there in dignity and with the rights and duties of a citizen, which exist in all the free and civilized countries. If I must die in exile, as many great and honorable Spaniards have done, I will die with dignity and pride at not having knelt before the tyranny in my country."

Even in 1983, 8 years after the death of Franco, Martin M., gives voice to the feelings of many exiles. He wrote to me: "As

15

to my return to Spain, at my age, seventy-five, Spain has lost the attractions it had in my youth. Like all of us I am bound to it by sentiment, through the bonds of the past, for its tragic history, but without any family to tie me to our dear land, I fear I will be condemned to die without seeing it, like so many others among us who form the enormous legion of the forgotten."

Preface

This strikes me as the story of a vocation—a calling, such as happened to figures in religious history. It was a surprise for me to read in these pages that Spanish Refugee Aid only got started in 1952; one had the impression that Nancy Macdonald and a small committee in the Union Square neighborhood had always been helping Spaniards. That is, the hundreds of thousands of Republicans left over, as it were, from the Spanish Civil War when it ended in 1939 with Franco's victory, turning what was a trickle into a tide of refugees that poured over the border into southeastern France. I remember our first leaflet—*Forgotten People*—written by Dwight Macdonald, but with many editorial suggestions from the rest of us, who wanted to do something to help. I would have dated it much earlier, perhaps 1948. I am mixing Spanish Refugee Aid up, evidently, with the package fund of Dwight's magazine, *politics,* which it grew out of and for which Nancy had done most of the work.

The *politics* clothes barrel (Dwight insisted on the small p) was famous in our circles of the 1940s and early 1950s: old clothes were collected from sympathizers by Nancy and her helpers for mailing (after due cleaning) to needy European intellectuals. Anyone who wanted a suit of clothes or a jacket could buy one from the barrel and the money—more efficiently—sent in its place to Europe. The barrel could be examined in the *politics* office or in the Macdonald apartment.

There was a time, as I recall, when Dwight dressed almost exclusively from the *politics* barrel, choosing various plaids, stripes, and checks he found there that suited his Scotch taste. I remember, in particular, a suit donated by C. Wright Mills, the writer, which Dwight was greatly taken with—a perfect fit and without a sign of wear. I see it as a three-piece gray tweed, belted in back like a Norfolk jacket. But I may be confusing things, and maybe it was not even Dwight but another of our contributors who bought the C. Wright Mills suit and wore it with pride. There were ladies' clothes in the barrel, too—I certainly gave quite a few—but for some reason there was less demand for them than for the old suits, shirts, jackets, and ties of male intellectuals.

In any case, that was long before Spanish Refugee Aid, though already, of course, some Spanish refugees were among the recipients of funds, food, medicine, and clothing collected by Nancy for *politics*. Two things happened by 1952: the magazine ceased to exist (hence no more barrel), and the aid, from then on, was concentrated on the Spanish victims of Franco. In keeping with that, the material character of the articles sent changed to reflect the situation of the donees. Though we still sent CARE packages and other food, as we had in the days of the barrel, when our shipments had been going to Germany, Italy, Austria, France, for another type of refugee (they were mainly from the East and known as "displaced persons") and for some hungry native-born citizens, we were now sending sewing machines, hearing aids, crutches, eventually an electric wheelchair—no longer goods to be consumed, but work tools for survival at the bottom of the economy. These came to include transistor radios and a saxophone. And, though Nancy continued to collect and ship clothes, the emphasis was now on warm clothes for heatless winters, and these were sometimes bought new over there.

The slogan used by Dwight, "Forgotten People," was true. Until Nancy's mailings—signed by Jim Farrell, by Dwight, by Hannah Arendt, for a couple of years by me—began to reach their natural U.S. public of liberals and politically interested people, the Republican veterans of the Spanish Civil War surviving in France had simply dropped out of sight, as far as the world was concerned. History had "passed them by." The last the world heard of them was probably Koestler's *Scum of the Earth*. Thanks to that book, it was vaguely understood by more alert liberals that remnants of the Spanish Republican Army had been interned in French camps where conditions were far from good. But what had happened to them afterwards no one seemed to know. The comfortable idea that they might have been "absorbed" by the French economy hardly fitted in with the reality that, like many war veterans, large numbers of these were war cripples—legless, armless, blind, deaf, tubercular. Among the stories told in interviews in the pages that follow, almost the worst have to do with incompetent surgery, above all, with amputations.

Yet just because no one seemed to know what had become of them after 1939, Nancy's appeals were welcomed. As checks were mailed in, cash pulled out from a pocket or handbag, people expressed positive gratitude for having been told about these forgotten people and hence given a chance to "remember" them materially. Gratitude is an unusual response to a charitable plea, but that is how it was and continued to be with Spanish Refugee Aid (or "Spanish," as the refugees called it—"Spanish has sent me eyeglasses"). Mysteriously, year after year, contributors "discovered" the Spaniards and wrote in to thank our committee for the opportunity of helping them.

This was one of several peculiarities of Nancy's organization, the greatest of which, for a charity, was its extremely low overhead. An *abnormally* high percentage of the money sent in went to the recipients. I forget now what the figure was when we made the calculation during one of my years on the board, but it was something like 75 percent—unheard of. Our greatest outlay, I think, was for postage, and Nancy managed to save even on that by the policy of "adoptions." In "adopting" a refugee, the contributor took on the postal expense of helping him; moreover, adopters, who signed up on a regular basis, did not have to be solicited by mail, like the rest of us, for an annual contribution.

Nancy's vocation, or "calling," to these Spaniards must have carried with it a natural gift for low overhead—a gift already exercised as business manager of *politics* and, before that, of *Partisan Review*. This, in turn, was related to a native simplicity and directness characteristic of Nancy, of her committee and those who worked for it, in New York and in France, and finally of the recipients themselves. One could see that from the letters they wrote and the kind of requests the letters contained—for seeds, for instance, or that saxophone. The instinctive attraction she soon noticed in herself—and describes in these pages—to anarchist and other libertarian groups is evidently related to a straightforward, open, direct mentality—low overhead. There is a sort of innocent logic typical of libertarian natures when they deal with property relations (the thinking is based on the help-yourself principle, both receiving gratis from a common store and contributing, through work or a surplus of goods); this logic creates bonds, as if by natural selection. A good example may be seen in the interview with the CNT sailor Mariano Puente when he tells how they organized the town of Puigcerda on strictly libertarian principles. It was inevitable that "Spanish" would be on the side of the POUM, the CNT, the FAI, Orwell, and Camus, rather than on that of the freedom-detesting Communists and their allies who were the bureaucratized Socialists of the Republican government.

To illustrate the libertarian strain in Nancy's own nature, I can cite a small episode from my personal life that had nothing to do with Spain but only with a piece of furniture. In the late 1940s, when Bowden Broadwater and I bought a farmhouse in Rhode Island, we owned very little to put in it in the way of chairs, tables, and so on. At the same time, through some deaths in her family, Nancy had come into possession of some nice antique pieces, and to her mind this coincidence spoke with an irrefutable logic: I must take some of her things. There was a desk, in particular, a fine piece of eighteenth-century American cabinet-making, in cherry, if I remember right, with many compartments. I also seem to remember a Sheraton-ish sideboard, not mine, that we had in the dining room, but that may have come from a different source besides not being as nice. When I try to analyze Nancy's motives in shipping that desk to me (we were friends but not close friends), it seems to me that they were two-fold: she was killing two birds with one stone, helping us out and giving it a good home for an indefinite period. It was a loan that I was to keep as long as I had a need for it. The desk stood for a number of years in a prominent corner of the house on Union

Street, Portsmouth, and was invariably admired by anybody versed in eighteenth-century furniture—evidently I had not realized how good it was. The time finally came when I had to give it back (we sold the house), and Nancy took it away with the same placid good nature as when she had given it in the first place. The anarchist maxim that the coat I wear is not really mine as long as someone lacks a coat was reflected in her matter-of-fact attitude throughout that transaction, while on my side, I confess, I hated to give it back, having come to feel that I owned it, even though I knew better.

When I think of Nancy's destiny and the role of Spaniards in it, I say to myself that maybe there were other needy libertarians in the world that she could have felt "called" to help. Yet only on Spanish soil would such large groups of them have originated; there are historical reasons for that, but, as always, there is also a mystery. Bakunin's doctrine arrived in Spain by some kind of miracle, like the scallop shell of St. James the Greater washing up at Compostella. In Nancy's own story, I see, chance played a considerable part, as commonly happens in stories of vocations. A predilection for Spain went back to courses she took at Vassar with Agnes Rindge—she was an art major, and Miss Rindge had a strong liking for Spanish art. So, immediately after graduation, Nancy and two classmates, following Miss Rindge's indications, traveled to Spain, starting with Burgos and its Cathedral—the apogee of Spanish Gothic. Being at that point totally apolitical, she scarcely knew that King Alfonso had fallen and been replaced by a republic during her junior year, to the great excitement of Miss De Mayo in the Spanish department. Nancy knew no Spanish; at Vassar, if I remember right, the language she took was Italian. Nonetheless she found Mallorca that first year, returned to it briefly the next year on a trip she made with her mother, and again on her honeymoon with Dwight. They spent a month on the island; by that time, I suppose, she was "hooked." In a couple of years, however, the uprising of the generals under Franco occurred. The Civil War began, and she was cut off from Spain, though not, as it turned out, from Spaniards, for 45 years. The first Spanish refugee she helped was a

POUM militant, Juan Andrade, who had been jailed by the Vichy government in Montauban for maintaining an illegal organization—that was in 1941. When the Nazi occupation finally ended, in 1945, there would be many other POUMists needing help. The first portable typewriter, like the first spring swallow, was sent, and the first money for drugs—insulin.

The pages that follow, mingling reporting, reminiscence, extracts from letters, and taped interviews, constitute a remarkable history of the Spanish Civil War, much more evocative than such respected "objective" histories as Hugh Thomas' and, as far as I can judge, very accurate in terms of dates, order of events, leading "personalities," political interplay of groups and factions, and estimated casualties. Here, for the first time, I have read about the Spanish Republicans in the French Resistance and in the Nazi deportation squads.

Of course it is "one-sided" in that the interviewees belong or belonged for the most part to libertarian organizations—a few are nonpolitical. There are no spokesmen here for the Communists nor for Largo Caballero's Socialists, to say nothing of Franco's people. Yet the tone is curiously free of bias; the chief feeling expressed is, simply, grief: many of these men break down and cry as they speak. Nor is humor lacking; one of the book's charms is the sense of amusement at a bitter human comedy that it conveys. A good example can be found in the very first interview, the one with Juan Andrade, who was still locked up as a POUMist in a government (Republican) jail in Barcelona while Franco's troops were approaching the city and the population was fleeing toward the French border. His jailers, from the warden on down, were eager to join the exodus and save their own skins. Not wishing to release the prisoners (illegal!), they hit on the simple expedient of moving the jail with the prisoners in it closer to the frontier. In the end, with the help of the prisoners (an example of Kropotkin's mutual aid), they moved it twice, by truck, until it was practically in France. Spanish logic. Naturally it could not be effected without the cooperation of the prisoners, who went through the forms of letting themselves be installed in the new place of confinement—in both cases a disused factory—a jail in name only, since they were now free to move around as they wished. Their only worry was to be careful to avoid a swarm of Communist troops, who had arrived at the frontier, too—a familiar menace. This amusing account jibes precisely with fearful stories I hard in Spain itself 30 years later, of Anarchist prisoners in Catalonia deliberately left under lock and key by their jailers (who had themselves run off), to be captured and usually executed by Franco's troops—I had asked why you did not hear of anarchists any more, and that was the answer, in a nutshell. For a sense of Spain and Spaniards in the Civil War and its aftermath there could be no better introduction than the story of "Spanish"—*Homage to the Spanish Exiles*.

Mary McCarthy
Paris, 1986

Prologue

I returned to Spain in June 1977. Forty-five years had passed since my first visit as a young Vassar graduate in 1932. Franco had been dead for a year and a half. (His widow was receiving a pension of 290,000 pesetas a month: about $1,740). Madrid, set in the bald central plateau, like a mirage, was now enormous and polluted. It was no longer the city I had visited in the thirties, where looking out of our hotel window one day, I had seen sheep being herded up the Paseo del Prado.

My visit in 1977 combined two purposes. I would see again the art that had meant so much to me long ago as a young art major. And I would make new contacts for Spanish Refugee Aid. In Madrid I stayed with Carmen Aldecoa. She was a sponsor and one-time board member of SRA. After the death of her husband, Jesus Gonzales Malo, in New York in 1965, she and I had become close friends. Carmen now lived with her sister Pilar in the apartment they owned in the central part of Madrid. Surrounded by family furniture and portraits, plants and bric-a-brac, Pilar sat watching TV from morning to night, with breaks for meals and going to mass. Except for one brother who had died during the Civil War, and her father, Carmen's family had been pro-Franco. When Carmen married an anarchist worker of the CNT, her brothers and sisters disowned her.

On the death of Franco there were high hopes for the triumphal return of the Spanish exiles. But things did not look propitious. There were still 40,000 political exiles in France—to say nothing of 530,000 Spanish immigrant workers. Old age pensions in Spain were lower than those in France. Of the three and a half million over the age of 65, a quarter of a million received no pensions at all. In Spain there was also a housing shortage, and, unlike France, no free medical aid for the aged.

Carmen and I visited the headquarters of the Socialist, UGT. Their welcome was most friendly. They showed us their new building, then being remodeled. We got to talk to several of their members, one of whom had been himself an exile. Then they took us to lunch in their building. But it became clear that fraternal well-wishes would be the extent of any collaboration. They told us there was very little they could do to help the exiles; but that we should carry on.

Carmen had organized a gathering in my honor, given by the Asociación Española de Mujeres Universitarios (the Spanish Association of University Women) where she and Professor Juan Marichal of Harvard and others spoke about SRA and me.

But Spanish art was unchanging. Carmen and I visited two beautiful ninth century churches in the hills of Oviedo and also the flamboyant one at Santiago de Compostela. And of course I went over and over to the Prado to see once more the paintings of Bosch, Goya, Greco, and Velasquez. On one visit, I was followed up the entrance steps by a soldier with a machine gun aimed at my knees. A holdover from Franco's days?

PART I

1. My mother arranged for my brother and me to "adopt" two French orphans, Carmen and Renée Coinces, after World War I.

students went there to see for themselves what she had made so vivid.

I travelled with two college friends, Mildred Aiken and Clara Lyman. We spent our first night in Burgos, the three of us in one room with two beds and a bathtub. It was cold, and we struggled with a dictionary to figure out how to ask for blankets—not daring to point to the beds. Breakfast included a big bowl of milk spiked with coffee. We visited the very ornate cathedral, where we were chased around the altar by a lecherous priest. We made a trip by bus to see the beautiful cloisters at Silos, and from Burgos we went to Avila, Salamanca, Valladolid, and Madrid. Our hotel in Madrid, the Nacional, was near the Prado, where of course we spent most of our time. I wrote my mother, "The Prado is breathtaking, better than any other museum I have ever seen." We made trips to the Escorial and Toledo. I was impressed by El Greco's beautiful burial of Count Orgas. In Barcelona, I especially admired the soaring hall churches. Rindge had recommended a photographer near the Cathedral from whom we bought photos of early Catalonian painters. The night boat took us to Mallorca. To save money we slept on the deck.

On this island, it was $2 a day for room and board at the Hotel Victoria, on the outskirts of Palma, and 75¢ a day in provincial Alcudia. A suitcase cost 56¢, espadrilles 16¢, a hat 30¢. We rented a car for a week and were attended everywhere by Paul de Havesy, Minister of Hungary to Spain, a friend of Mildred's family, who made passes at the three of us in rotation. Mildred and I made a flying trip to Italy, but after very hot visits to Siena for the Palio and to Borgo San Sepolcro and Arezzo to see the Piero della Francescas, we took the boat back to Palma. As we sat talking together, a Spanish artist sketched us and said he was a "friend of Pablo Casals, *violinist.*"

At that time I had no interest in politics. I was only vaguely aware that a Republic had been established in Spain the year before, on April 14, 1931, and that King Alfonso XIII had gone into exile. Municipal elections had been held for the first time in 8 years. The vote for a Republic was overwhelming. Many anarchists voted, hoping to free their 30,000 imprisoned comrades. In the Hotel Victoria where we were staying in Palma de Mallorca, Juan March was pointed out to me as one of the richest men in Spain. He had made his money smuggling tobacco, and was later to become one of the main backers of the fascist movement. (He died in November 1973). In the lending library of El Terreno (the suburb of Palma where I lived), I found Trotsky's

Autobiography. This was a strong influence on my later political beliefs. In a local paper I read that Trotsky was leaving Alma Ata, Turkey, and would perhaps become an exile in Mallorca. (Actually, he went to France on July 24, 1933). In Mallorca I fell in love with a handsome German making a living as a masseur. He lived in the apartment of a native Mallorquine woman, the first Spanish peasant whom I came to know—warm, affectionate, and very open.

In 1933 I returned to Europe with my mother and we spent several weeks in Evian, where the eldest son of Alfonso XIII was also staying. I remember his jaw, right out of Velasquez's portrait of Philip IV. On the 14th of July there was a display of fireworks in his honor. Earlier in the summer I had gone back to Mallorca but learned from Dona Emilia that my German friend had been recalled to Nazi Germany.

My third trip to Spain was in May 1935, shortly after I was married. My husband, Dwight Macdonald, and I spent a month in Mallorca. We came with a trunk full of books. He was going to write a book about modern dictators and I was contemplating one on Oriental art. For $24 a month we rented the Villa Soleil on the outskirts of Palma at Porto Pi, owned by an English couple, who spent their winters there. It was in the country overlooking the Mediterranean and we had a small garden with a lemon tree and carnations. Dona Antonina, who lived next door, came every day to clean, market, and cook our lunch; we paid her 11¢ an hour. She cooled the house by wetting and sanding the tiled floors, bought one or two eggs and half a chicken when she went to market for us. There was no refrigeration; the eggs were in a wire basket hanging from the ceiling and the food was put in wire cupboards, all to be consumed rapidly. Antonina climbed up in the hills behind our house to pick up brushwood to start the wood stove. She often cooked us a wonderful peasant soup and taught us how to light the stove at night. We slept under magenta colored mosquito nets which were always developing holes, and our water, drawn from a well with a bucket, appeared on careful observation, to be full of tiny living creatures. With that and the goat's milk, which was left at our door every morning in

2. *Dona Antonina, who lived next door, came every day to clean, market, and cook our lunch.*

a can, I'm not sure why we stayed well. I wrote my mother: "... happiness of this sort is difficult to describe, perhaps that is why I haven't . . . ."

A cable from Henry Luce of *Fortune* magazine cut short our European trip. He wanted Dwight, who was one of his editors, to return and work on an article about the steel industry. When we left Mallorca in August 1935, Dona Antonina came in her best dress, her head covered with a piece of lace, to hug us and say goodbye. That was the first of many *abrazos* I have received over the years. I have often wondered what happened to this kind, warm woman and her family during the bloodbath on the island of Mallorca under the Italian occupation.

2

Background to the Spanish Civil War

*T*o understand the stories of the refugees it is essential to understand what happened in Spain during the Civil War. This brief account is written from my own bias. My sympathies are with the libertarian Anarcho-Syndicalists and members of the POUM, and I have tried to show where they stood, and why. Most of the histories of the Civil War, on the contrary, refer to them as uncontrollables, or even bandits; or do not mention them at all. But these libertarians are the men and women to whom I feel closest—the people who were not interested in power and material things, but wanted to create a better and more equitable society in Spain. Although many of the taped stories are told by libertarians, some are also told by Communists, Socialists, and people with no political affiliations. (The bibliography offers sources for a fuller history.)

On April 12, 1931, the people of Spain, in free municipal elections, voted overwhelmingly for a Republic, which was proclaimed on April 14. The King, Alfonso XIII, went into exile; but he did not abdicate. For the next 5 years the country struggled with its desperate problems. Manuel Azaña became Prime Minister, and a Cortes was elected on June 28, 1931. On December

9 a new Constitution was adopted. It gave the vote to women for the first time in Spain and enacted a divorce law. A statute of autonomy for Catalonia was promulgated in September 1932; but not for the Basque region until October 1, 1936. Reforms were introduced in the Army and Civil Service, separation of Church and State, and most important of all, first steps were taken to address the agrarian problem.

These measures were timid, yet aroused strong antagonism on the Right, which came to power in November 1933, after an electoral defeat of a divided Left. Alejandro Lerroux of the Radical Party became Prime Minister and was backed by the CEDA (Confederacion Española de Derechas Autónomas) headed by José María Gil Robles. During the two "black years" (*bienio negro*) under this Center-Right Government, many of the reforms passed by the Left Republican Government of Azaña were repealed. It was a period of unemployment, strikes, arrests, and imprisonment. An uprising in the Asturias in October 1934 was put down with great brutality by Moors and the Foreign Legion sent in at the recommendation of Generals Franco and Goded. In October 1935 Lerroux resigned. The Cortes was dissolved in January 1936. In February the Popular Front won the election and a Left bourgeois government was formed with Azaña as Prime Minister.

In 1936, out of a population of 24 million, four and a half million were farm workers and only 2 million industrial workers. Forty seven percent of the country was agricultural and 84 percent of the farm workers didn't make enough to live on. Two million had no land, while 50,000 proprietors owned half of Spain. Before the Civil War the peasants in a number of areas had taken matters into their own hands and started to expropriate the land and work it collectively.[1] There was unrest among the urban workers as well as strikes in almost every trade and province. According to Bolloten (1961) there were "mass meetings and demonstrations, arson and destruction, the closing of party and trade union headquarters, seizures and attempted seizures of property, rioting and bloody clashes with the police, and assassinations and counter assassinations . . ." (pp. 23-24).

On July 12, 1936, Lieutenant José Castillo of the Republican

Assault Guards, a Socialist, was murdered on the streets of Madrid by a group of Falangists, the right-wing followers of José Antonio Primo de Rivera. [He was the son of Miguel Primo de Rivera, dictator of Spain from September 1923—January 1930, during the reign of Alfonso XIII. José Antonio was tried and executed by the Republicans in Alicante on November 20, 1936.] On July 13, in retaliation, José Calvo Sotelo, leader of the Right wing and Finance Minister under Primo de Rivera, was assassinated by Assault and Civil Guards. On the 16th, the Army in Spanish Morocco revolted and occupied Ceuta and Melilla. General Francisco Franco was flown in from the Canary Islands by a British pilot to take command. Throughout Spain, the officers of the garrisons rose against the Republican Government. Much of provincial conservative Spain also fell into rebel hands. The Spanish Civil War had begun.

This revolt of the Army was not unexpected. A military uprising in Seville, led by General Sanjurjo, had been put down in August 1932. The General was sentenced to a long prison term and his followers exiled. Then in 1934 the Centrist Government of the Bienio Negro amnestied Sanjurjo and his followers. He was to have led the new uprising. But en route from Portugal to Spain he died in a plane crash.

The Republican Government knew of the plots against it, but feared revolution by an armed Left if it took action. As late as June 1936, when Francisco Largo Caballero, Secretary of the UGT (the Socialist trade union organization), asked for arms for the workers, Manuel Azaña, President of the Republic, refused. Even when the revolt started, it was only on July 18 that arms were issued to the people to defend themselves and the Republic; and often, even then, weapons had to be seized from the authorities.

Support by Italy for a fascist coup in Spain was solicited as early as 1932, and in March 1934 Spanish Monarchists visited Mussolini to seek the backing of the Italian Government. Once the war started, massive support—70,000 men, 700 planes, and 14 milliards of liras (only part repaid)—was forthcoming. The Italians wanted supremacy in the Mediterranean and the Island of Majorca became their aviation base for bombing Barcelona, Valencia, and the coast.

General Sanjurjo went to Berlin in the early 1930s to ask Hitler's support, but was unsuccessful. An emissary from Franco in Morocco had better luck. When the war started the Germans supplied only 10,000 men, many of them officers and technicians. German planes were in action during the first few weeks of the war, and the Condor Legion, which destroyed Guernica, and whose last commander was Von Richthofen, was a formation created for Spain. However, most of the Nationalists' armaments came from Germany; and throughout WW II Franco's Government sent minerals to Germany to compensate for the 500 million reichsmarks spent in Spain during the Civil War. Franco also sent the Blue Legion in July 1941 to fight with the Nazis against the Russians on the Eastern Front.

England and France signed a nonintervention pact on August 15, 1936, and offered the Republic hardly any arms or aid. The United States also declared itself neutral and gave the legitimate Republican Government of Spain no aid at all. Individuals, however, came from all three countries, crossing the borders illegally to fight in the International Brigades. (They also came from many other countries and fought valiantly for the Republic until they were withdrawn from Spain in November 1938.)

The workers in Spain had two powerful trade union organizations, the CNT (Confederación Nacional del Trabajo) and the UGT (Unión General de Trabajadores). The UGT, founded in 1888, was affiliated with the Spanish Socialist Party (founded in 1879). The UGT had a little less than a million and a half members at the time of the Spanish Civil War, with its main strength in Madrid and Bilbao. The Socialist Party advocated parliamentary and municipal action and a strong central government. Largo Caballero, as Secretary of the UGT, became a Councillor of State during the later years of the monarchy. He was also Prime Minister of the Republic from September 4, 1936—May 15, 1937.

The CNT, founded in 1910, was Anarcho-Syndicalist, with over a million and a half members at the start of the Civil War. Its most militant members belonged to the FAI (Federación Anarquista Ibérica), founded in 1927. Their main strength was among the industrial workers of Catalonia and the agricultural workers of Andalusia. The CNT believed in libertarian communism and freedom for the individual as well as in control from below, and abolition of capitalism and of the state. It opposed elections; its strategy was the general strike, to be followed by expropriation and collectivization. As early as 1922 the CNT had refused any connection with the Moscow International.

In July 1936, the POUM (Partido Obrero de Unificación Marxista) was a small Marxist revolutionary party of not more than 3,000 militants, former Communists or Trotskyists, most in Catalonia. They opposed the Popular Front and denounced the Communists who backed it. They favored socialist revolution and the dictatorship of the proletariat.

A small Spanish Communist Party, founded in 1921, had only one deputy in the Cortes by 1933. In 1936 it had 30,000 members and 17 deputies, but by January 1937, 200,000 adherents. The Communists favored a bourgeois democratic revolution in Spain, and gave priority during the Civil War to a military victory. They favored centralization of power and violently opposed the CNT and the POUM, which were fighting not only for the defeat of Fascism, but also for a revolution.

The Communists gained power as the war went on because of the intervention of the USSR, which supplied arms to the Republic, the first in October 1936. For Stalin, Spain was an arena to test new weapons (over 50 percent of the planes received and most of the tanks were Russian). On the other hand, often old and useless arms were dumped in Spain, some dating back to the Crimean War. All came through dealers controlled by the Kremlin and were paid for in advance with Spanish gold, 500 million grams (about 578 million dollars or over half the gold reserve) being sent to the USSR in October 1936. No accounting was ever made, and none ever returned.

While arms were being supplied, a section of the NKVD (the Russian secret police) was installed in Spain under the direction of Nicolsky (alias Orlov). Almost all the political commissars in the Army became Communist Party members. The Communists controlled the subsecratariat of Propaganda, the Cypher Bureau, and, except in Madrid, the Spanish political police (SIM—Servicio de Investigación Militar). They had their own prisons and police, run by the Russian NKVD. W.G. Krivitsky, chief of Soviet Military Intelligence in Western Europe, records in his book *In Stalin's Secret Service* that Stalin aimed to be master of the Spanish Government.

Two thousand Russians went to Spain; but only the pilots and tank officers fought. The rest were technicians. They were segregated from the Spanish, and closely watched by the NKVD. Five or six hundred foreign refugee Communists were sent from Russia as a nucleus for the International Brigades, not a single Russian among them.

To appreciate the story told in this book by Mariano Puente, it is important to understand what happened in Catalonia at the beginning of the Spanish Civil War. The CNT and the Anarchists were strong in Catalonia and thanks to them and the POUM the Fascist uprising was put down. Catalonians wrested arms from the local government, headed by Luis Companys, in order to defend themselves. Groups of militiamen took over factories and businesses and ran them, as well as collectivizing towns and villages. A Central Committee of Militias was formed of representatives of the various trade union and political groups. The Committee had power in its hands—but there was dual power, because Luis Companys remained as titular head of the old government.

This revolutionary period lasted from July through September 1936. Then the counterrevolution began. In the early stages of the war the Republican Government in Madrid had refused financial aid for collectivized industry or agriculture in Catalonia. Raw materials, food, and munitions soon ran short. The attempt to free Saragossa from the Fascists on the Aragon front failed because the Republic would not supply the arms. Saragossa was not only a former Anarchist stronghold but strategically crucial, lying between industrial Catalonia and the northern front, which consisted of the Basque region and Asturias, cut off from Republican Spain by the Fascists. These two regions were indispensable for their raw materials and munition factories. But the Central Government, backed by the Communists, refused to arm the people to defeat the enemy on the Aragon front unless it controlled them completely. Threatened with withdrawal of aid from the USSR, the Central Government gradually destroyed the collectives and restored control to Madrid.

In January 1937 the CNT-UGT Committee for Supplies was dissolved. In February the collectivized milk industry was declared illegal. In March the collectives around Valencia were attacked. On April 17, 1937, carrying out the orders of Juan Negrin,[2] Finance Minister of the Republic, always backed by the Communists, the Carabineros began to reoccupy the customs stations on the French border, which had been held by the Anarchists since the beginning of the Spanish Civil War.

The Communists in Catalonia had brought various Socialist groups in the area together in the PSUC (Partido Socialista Unificado de Cataluña), affiliated with the Comintern. The PSUC opposed the CNT and the POUM. On May 3, 1937, the Councillor for Public Order, Rodriguez Salas, a member of the PSUC, came with a detachment of police to take over the central telephone building of Barcelona. This key building had been captured in July 1936 by the workers and had since been controlled by a committee of the CNT and UGT; but most of the employees were CNT members. They mounted armed resistance to Salas' attempted takeover and local defense committees throughout the city put up barricades. The POUM wanted to seize power; but the CNT, already compromised by having had four members[3] in the Caballero cabinet, favored concessions. A truce was called until May 6 when the Republican Government in Madrid sent 5,000 Assault Guards withdrawn from the Front to put down the uprising in Barcelona. They were commanded by General Pozas, formerly a commander of the Guardia Civil, and now a Communist. In the fighting that followed, 500 people were killed and 1,000 wounded. Among the many revolutionaries murdered at this time by the Communists was Camilo Berneri, an outstanding Italian Anarchist intellectual, who was arrested and shot by the Communist-controlled police on May 6. With the Barcelona "May Days," as they were called, dual power came to an end in Catalonia.

On June 16 all the leaders of the POUM were arrested and charged by the Republican Government, instigated by the Communists, of seeking its overthrow. They were further accused of treason and of collaboration with the enemy. Their main theorist, Andres Nin, was abducted and taken to the NKVD prison in Alcala de Henares (near Madrid), where he was subjected to torture to extract a "confession" from him.

Nin did not "confess," and the trial of the other leaders did not follow the lines laid down in Moscow.[4] Nin was assassinated, and the others drew prison terms for their revolutionary aims. The charge of spying and being agents of European Fascism had to be dropped. Juan Andrade, whose story will follow, was one who received a 15-year sentence.

The last round of the counterrevolution was now to be played. On August 10, 1937, the largely Anarcho-Syndicalist Defense Council of Aragon, which coordinated all municipal councils, was dissolved by the Central Government, and in September the Communist, Enrique Líster,[5] went with his 11th Division to break up the remaining local committees and collectives on the orders of the Governor General of Aragon, José Ignacio Mantecón, a Communist sympathizer.[6] As Chomsky (1969) narrates it, "The last Anarchist stronghold was captured with tanks and artillery on September 21" (p. 104). More than 600 organizers of collectives were arrested; land, animals, tools, and harvest were given to individual families, or even to Fascists who had been spared by the revolution. This was the end of the collective movement and of the revolution in Spain.

While the revolutionary movement in Spain was being crushed, the war on the fronts was taking its course. By October 1936 the Nationalists held Spanish Morocco, Cadiz, Seville, Badajoz, Toledo, and most of the Northwest of the Peninsula. Madrid was besieged by the Insurgents beginning October 29, but was successfully defended by the people in arms, though deserted by the Government, which fled to Valencia. The Republicans also successfully routed the Italian forces at Guadalajara in March 1937.

But Malaga had fallen to the Nationalists in February. The destruction of Guernica by the Nazi Condor Legion followed. Then Bilbao, Santander, and Gijon fell. The Republicans held Teruel briefly, but lost it in February 1938.

The Nationalists reached the Mediterranean on April 15, 1938. Now cut in two, the Republican forces made a final stand at the Ebro river, crossing it on July 25, 1938, and swept back on the 15th of November (the POUM trial had ended November 1). Barcelona fell on the 26th of January, and a stream of refugees started their flight towards France. About 500,000 would become exiles there. A last struggle between the Communists and the CNT in Madrid went on for 3 weeks before the Nationalists marched in on March 28, 1939, ending the Spanish Civil War.

3. *A total of about 500,000 refugees would become exiles in France.*

NOTES

1. Agricultural and municipal communes have a long tradition in Spain. Some of the former are said to date back to the early Middle Ages. At the start of the Civil War, in Aragon alone, with a total population of about half a million, 510 towns and cities had collectives established by the people.

2. Negrin has been called the "ambitious and docile tool" of the Communist Party in Spain. In order to continue receiving aid from the Soviet Union, he was ready "to go along with Stalin in everything, sacrificing all other considerations to secure this aid" (see Krivitsky, pp. 100-101); and "he was more responsible than any one Spaniard for the later success of Communist policy" (see Bolloten, p. 121, footnote 9).

3. In November 1936, Juan García Oliver, Juan López, Federica Montseny, and Juan Peiro became ministers in the government headed by Francisco Largo Caballero. This decision to enter the Cabinet was contrary to Anarchist principles and, in addition, was taken without consulting the rank and file of the CNT.

4. The first of the Moscow trials took place in August 1936 and Kamenev and Zinoviev were executed on the 14th.

5. After the 1934 rising in the Asturias, Enrique Lister, a militant Communist, took refuge in the USSR where he studied at the Frunze military school. Later he became head of one of the Moscow-oriented Spanish Communist Parties.

6. He joined the Communist Party when in exile.

3

Juan Andrade and Victor Serge
"First Refugees"

ANDRADE—A DON QUIXOTE

In July 1937 I went to a rally for the Loyalists in Madison Square Garden. It was attended by 20,000; the speakers were Earl Browder and Norman Thomas. If I had known more about what was happening in Spain I would have gone to the smaller meeting (300) in Union Square, where Liston Oak exposed the Stalinists' role in the Civil War. Oak, an American who had worked for the Spanish Republican propaganda office and had "asked too many questions," had to flee Spain, disguised as John Dos Passos' secretary.)

It was only after the Spanish War was over that my tenuous connection with Spain and the Spanish people began to strengthen. I was Business Manager of the literary magazine, *Partisan Review* (PR), of which my husband was an editor. Originally, PR had been founded as a magazine of the John Reed Club of New York, and was close organizationally to the Communist Party. In 1936 it suspended publication, and came out again at the end of 1937 with a new editorial board and a new policy of independent Marxism. The other editors were William Phillips and Philip Rahv (who had been on the old board) and Fred Dupee,

44

Mary McCarthy, and George L.K. Morris. My job as business manager was filled by a friend, Laura Wood, around the interval of my son Michael's birth in April 1938.

Among our European writers, Victor Serge, the Belgian journalist and novelist, had been writing for PR. In 1941 he wrote from France to ask if we could help a Spanish refugee, Juan Andrade, suffering with tuberculosis in the prison of Montauban in Vichy-ruled France.

I knew the name Andrade. In *Class War in Republican Spain* published in the *Modern Monthly* (September 1937), Anita Brenner wrote: "On July 29 (1937), the Ministry of Justice announced that trials under the espionage act were being prepared for 10 members of the Executive Committee of the POUM as follows: Andrade, Escuder, Bonet, Gorkin, Rebull, Palomo, Arroyo, Iglesias, Ruiz, Jimenez. With them would be tried—note the typical trick of amalgam!—a Fascist named Golcin." (Andres Nin, General Secretary of the POUM, had already been kidnapped and assassinated by the Communists.) Andrade and the others were put on trial by the Republican Government in October 1938 and condemned to 15 years in prison for attempting to overthrow the established government.

Andrade, Serge now wrote me, had along with 13 other militants of the POUM (Partido Obrero de Unificación Marxista), been "condemned by a military tribunal of the Vichy Government, sitting behind closed doors, for having maintained an illegal organization with connections in Spain." The trial took place in the Palais de Justice in Montauban on the 17—18 of November 1941; Andrade was sentenced to 5 years. Among the 14, wrote Serge, "Andrade is the most cultivated, the most mature, a good head but with health broken; his life since the defeat of Spain has been a real little hell, exhausting. Almost all of them have had long stays in the Stalinist prisons in Spain. . . . The most urgent problem is to keep them from dying of hunger in prison." Serge gave the address of Andrade's wife, Maria Teresa. We, and some American friends of the Andrades, John and Jane Pontormo and Willmoore Kendall, were able to send some food and money before communications with France were broken by the Nazi takeover.

Andrade was forty-five at the time of the Vichy trial. He was in prison from February 25, 1941 to August 23, 1944, when he was freed from the prison of Bergerac by Spanish *maquis*. In 1945 I was in renewed contact with the Andrades when he asked us to help some comrades in special need: Ignacio Iglesias and Pedro Bonet, and a comrade who had been forced to return to Spain and needed insulin for diabetes. Andrade wrote that he would send more names, and all would be members of the POUM, since they got no help from other organizations which were "in the hands of the Republicans, Socialists and Communists." The Andrades themselves were receiving packages from Willmoore Kendall. At the end of his letter Juan added, "Oh! yes, it is really a tragic situation when a writer has no typewriter." We found a portable and sent it to him in Toulouse by a friend bound for Europe. By 1947 Marguerite and Alfred Rosmer wrote that the Andrades were in pretty good shape, selling books imported from the Argentine, but that an occasional package of rice, coffee, and tea wouldn't come amiss.

After they moved back to Paris, I met Juan and Maria Teresa a number of times. He was the Don Quixote type, tall, gaunt, and idealistic. Maria Teresa was his Sancho Panza, short, lively, and down to earth. When I taped them in 1967, I questioned them in French and they answered in Spanish.

Andrade: "When Barcelona fell (January 26, 1939), we were in prison and we came to an agreement with our jailors to leave and go to France together. Our group consisted of those who had been in the Barcelona prison, the executive committee of the POUM and a few comrades who had been arrested for their activities connected with the party.

"In reality the story is rather picturesque and special. The troops of Franco were nearing Barcelona and most of the inhabitants were leaving. And the jailers and the director of the prison wanted to flee from Spain too and see if they could cross the frontier. And then in agreement with us, they pretended to transfer the prison to Gerona and all of us left together in a truck. In Gerona, the prison of Barcelona was installed in an old fac-

tory. But naturally there was what one might call a sort of camaraderie between the jailers and us. Because all we wanted to
do was to cross the frontier and go to France. Well, as Franco's
forces continued to advance, we decided to move the prison once
again from Gerona to Agullana, which was a town very near the
frontier. And here again we found a place which must have been
a factory, and here the prison was installed again. But we were
able to go out freely and do what we liked.

"The second day we went out, we were very surprised to discover that the Army Staff of the Communist Party and the big
military powers had established their headquarters in Agullana.
And so we decided to leave immediately because we feared the
worst. That night, at 4 or 5 in the morning, all the comrades left,
but this time without our guards. We went silently and crossed
the border and started walking towards the interior of France. But
in the first town we came to, there was a police barrier. They arrested us, put us in a truck and took us to Le Perthus, and made
us cross the frontier into Spain.

"Again, fearing that the Communists would recognize us, we
decided to go to the mountains to try and cross the frontier in a
spot where there wouldn't be such an abundance of people fleeing
from the Spanish war. There were difficulties; we slept for 2 days
in the mountains, we had no food, and there was no place to find
any. I remember well the acorns and chestnuts we ate. Then we
decided to send two comrades as delegates who, hiding and
avoiding the French police, went to a bar in the French town
nearby to telephone to Paris. Our comrades in Paris sent a truck
to pick us up and they brought with them bread and cold cuts,
enough for a big meal. We were half starved, so the first thing we
did when they arrived was to sit down and eat.

"The trip to Paris wasn't easy, because police were stationed
along the way and the truck was stopped frequently. They were
arresting all the Spaniards and taking them to concentration
camps. But the comrades in Paris had taken precautions and we
were successful in passing all the police barriers. They had an
official document made which said that we were ill and they were
taking us to be hospitalized in Paris.

"We were all very weak and I was in the worst condition because I was already weak when I left the prison. After 2 nights of rain in the mountains my weakness became extreme. During our trip, because of exhaustion I had been unable to carry anything, and left everything behind. I had started writing two books in prison and they were the principal thing I had taken when we left the prison in Barcelona. Although they couldn't have weighed much, being paper, I abandoned them in the mountains because they hindered my walking.

"When we arrived in Paris, we were placed in various homes of comrades, or sympathizers of the Spanish Republic. First I spent several weeks in the home of a woman who belonged to the classic French bourgeoisie. I was very well received, mainly because her son, a doctor, sympathized very much with our movement. But later, since there were some difficulties in my staying there, I asked to be moved. So I was sent to the janitor's apartment in a house in the well-known workers' district of St. Paul. And there I was received like a real son of the caretaker and like a comrade by her nephew, who was the one who had asked for a Spanish refugee. I stayed there for a number of months.

"At first it was I alone who received the solidarity of those who took me in. My companion, Maria Teresa, had stayed in Barcelona. She was imprisoned like me and she left prison only when the Fascists were marching through the streets. She was in a really difficult position. But finally, thanks to the solidarity of a comrade, she found a place to be free from the persecution of the Fascists. And I was running all sorts of risks to try and get in touch with her, as we were cut off. I had the idea of writing a card in a special sort of way, sending it to her address where we used to live. Sending this card was a shot in the dark and I was really lucky. The card arrived and the caretaker, whose husband belonged to the CNT, took the card from the postman. She knew Maria Teresa's address and immediately took it to her."

Maria Teresa: "The police had detained her for 48 hours to try and force her to tell where I was hidden in Barcelona. The poor woman, who was neither militant nor anything, denied over and over again that she knew where I was. When the card came, she brought it to me, a really extraordinary act."

Juan: "Naturally, this served as a means of reestablishing contact, in veiled language, but that was enough. Almost all of the comrades here in Paris said I was crazy and that I was losing my time. But after a few days I received a card from Maria Teresa at the headquarters of Pivert's party [Marceau Pivert (1895-1958), co-founder with Daniel Guerin of the PSOP (Workers and Peasants Socialist Party)].

"We started a correspondance, and perhaps I was stupid in interpreting the words, because she needed money to cross the frontier and I hadn't understood. Perhaps I wouldn't have been able to send money, because at that time it was very difficult to send it to Spain. So we continued our correspondance until 11 July. I will always remember the date, when a French friend of mine, Alfred Rosmer [Alfred Rosmer (1877-1954), a founding member of the French Communist Party and in the Trotskyist movement (1924-1930)] who was the one who received letters for me, got a telegram from Maria Teresa saying: "I am in Perpignan." And a comrade picked up the telegram and brought it at 11 in the evening to the porter's lodge where I was living. It was an occasion of great joy. The concierge opened a bottle of wine to celebrate and we started immediately to make preparations in the lodge for her arrival.

"We had a comrade with an automobile, who promised to take me to Orleans the next day where she had asked me to meet her. We went to Orleans and Maria Teresa wasn't there. Our contact in Orleans was the principal of a school. We left him some money to give her when she arrived, and gave him our address in Tours. Maria Teresa was very apprehensive during her trip, because already there was danger of war. A number of precautions had been taken in France, and on all the trains they asked for papers. Maria Teresa didn't have a single document that might have served as identification. When she got to Orleans, she went to the school and was received magnificently. I believe they also gave her breakfast and she took the first train for Tours. But, unfortunately, the friends who took me to Tours, and those who received us there, wanting to show me the city, took us for a long drive and we arrived at the station after Maria Teresa. But we did meet her, spent a few hours in Tours and returned to Paris. It was the 14th of July when everyone was celebrating in Paris and everyone was happy.

"We lived there with difficulty, not knowing what to do, finding no work, and suffering all the persecutions with which the French police tormented the Spaniards. Until one day we were told that in Chartres we could legalize our situation, where the Police Prefect was Jean Moulin. (Later he was a great hero of the Resistance, a Maquis chief tortured and killed by the Nazis in June 1943.) It was the only department in all of France where they legalized the situation of the Spaniards. But finally this stopped because the news spread among the Spaniards, who went en masse from Paris and all the departments. And naturally, a time came when Jean Moulin could do no more. I had gone there to see if it was easy and actually my situation was legalized and I received a *"récépissé"*, (the alien's registration card), which was what all of us hoped for. I returned to Paris and told Maria Teresa that she could go too. But when I arrived at 7:30 or 8 in the morning, we heard on the radio that Hitler had attacked Poland. All our joy was muted, because we knew that this was war and that once again there would be all sorts of difficulties. In spite of this, Maria Teresa went to Chartres and also succeeded in getting a passport.

"We returned to Paris for a few days. The owner of the house where we were living didn't want us to leave under any circumstances. She was ready to keep us there illegally and hidden. But we didn't want to weigh her down with this responsibility and decided to go to Chartres. Once there, we had great difficulties in finding a place to live. As soon as we announced that we were Spaniards and refugees, no one would rent us anything, because Chartres is a very Catholic and reactionary city. But one day Maria Teresa in desperation asked at a café where we went if they knew of some place we could rent. She sent us to a big grocery store whose owner was a Parisian from La Villette, fat and with a very ugly face, but with an extraordinary spirit. We were very surprised when, screaming at the top of her lungs, because she always spoke in a scream, she said to us: 'Yes, I have a lodging. Take the key and do what you like with the place'. That was our salvation. We bought some pots and we stayed there until the French defeat.

"The landlady worried about us and liked us very much. In the most difficult times in France, we were very lucky with the people who took us in."

Maria Teresa: "Mme. Dobiler saved the lives of an enormous number of Jews in Paris and hid them until they were able to leave. And Mme. Emery of Chartres did the same, hiding and saving a great many people. They were extraordinary beings."

Juan: "We stayed there until the Germans began to advance in France. One day, everyone, the French and, above all, the foreigners, were being mobilized in Chartres to go and make trenches and fortifications in the North. The majority of the Spaniards in Chartres who had experienced the Spanish war presented themselves. We were taken in trucks to Evreux. There we were lodged in a school, the French and a few Spaniards. They told us nothing about what we had to do but said they would give us instructions on the following day. We went to sleep and at about 4 in the morning, an Andalusian peasant, who was very ignorant but very clever, with whom I had become friendly, woke me and said: 'Listen, this is the defeat, the Germans are advancing and the French are leaving. Let's go. Are you coming with me?' He understood that the noise meant the retreat. He knew it and insisted, saying: 'You're stupid, they'll catch you here.' But I stayed, not out of heroism, but because I didn't believe that the defeat would come so fast. When we arrived in Evreux, the Germans had been 94 miles away.

"In the morning we went to the committee at the Town Hall and there was no one there. And there was no one in the town— no one. The Andalusian was right. While we slept, everyone fled. Only the farmers stayed. And now I had the problem of being separated from Maria Teresa. The Germans were advancing and at all costs I wanted to reach her in Chartres, 56 miles away. I started walking, and I didn't dare hitchhike. At that time there was much hostility toward foreigners, who were regarded as spies and German parachutists. So I decided to join two Spaniards who were going on foot. But I didn't have much confidence in them, because they were talking a lot, and shouting. I noticed that when we went through towns, everybody looked at us and were suspecting that we were spies—to such an extent that I feared the consequences. So when we came to a certain town, whose name I don't remember, I said to the Spaniards: 'The best thing for us to do is to separate. You can go your way and I'll go alone on mine.' So we separated.

"When I had gone about a half a mile and was in the country, I saw all the people from the town coming, some on bicycles and others running. They stopped me and said: 'Listen, do you have papers?' I had my mobilization papers, but still they said: 'Although you have this paper, you must come to the police station.' We walked to the police station with all of them behind me muttering: 'Parachutist, parachutist.' And I didn't know how things were going to turn out. Well, there are always comic notes in life. When we entered the office of the police there was a brigadier there. And he said: 'Once again, a parachutist!' He asked me: 'Mister, do you have your papers!' And I said: 'Yes, here.' And he said: 'Listen, they are idiots in this town. They see parachutists everywhere. Go along.' So I left, and at the door, all the townspeople, seeing me free, were really astonished.

"Then again I started walking, and luckily I reached Chartres, but in a deplorable condition, my feet mangled. Thinking back, it seems impossible that I made 56 miles in a day and a half. I arrived in Chartres at about 6 in the morning, and by coincidence, when I arrived, Maria Teresa wasn't there. The landlady had decided to go to the country away from the danger of bombardments in Chartres and had taken Maria Teresa to sleep there. So when we arrived, I was dead tired and had no money. Fortunately, Maria Teresa arrived soon afterwards and we stayed there a few days more—until the retreat started, when everybody left

Chartres. And we began a journey which was very complicated and very long."

(Juan was writing an autobiography; so what they told me in Paris in 1967 is only a fragment of his political life. In April 1980 he returned to Spain for what was to be his last year of life. He died there on May 1, 1981.)

SERGE:
> *"We were so tired . . . we slept through an entire bombardment."*

Juan Andrade was my first *Spanish* refugee. But Victor Serge (Kibalchich) was my first *refugee*. Born in Belgium in 1890, active in the anarchist movement in pre-1914 France, revolutionary, novelist, journalist, Serge went to Barcelona to take part in the 1917 revolution. In 1919 he went to Russia and joined the staff of the Communist International. In 1933 he was accused of being the ringleader of a Trotskyite conspiracy. He was deported to Orenburg on the Ural River, where he spent 3 years with his wife Liuba (who was periodically confined in mental institutions) and his son, Vladi. His best known novel, *S'il Est Minuit dans le Siècle,* is about these 3 years of exile. An intense protest, the "Victor Serge affair," was headed by André Gide and Ignazio Silone, and signed by André Malraux, Romain Rolland, and Boris Souvarine.[1] Romain Rolland was invited to Moscow where he talked with Stalin, who promised that Serge would be released. Serge was the last intellectual to be rescued from the USSR before the Moscow trials. He left Russia in April 1936 after spending 17 years there. When Pierre Laval denied him entry into France, he was granted asylum in Belgium for 3 years. From Belgium he moved to France where he worked as a proofreader and was active in the protests against the Moscow trials, and in defense of the POUM which was being persecuted in Spain.

When Paris fell to the Germans on June 13, 1940, Serge and his companion, Laurette Séjourné [Victor's wife Liuba confined in a mental institution, survived the Nazi Occupation] and his son, Vladi, started their flight to the South in a "providential taxi

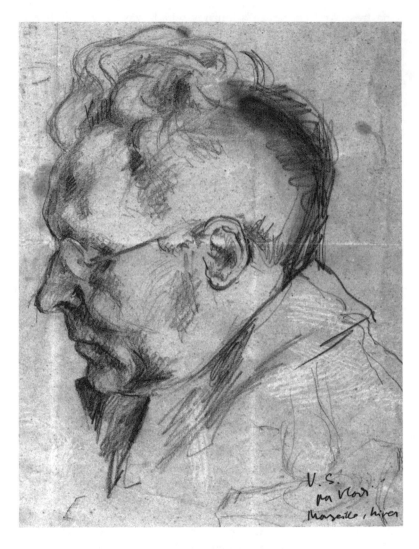

4. *A portrait of Victor Serge by his son, Vladi, in Marseille, winter of 1940—1941. Victor was in great danger because he had written a number of books exposing the Communist realities and horrors and, naturally, he was also an anti-Fascist.*

with a one-eyed driver.'' Serge, who had written for *Partisan Review,* wrote us from Fenlac in the Dordogne asking us to help him and his family:

> By some luck I managed to flee Paris at the very last minute. We have been traveling in freight trains, spending nights in the fields. In a little village in the Loire country we were so tired that we lay down behind some stones and slept through an entire bombardment. Nowhere, in this completely chaotic world, were we able to find any asylum. Finally the roads were barred and we were stranded in the small village in the south from which I am writing you. I do not think I will be able to remain here since I know no one and have neither roof nor money nor chance of earning anything.
>
> Of all I once owned—clothes, books, writings—I was able to save only what my friends and I could carry away on our backs in knapsacks. It is very little, but fortunately includes the manuscripts which I have already begun. This letter is a sort of S.O.S. which I hope that you will also communicate to my known and unknown friends in America. I have no money for stamps; I will be able to send off perhaps one or two letters, but that is all. I must ask you to immediately undertake some action of material aid for me. I have scarcely a hundred francs left; we are eating only one meal a day and it is a very poor one at that. I don't at all know how we are going to hold out.

We answered this appeal by setting up the *Partisan Review* Fund for European Writers and Artists. Serge was in great danger because he had written a number of books exposing the Communist realities and horrors and, naturally, he was also an antifascist. But since he had once been a member of the Communist party, he was not allowed to come to the U.S. Dwight and I made every effort to persuade the State Department to grant him a visa. When we were told Ed Prichard in the Justice Department would be sympathetic, we made a special trip to Washington to see him, but with no success. Prominent Americans including Max Eastman, John Dewey, Eugene Lyons, Sidney Hook, Meyer Schapiro, and James T. Farrell backed our appeals. Finally, in December 1940, Victor and his son Vladi received Mexican visas. This was due in part to Dr. Frank Tannenbaum, a personal friend of Lazaro Cardenas, the president of Mexico.[2] Tannenbaum made a special appeal on Serge's behalf. To reach Lisbon, it was necessary to obtain an American transit visa because there were no diplomatic relations between Spain and Mexico. Again we were up against a stone wall. At one point we advised Serge to get a visa for emigration to China.

Finally, on March 25, 1941, Serge and Vladi sailed on the *Captaine Paul Lemerle,* the first of 5 boats to transport refugees from Marseille to Martinique via Ciudad Trujillo. On their way to Mexico they were held briefly in a Cuban detention camp. After more protests, they arrived in Mexico in September 1941. Victor's companion, Laurette Séjourné[3] and his four-year-old daughter, Jeannine, joined them in March 1942. Through the *Partisan Review* Fund, which helped 40 different refugees, we raised $800 for Serge and his family. But Dwight and I financed a good part of his trip ourselves and kept him going with cash after his arrival, until he and Laurette were on their feet. Trying to help Serge, I learned on a small scale many points that would be of later use in helping Spanish refugees.

Serge died in Mexico in November 1947. His funeral documents registered him as a Spanish national. He had been in Spain in 1917 and was a close friend of Andres Nin (see Chapter 2) in Moscow, and was in political affinity with the POUM and its members.

NOTES

1. Malraux fought in Spain and wrote a novel, *Man's Hope,* about the Civil War. Souvarine, the author of the biography *Stalin,* was the brother-in-law of Joaquin Maurin, one of the leaders of the POUM, who was a prisoner of Franco from the beginning of the war until he was released in 1946. Born in 1895, Souvarine, until his death in 1984 was still writing about his experiences in the early days of the French Communist Party of which he was one of the founders.
2. President Lazaro Cardenas saved thousands of Spanish refugees by granting them visas to Mexico. He was Honorary Chairman of Spanish Refugee Aid from 1953-1961. Mexico never recognized the Franco Government. It maintained diplomatic relations with the

Spanish Republican Government-in-Exile from 1939-1977. Mexico reestablished diplomatic relations with Spain and the Government of King Juan Carlos I on March 28, 1977.

3. Laurette was the first of our contributors to adopt a Spanish refugee from SRA at $10 a month, and continued this for 31 years. After Serge's death she married and became Laurette de Orfila.

4

A Dozen Years,
a Half-Dozen Committees
1939-1952

NEW WORLD RESETTLEMENT FUND

During the 1940s, I was not only Business Manager of *Partisan Review* and then of *politics,* but was involved with various committees. In 1941 I was already beginning to think in terms of special aid to the Spanish refugees. I wrote Serge that I felt they had been "shamefully neglected." "The problem is so vast that I don't know where to start." Serge replied that refugee work is *"une des formes de la bataille necessaire."*

An organization called the New World Resettlement Fund (NWRF) had been founded to resettle several thousand Spanish refugees in the Simon Bolivar Colony in Ecuador. Oswald Garrison Villard was President and in 1940 John Dos Passos was secretary of the NWRF and travelled to Ecuador and the Dominican Republic to help select Spanish refugee families for resettlement. But funds for their survival were nonexistent. I urged America Escudero, NWRF's executive, to campaign for contributions for the Spaniards; but she was pessimistic.

PARTISAN REVIEW FUND FOR EUROPEAN WRITERS

Among those in greatest danger were Olga Nin and her children. The widow of Andrés Nin, assassinated in Spain by the Communists, wrote from Marseille: "We are in despair, every day our situation is worse. We receive no money. . . . Packages from Lisbon no longer arrive. . . . No work to be found. . . . I am fearful of the coming winter." I wrote Serge that our committee, the *Partisan Review* Fund for European Writers and Artists, could send her a small stipend each month. The Nins, thanks to Indalecio Prieto, were granted visas to Mexico. By May 1942 we were still collecting funds for the Andrades and I was reflecting whether "some sort of general committee could not be formed to help Spaniards in France." Then, when the Nazis took over the whole of France in December 1942 I lost contact with these Spaniards.

COMMITTEE FOR EMERGENCY AID TO REFUGEES

While I continued to work as Business Manager of *Partisan Review,* I was gaining experience with refugees, running the Trotskyist Committee for Emergency Aid to Refugees. In 1939 with my husband, Dwight, I had joined the Socialist Workers Party (Trotskyite). (Our party names, chosen by Dwight, were James Joyce and Elsie Dinsmore.) This was at the time of the split between the Schachtmanites, who held that the Soviet Union was no longer a Workers' State, and the Cannonites, who agreed with Trotsky that it was. We sided with the first group, led by Max Schachtman, James Burnham (an old friend of Dwight's), and Martin Abern. For many hours we'd listen to the "leaders" expounding their views on this question, go to meetings and fundraisers, and distribute and sell papers and pamphlets on the streets. My first attempt to sell the Schachtman paper, *Labor Action,* was promising—I was given $1 for a 5¢ item.

I was made executive of their Committee for Emergency Aid to Refugees, to help Trotskyite and dissident refugees in Europe. The novelist James T. Farrell was Honorary Chairman, and Cuthbert Daniel, a physicist and friend of our comrades was Chairman. My job was to find people who would give money and affidavits of support. I also had to write up biographies (sometimes fanciful) to assure the authorities that these refugees would make good citizens.

I left the party in 1941 because of its bureaucratic nature. But I took the committee with me. The party assigned one of its members, Stanley Plastrik, to keep a check on me and make sure I was doing right by the comrades, which led to some angry interchanges. This committee managed to save some good people. Our most difficult case was Anton Grylewicz, the leader of the Trotskyites in Germany, who was too well known to be allowed into the U.S. (former members of the CP were barred). We planned to buy him a Cuban visa for $1,000. He being an orthodox Trotskyite, we thought the Cannonites should help. Farrell, Mary Green (my most active helper), and I went to see George Novack at their headquarters on 13th Street and University Place, but discussion got nowhere. Then I suggested to George that they skip two issues of their magazine, the *New International,* to pay for the visa. Novack was appalled, especially at my chutzpah in telling him how to run his magazine. We did manage to raise the money to save Grylewics; no thanks to the "comrades." Annemarie, his wife, received her visa for Cuba in Berlin in spring, 1950. Another Trotskyite, Walter Held, who sided with the Cannonites, decided it would be safe to leave Sweden via the USSR. He was never heard from again.

The Lynn Committee to Abolish Segregation in the Armed Forces

During this same period I was learning more about fund-raising and committee work as the executive secretary and treasurer of The Lynn Committee to Abolish Segregation in the Armed Forces. Winfred Lynn registered for the draft but refused to serve in a segregated army. His brother, Conrad, a lawyer, backed his suit. The American Civil Liberties Union assigned a lawyer to the case. (We were horrified to discover he was from Texas, but he proved very sympathetic.)

We started our work in 1943 under the aegis of A. Philip Randolph at his office of The March on Washington in the Hotel Teresa on 125 Street. We soon found that sharing quarters was a mistake; we could not be independent. We moved to our own office at 1 West 125 Street. Our committee was headed by Wilfred Kerr, Chairman, and its members included Gene Clemes, Richard Parrish, Mary Green, Maude Brown, Dorothy Brumm, Dwight Macdonald, A.J. Muste, Selma DeKroyft, Bertha Gruner, John Becker, Layle Lane, Henry Pelham and Isaac McNatt (one of 19 Seabees who were fighting their discharge from the Navy as "undesirable by reason of unfitness"). I continued as Treasurer of the Lynn Committee until the birth of my son, Nick, in October 1944. We got out publicity, raised money, gave parties, wrote to Winfred to keep him informed, and dealt with lawyers. Among these, Arthur Garfield Hayes wanted to fight the case on technicalities rather than on the question of segregation. We refused. Winfred's case was declared "moot" when he was shipped off to the Pacific.

While running both the refugee organization and the Lynn Committee, I continued active as Business Manager of *Partisan Review*. Then, in 1943, William Phillips and Philip Rahv "wanted to reduce the magazine's political content and concentrate on literary criticism." Dwight wanted "to continue the mixture as before."

Dwight's letter of resignation appeared in the July-August 1943 issue. At the end he notes: "Finally, I should add that Nancy Macdonald, who has functioned in the demanding capacity of business manager of *Partisan Review* for the greater part of the past 5 years, is also severing connections with the magazine. Her reasons are about the same as those indicated above, and she will work with me on the new project. Both of us wish the new *Partisan Review* the best of luck."

Politics magazine was started in February 1944. Previously, we went to the PR offices to talk about using the list of contributors to see if some might be interested in our new venture. The first thing we discovered was that Phillips and Rahv had changed the locks. When we were admitted, we asked Rahv for the use of the list. He flatly refused. I could only think how Dwight had been the main editor of PR for years, doing layouts, proofreading, correspondance, to say nothing of editing, how I had been what Dwight termed "the Unknown Soldier of the little magazine world." And now this was the friendship and trust for the Macdonalds.

I was sitting on the radiator in the tiny PR office. I told Rahv that I'd sit there until they gave us their list for this one-time use.

Rahv said, "I'll call the police."

"Go ahead!" I told him.

When we left, we had what we had come for. We never had any idea of pirating the list. But there was no telling Rahv this. We got off lightly. We didn't arouse him to a lawsuit, such as he had brought against Mary McCarthy over her spoofing him in the *Oasis*; or the one against William Phillips in 1965 when the editorial board of PR voted to list William Phillips as editor-in-chief.

Many European refugees wrote for *politics* magazine. Once the war was over, they were in touch with friends in Europe who had been persecuted for their beliefs or had been in Nazi concentration camps. Hannah Arendt, Nicola Chiaromonte, Lewis Coser, Paul Froelich, Paul Mattick, Victor Serge, Boris Souvarine, Herta Vogelstein[1] and others supplied us with the names and addresses of people who needed money, food, clothes and medicines. And so in October 1945 we started politics packages abroad (PPA).

POLITICS PACKAGES ABROAD (PPA)

We were asked to help people like Pierre Monatte; "A veteran syndicalist fighter of great quality, who was very courageous in the first world war and never changed, he desperately needs a pair of high shoes, size 39"; Yvon, "the author of a well-known book about Russia"; Goldman "spent a term of 5 years imprisonment in a Polish jail"; Simon Roth, "engineer, came from Mauthausen concentration camp, now unemployed"; Mrs. Emmy Gotzmann, "who is sixty-five and her old mother, ninety-three, both were active anti-Nazis and deserve help"; "a list of Russian Jews, most important, Mme. Sholem Schwarzbard, widow of the famous Sholem, who killed Petljura in the twenties in Paris and was acquitted".

Then there was Samorei, "crippled in WW I but his spirit never broken. Leader of Ruhr miners. Under the Nazi terror was caught and tortured, sentenced to hard labor. After 10 years of prison came out almost paralyzed but with his old fighting spirit. I think he deserves help!" There was Victor Brauner, "great surrealist painter, Leftist, Jew, years in underground"; a remarkable Greek militant, Theo Sgourdellis and his wife, Helen; Paul Ciliga, the nine-year-old son of Anton, the author of the first book about the Gulags. Paul living with his sister in Paris, mother deported and died in Germany. Anton suffered a lot during the occupation."

And we had two letters from Mr. and Mrs. E. Cohn-Bendit (parents of Danny the Red, famous for his role in the student strike in Paris in 1968), who were administering a camp in Normandy for 69 children of deported parents, asking us for clothes and food. "These children have next to nothing to put on."

The first appeal for *politics* Packages Abroad appeared in the October 1945 issue of *politics*. Dwight wrote that this project expressed "at least a token of fraternal feeling across national boundaries. The idea of corresponding with individuals abroad, furthermore, seems to appeal strongly to people. The human ties, whose formation the arrangement makes possible, may turn out to be at least as important as the material help provided."

Victor Serge wrote, "Dear Nancy, Your good letter put me in a difficult situation. We have the feeling that *all* our friends in France need help, even if they are working, but we must concentrate the solidarity in favor of the most disarmed or disabled." Andrade wrote in November about three comrades. I was expecting a list of 50 or so "POUM people to whom we will try and send food. I feel specially strongly that they should be helped and well because it seems to me that they were horribly neglected before." I wrote Serge "I've been terrifically rushed because of this package business which I vowed I wouldn't get involved in but of course I have." In February 1946 I wrote him, "We have 400 people on our lists."

5. *Ramon Dwight Vallecillos, one of PPA's Spanish refugee children, was named after Dwight.*

From 1945–1950 *politics* Packages Abroad got many individuals and families abroad "adopted" by contributors in America. Individuals sent cash and clothes directly, and we also sent great quantities of clothes packages from our office. In spring of 1949 we raised money through a lecture-discussion series at the Rand School in New York. Bertram D. Wolfe spoke on "Josef Stalin, The Man and his Place in History." Karl A. Wittfogel's subject was "The Historical Meaning of Chinese Communism." Arthur M. Schlesinger, Jr. spoke about "Truman—Heir or Epigone of the New Deal?" Dwight's speech was titled "Goodbye to Utopia." In its first 3 years PPA raised over $23,000 and sent 20,000 packages to Europe.

I became an old-clothes expert. I never returned from a dinner or party without a bagful. Once or twice a month a group of friends—Bertha Gruner, Abe Bienstock, Anthony and Nika Standen, Francoise Souvarine, and Elizabeth Klintrup, came in the evening to our office in the old Bible House across from Cooper Union on Astor Place. We tried on clothing, speculated on European shoe sizes, and attempted to make the contents of the packages both useful and attractive. Once we managed to send a left shoe to Italy and the right one to France. When the packages were ready, measured for size-limit, and affixed with their proper customs labels, we would go off to the General Post Office to mail our 20 to 25 packages before midnight.

When *politics* Packages Abroad made its first appeal, the *Socialist Call* accused us of stealing the idea from their International Solidarity Committee (ISC). Our organization started about 3 weeks after theirs. But I had already been getting personal friends to send packages abroad during the summer, and neither Dwight nor I knew about the ISC. Philip Heller,[2] who ran the ISC, was invited to PPA's first meeting but could not attend.

At this meeting we decided not to join with them when we learned they were mainly helping Socialists. Our interests were broader, there were many dissidents we wanted to help. We also felt that a smaller group was better, and we wanted to keep in touch with our kind of people. PPA aided anti-Communists of all varieties and nationalities—Italians, French, Belgians, Poles,

Germans, Czechs, Dutch, Austrians, Greeks. And we didn't forget the Spaniards. Andrade put us in touch with Pedro Bonet, also a militant of the POUM, who gave us the names of many more needy Spanish exiles.

INTERNATIONAL RESCUE COMMITTEE (IRC)

In the winter of 1949-1950, Dwight wrote in *politics* magazine: "This has been a one-man magazine . . . . and the man has of late been feeling stale, tired, disheartened and—if you like—demoralized." Also, the rising costs of printing and our falling bank balance meant that Dwight would need to go back to writing for a living. And he was no longer as interested in political writing, but rather in social-cultural reportage.

Politics Packages Abroad also slowly closed down. In 1951, out of a job, I went to work as a volunteer for the International Rescue Committee. I had a number of friends there from earlier refugee work. They included Charles Sternberg, who had worked for the International Relief Association (IRA) in Marseille. I offered to work for him without pay. Later he gave me a paid job, mostly getting affidavits of support for refugees who wanted to come to the United States and, for a while, as secretary to Rainer Hildebrandt, a one-man-movement-resistance-fighter from West Berlin.

The International Rescue Committee (IRC) was the amalgamation of two organizations, the International Relief Association and the Emergency Rescue Committee (ERC). The first was founded early in 1933 to help people fleeing Hitler's Germany and those who continued to work in the underground. The second was started shortly after June 1940 by a group of Americans to spirit out of France those intellectuals and political refugees who were on the Nazi wanted list and were to be "surrendered on demand." In March 1942 the IRA merged with the ERC to form the International Rescue and Relief Committee (later abbreviated, to be called International Rescue Committee). Immediately after Paris was liberated, IRC opened an office there.

Hanne Benzion worked for IRC from May 1945 until January 1974. She started as a receptionist-typist but was soon involved in all aspects of refugee work. When I first met her in 1952, she was the Director of IRC in France. We became friends and she was an invaluable one, finding me an inexpensive hotel, forwarding my mail, taking me on trips and picnics, giving me books, and introducing me to her friends. Among them were Czeslaw Milosz and his family; Mika Etchebehere, an Argentinian journalist who wrote a wonderful book on Spain, *Ma Guerre d'Espagne a Moi,* about her experiences as a Commander of a Spanish batallion during the Spanish Civil War; Mme. Selma Weil, the mother of Simone; Baladin, who had been a close friend of Rilke and was the mother of the painter, Balthus, and the philosopher, Pierre Klosowski; Muriel Gardner (Buttinger), who wrote a fascinating book about her experiences in the Austrian underground and another about patients she had treated as a therapist.

Hanne Benzion (nee Back) was born in the Sudetenland on May 29, 1896. She received her Doctor of Philosophy degree in Vienna for her thesis on Thomas Mann, which was published by Phaidon Verlag in 1925 for Mann's fiftieth birthday. She came to France in 1930. Hanne gave German lessons and one of her students was a very wealthy American woman, Mrs. H.P., who in 1934 invited her to go on a trip to Russia. Recalling this, Hanne said, "I think of the time Trotsky sat in that chair you are in now!"

I exclaimed: "How did he get here?"

It seemed that Mrs. P. contributed heavily to Trotsky's transfer from Turkey to France. When he arrived, he needed a place to meet friends and Hanne offered her apartment through Mrs. P. and mutual friends, Alfred and Marguerite Rosmer. Hanne told me that the Trotskys spent several days with Simone Weil and her parents, and he found Simone an excellent arguer and "devil's advocate." Hanne recalled that Trotsky was a big man, polite, who kissed her hand in greeting. She became great friends with Natalya after Trotsky's death.

When Hanne returned from Russia, she met a Frenchman, Al-

6. Hanne Benzion in 1957. "We soon became friends and she was an invaluable one for me."

exandre Benzion, and they were married on June 2, 1936. He was trilingual and did translations for broadcasting and was also a film writer. He lived in Hollywood for a year (1936—1937) where he had a contract with the actress, Anna Sten, met Greta Garbo and others, and worked with Pabst.

During the occupation of France by the Nazis, Hanne and her husband were hidden near Bergerac by Elie Faure and her family. Elie became Hanne's closest friend. They were in the South of France between the Gironde and Dordogne rivers. When the Germans were on the prowl, the Benzions were rowed across the Dordogne and hidden on the other side. The peasants of the region were marvelous to them, bringing them all sorts of food in great quantities.

When the war was over, Hanne and her husband spent 2 years on the sixth floor of a bordello. They went there by chance when they returned to Paris. They had to sue to get back their apartment, but finally won. The proprietor of the bordello wept when they left. In 1943 Hanne learned that all her family had been deported from Czechoslovakia by the Nazis in 1942 and all had perished. Alexandre died on January 1, 1949. In her eighties, though with failing sight, and housebound, Hanne continued as concerned as ever about what was going on in the world—the world now brought to her by her devoted friends.

Much of the International Rescue Committee's work after 1945 was made possible by funds contributed by the International Refugee Organization (IRO). IRO had been created by the General Assembly of the UN on December 15, 1946 and terminated December 31, 1951. Its funds for distribution amounted to $25 million realized from the sale of nonmonetary gold captured from the Nazis, 90 percent of which was designated for Jewish victims and 10 percent for others. IRC distributed $819,000. From 1945 to 1952 the IRC in Paris, headed by Hanne Benzion, included a Spanish section run by José Rodes. But by the early fifties IRC's main focus was Iron Curtain refugees and their Spanish program was being phased out. Rodes, aware of my interest in Spanish refugees, besieged me with pleas to "do something."

Rodes was born in 1893 in Lerida and died August 23, 1968 in

Paris. He was Mayor of Lerida for 10 months during the Spanish Civil War. Condemned (along with Juan Andrade), by the Petain Government to 15 years forced labor in 1941, he spent 3 years in Vichy prisons and 1 year in the Nazi concentration camps of Dachau and Allach. He was an active member of the POUM from 1928 until his death 40 years later.

In his last years Rodes worked for the Federación Española de Deportados e Internados Politicos (FEDIP) and arranged the papers of many Spaniards seeking indemnification from the West German Government. He wrote me in March 1963 that the FEDIP had been able to get indemnification for some 3,000 families living in Spain. All the widows, sons, and parents of the Spanish Republicans who died in Nazi concentration camps had received pensions and indemnification. For a widow this meant about $8,000 plus a monthly pension of about $75—"a fortune for these poor people." A pact between Franco and the Federal Government of West Germany granted indemnification to the widows of the men in Franco's Blue Division. These men had fought for the Nazis during WW II on the Russian front. But the Spanish refugees, who were in the French Resistance and the Maquis and who took up arms for France against the Germans had no right to this indemnification. They had fought *against* The Germans. Only those who resisted Nazism on an ideological plane were indemnified. Eventually, those who had been in the punishment camps of Vernet d'Ariège and Nŏe, or were deported to the Channel Islands, or who had been used as forced laborers by the Nazis on the Atlantic Wall fortifications were also indemnified.

A second indemnification bill was voted by the West German Government in August 1981 to benefit the gypsies. But since so few survived, the remaining funds were used for Spanish refugees who had been in the camps of Argeles, St. Cyprien, Bram, Septfonds, Gurs, and Barcares between 1940 and 1945. Each person was to receive 11,500 NF (c. $1,440) and perhaps more later. Requests were channeled through a Spanish committee in Paris with a German lawyer and they retained a commission ranging from 1.500 to 3.250 NF. Suits were brought to recover part of these often outrageous sums.

OUT OF IRC AND INTO SRA:
"Une des formes de la bataille nécessaire"

In the spring of 1952 I lost my job at the International Rescue Committee when a large grant from the Ford Foundation was not renewed. In response to Rodes' appeal for the Spanish refugees, I suggested to IRC that I would continue to work without a salary and set up a special project within the committee to raise funds for these exiles. The IRC regarded this as a lost cause. However, if I wanted to set up a separate organization, they would help.

My feelings for the Spanish political exiles already ran deep. These were the people who had fought to keep their country free from Fascism; but the democratic countries had not helped. If the Spanish Civil War had ended differently there might have been no WW II. I thought that many people must feel guilty, as I did, at the failure of our country to help the Spanish Republic. Also, it puts me on my mettle to fight for an unpopular cause for which I feel strongly. I am always confident that one can succeed if the need is genuine and if one can present the facts realistically and in terms that "get to" people. So I decided to "do something." I also wanted to direct my energies and divert my thinking from my marriage, then breaking up.

To "do something" entailed two steps: to form an organization to raise money; and to find the people who needed help. I began by seeking further information in the US about these exiles; very little was available. Antonio Reyna at the International Ladies Garment Workers' Union (ILGWU) was said to have connections with the Spaniards in France. His suggestion was that all aid should be channelled through the Spanish Socialists at the UGT in Toulouse. They, he said, were impartial and helped everybody. On the basis of my own brief experience of political factionalism in the Trotskyite Socialist Workers Party in 1939–1941, I discounted this suggestion. (Later, my intuition proved correct.) The Spanish refugee in New York at this time was Jaume Miravittles. During the Civil War he had been a prominent member of the Esquerra, the Catalan autonomist party. He offered no specific information, only encouragement. (Miravittles was one of our original sponsors; but we dropped his name from our lists in 1954 when he was accused by Jesus de Galindez of being a Fascist, and of writing articles in favor of the US pact with Franco, and a paragraph honoring Primo de Rivera, the founder of the Falange.)

Federico de Onis was one of the world's leading Hispanic scholars. In 1950 he had helped bring into the United States a group of Spanish refugee children who had been sent to the Soviet Union at the end of the civil war. When I spoke to him at Columbia University, I was astonished to hear him say that the Spanish refugees were dead, or didn't need anything. (He died in Puerto Rico at the age of 80 in 1966.)

Celine Rott de Neufville told a different story. She was one of the people who strongly urged me to start SRA. I met her only once, but I feel a debt to her. She got in touch with me through one of PPA's "adopters," Lionel Anderson, and told me that there was much individual need. She particularly asked for help for the Spanish Republican Red Cross Dispensaries in Toulouse and Montauban, which desperately needed funds.

Celine was an immigration inspector in Venezuela in the early forties, then worked for the Quakers in France. She had an adopted son, Ed, who was a diver by profession and lived in California. She was born in Paris; her father was Swiss and owned silver mines in Spain. When Celine inherited them, she couldn't take the money out of the country. So she went to live in Malaga in the fifties and used her inheritance to raise eight orphaned Spanish boys and one girl. She wrote me in 1955 that she was living in Malaga "with people I met last year and liked. He, Don Manuel Vallejo Barba, is a self-made man of fifty, who lives with his two sisters, also unmarried. They like me because I remind them of their mother, whom they recently lost. They are helping me in the work I have undertaken." She also wrote that a friend of hers, "Charity Willard, who taught Spanish at the University of Vermont, has accepted to take over the work when I am no longer there and is coming over in the fall." Celine died in the sixties in Madrid.

7. *Celine Rott de Neufville went to live in Malga in the 1950s and used the money she had inherited to bring up eight orphaned Spanish boys and one girl.*

The novelist James T. Farrell promised to be chairman of a new committee, and provided the Paris address of Victor Reuther, the International Director of the United Automobile Workers Union (UAW), who might be able to help.

In April 1952 I still vainly hoped that ADA and/or the Inter American Association for Democracy and Liberty would help me set up a committee. In May, before leaving for Europe, my friend Martha Hall and I were typing the names and addresses of IRC contributors who had been interested in Spanish exiles. Abe Becker, their director, had authorized this; but then decided we were transcribing too many. Dick Salzman, their fund-raiser, offered to pirate the remainder, but I declined. Eventually we were allowed to finish our list if we made short work of it. As Director of *politics* Packages Abroad I had also written an appeal for Spanish refugees, with my home address. There was no response to an ad in the *New Leader*; but I received $22 and two offers to "adopt" families through *Catholic Worker*. My friend Laurette Séjourné, in Mexico, also offered to adopt a Spanish refugee at $10 a month, and continued this for 31 years. She had started what later became our adoption program.

NOTES

1. Hannah Arendt was Chairman of SRA from 1960–1966 and on our Board of Directors until her death in 1973. In 1936 Chiaromonte served in André Malraux's squadron in Spain and he was the original of Scali in Malraux's *Man's Hope*; Lewis Coser wrote regularly for *politics* under the pseudonym Louis Clair; Paul Froelich's widow, Rose, started a German committee in Frankfurt in 1955 to help SRA, and still contributes although she is in her nineties. Paul was a friend and biographer of Rosa Luxemburg.
2. Heller ran the International Solidarity Committee from 1945–1949, was a close associate of Norman Thomas, and the educational director of ILGWU local 155. Later he worked for the Marshall Plan in Germany and Austria and then was in the Foreign Service until 1970. He died in December 1976. When SRA was starting to raise funds in 1953, we asked if we might use the ISC list in our search for donors. It was refused.

5

Travel Diary

PARIS: "A STRANGE STAGESET"

On June 4, 1952 I sailed for Europe on the Queen Elizabeth I, with my sons, Michael (Mike), fourteen and Nicholas (Nick), eight. We were funding the trip. Dwight, who stayed in New York, wrote:

> It takes all the running I can do to keep in same place here. . . . Money! Strange that, after so many years of lofty disregard of the stuff, now it becomes topic #1. (Could it be connected with the fact that our capital, except for the providential trust fund, is now exhausted ?????) Right now, WHAT a pinch (my poor bank account is black and blue)." (The trust fund was mine from my mother and yielded $250 a month and some extra in September, the month she died. Dwight was trying to find suitable subjects for biographical "Profiles" for the *New Yorker* magazine, just having completed two on Dorothy Day and Roger Baldwin).

In Paris where Hanne Benzion, the director of the International Rescue Committee had booked rooms for us next door to her apartment at the Hotel Istria I exulted to Dwight:

75

8. Dwight and Nancy Macdonald (photographed by Bertrand De Geofroy).

Paris is really wonderful and beautiful. Stepping out of the Gare St. Lazare seemed like stepping into a strange stageset, glistening, smelling delicious. The gray-tone buildings are beautiful and I am specially struck by the individuality of the life and people around. First of all, the traffic is completely mad. My first taxi ride was a chariot race. A man in a car next to us was determined to pass. He leaned over his wheel, veered towards us, leaped ahead, fell back, swept around behind and passed us triumphantly with a terrific rush. It is hard to cross the streets but one is "insured" if one crosses between the little lines of metal on the pavement (of course you may be dead!)

I have seen the Chiaromontes . . . . I talked to Nick about your reviving *politics* . . . . Went to a cocktail party at Sheba's attended by such characters as Koestler, Mannes Sperber (whom I talked to and liked very much), Gorkin, Raymond Aron, the Souvarines, Altman, Leon Dennen. Mannes Sperber and Camus have been talking about starting some sort of magazine. Sperber agreed that it would be an excellent time to start *politics* again and that many writers here would happily contribute. I do wish you would come over but I don't want to press you. I think you would benefit enormously by coming both from the stimulation of talking to people here and the surroundings. I think we were both crazy not to come before.

On the Spanish front, I wrote:

Hanne Benzion has given me the dossiers of 100 Spanish needy families. She seems 'une tipe serieuse' . . . . Maria Teresa Andrade popped in this morning at 10, kissed me on both cheeks and we were off at a gallop . . . . Pedro Bonet is a wolf, I had pictured him as a graybeard! . . . . Maximilian Rubel is starting a project to help recent Spanish refugees from Spain which is, of course, wonderful for my project . . . . Lunch with William Gausmann,[1] who told me that the Committee for Cultural Freedom is very definitely subsidized by the U.S. State Department. It's an open secret . . . . As to our Spaniards, he gave me a list of Spanish trade union groups from Victor Reuther's office.

Gausmann thinks if all the Spanish political groups would get together in one refugee aid committee that the American trade unions and specifically the International Confederation of Free Trade Unions (ICFTU), would help with money. However, I had already learned from Michael Ross, director of the International Affairs Department of the CIO in Washington that the CIO, when it makes financial contributions for the Spanish Republic, does it through the ICFTU, with whom the Spanish trade union groups in exile are affiliated. [Actually, as it turned out, it was only the UGT (Socialists), who were affiliated with it and not the equally important CNT unions (Anarchosyndicalist)]

In the course of my stay in Paris, I saw Rodes and the POUM people, the Basque Delegation at 50 rue Singer, Hanne Benzion, and Francine Camus. The Liga de Mutilados told me that "certain small sums used for special aid would be invaluable." I wrote Dwight asking him to send our first CARE package, with the money contributed by two *Catholic Worker* readers, to Martin Gruart Casanovas a 'grand Mutile' with two boys of eleven and seven, the oldest suffering from a nervous disorder.''

I next recorded

> . . . two long sessions with José Ester of the Federación de Deportados Espagnoles (very good fellow from whom I learned a lot) and the head of the Service Social d'Aides aux Emigrants (SSAE). They spend 80 percent of their funds for Spaniards but I gather from other sources that they are bureaucratic and take months to make decisions and don't really carry through as splendidly as they claim. . . . If I can survive the intricacies of personal and political feuds here, I'll be lucky!

SWITZERLAND AND UN "CHANNELING"

From Geneva:

> Had lunch with Alida de Jaeger, a young Dutch woman who runs the IRC here and is vey nice (later she became a close friend). She took me to the UN to the office of the High Commissioner for Refugees. Its first commissioner, Dr. G.J. van Heuven Goedhart, was appointed on December 14, 1950 and the Spanish refugees are under his mandate. We saw his representative, Aline Cohen, a rather pleasant woman who didn't seem to know much about the present situation of the Spaniards (thought I could inform her!) A younger man promised to get me some statistics and "seemed rather conscious of the fact that not much was going on in that monstrous pile called the UN (endless marble halls, with plushy offices). One has the feeling that these people have nothing to communicate and take a lot of time doing it. Anna says that this is called channelling." [Through Alida I met Heinz and Frieda Jacoby, who became devoted SRA supporters and friends.]

On Saturday morning July 12 we started off on our trek through France. I wrote: "I've never been through so many mountains. Switzerland seemed flat in comparison. The scenery was marvelous and spectacular. . . . We spent the night at Mendes, a small town in the mountains, very pretty and gay with the 14th of July celebrations. They were dancing in the street in front of our hotel. . . . The next day we stopped in a number of towns to look at churches, Le Puy, Rodez, and Albi (the latter quite famous, looks like a tremendous fortress outside, pinkish stone). . . ."

On the 21st of July, I left Arcangues for Toulouse (the children remaining with friends). I asked Dwight to send batteries for hearing aids for 8 deaf anarchists in Toulouse, to be sent to Solidarite Internationale Antifasciste (SIA). Dwight reported the cost was $68. I had collected $200 for Spaniards before I left New York, so that covered it.

MONTAUBAN, TOULOUSE AND PERPIGNAN

I reported

. . . a very rushed stay in Montauban where I saw a lot and where, I believe, the greatest need of the Spaniards exists. There's a Spanish Red Cross Dispensary which is doing excellent work but it is about to fold for lack of help (used to be subsidized by some Norwegian outfit). The woman who runs it, Teresa Palacios, and her husband, Manuel, took me around to see a lot of families. I gave her $60 to cover 1-month vacations for 3 Spanish children. The Dispensary in rue Lassus used to get 40,000 francs a month, if this help could continue, it would be wonderful. I found that quite a lot could be done with small sums like this to keep outfits going that are doing good work.

Another Republican Red Cross Dispensary in Toulouse at 4 rue Mondran is assisted in a small way by two of the Spanish solidarity outfits. The social worker there, Anne Marie Vitaller (nee Berta), hates red tape and by rushing around town from morning to night obviously helped many people enormously on tiny means (she gets 10,000 francs a month salary and to keep alive, works at night making corsets.) I saw both factions of the CNT. The Solidarite Internationale Antifasciste (SIA) people took me to the 3 Toulouse public hospitals where we doled out pears, chocolate, crackers, canned milk, and newspapers to any Spaniard who wasn't being helped. We saw a victim of silicosis who had been there for 10 years and had such a look of defeat and despair in his eyes. A woman with TB cried when we came by. She had been in the hospital for 30 months. . . . When the Spaniards are very ill, Catholic priests come around to perform last rites . . . . the Spanish refugees don't want this. They feel cornered and terrified in their helplessness.

I saw Federica Montseny, the leading light of the Spanish anarchists. I liked her, very friendly, intelligent-looking, and nice. A bit on the Ruth Fischer build but much more feminine and less calculating. Pedro Duran, a POUM man, and his wife Josefina ("Pepita") were marvelous to me. I had lunch with them every day and he made appointments for me, took me sightseeing . . . . A little working man who is part of a mattress making cooperative (I could almost make a mattress now), who was marvelously sensitive to art details. I've promised to take him to Albi where the Toulouse Lautrec Museum is and where there is a big exhibition now if I get back to Toulouse (imagine an American working man wanting to go to such a thing!—his eyes brightened when I suggested it and he said he would love to take a day off from work to see it.)

In Perpignan, I had every meal with Suzanne Chatelet and her man Francois Olivé, très chic, and used their bathroom (my hotel had only the hole in the floor kind—I thought how the Germans are said to have said of the French, "They certainly know how to eat, but they don't know how to go to the bathroom"). They feted me with champagne and I was given little gifts at the drop of a suggestion that I liked something. . . . Francois is full of vitality and good spirits, rides high, fanciful. Someone called him a poete manque . . . He is finished with politics. Says he couldn't go through another revolution. Wants now only to form good human relations. Suzanne, his wife, is the strong minded executive, takes care of him. She works as a masseuse (one day she gave me a delicious one). He is the accountant and general factotum in a cork factory."

COLONIE D'AYMARE

At Toulouse, the anarcho-syndicalists of Solidarite International Antifasciste (SIA) took me to see their Colonie at Aymare, 100 miles to the north.They desperately needed more water for cultivating and irrigating their 37 acres of farm and wood land.

It would take about $3,000 to build a reservoir and the Service Civil International offered free labor. They hoped that our new committee might be able to help. So Jacques Vive, who was the secretary of SIA, and I motored to Le Vigan (Lot), 100 miles north of Toulouse to see this farm community.

The property for the Colonie d'Aymare was bought by the CNT in 1939 and was to be administered by the CNT, SIA, and the Ligue des Mutiles (LM). It consisted of a 500-year-old chateau on high ground with a magnificent view in all directions. On one end of this chateau, which could house about 30 people, a pavilion had been built with funds from the IRO to house about 15 old, sick, or disabled comrades who were cared for by six able-bodied men. The IRO also bought furniture, and the pavilion had a modern shower and two toilets as well as electricity. Visitors to Aymare slept in a barnlike room on straw mattresses, or camped out in tents. While I was there they were preparing for a party with dancing, and a theatrical group was to give a show.

There was a barn—for horses, cows, and pigs, and another for sheep. Outbuildings housed the tractor, grain reservoir, tobacco-drying racks, carpenter's room, forge, and an oven for baking bread. There was also an ultramodern building for raising rabbits, with space for 70 and another for chickens (capacity 500). At the time of my visit they had four milk cows and one heifer, a horse, two sows and fourteen pigs, 130 sheep, and about 500 rabbits and 500 chickens. They also had various work tools, including a tractor, sewing, washing and macaroni machines and a portable forge.

From time to time, especially in the summer and at harvest, *nos copains* from the anarchist movement came to help with the work. During my visit a couple and their small daughter were there. He was a mason and was helping with work on new rabbit hutches and chicken coops.

The colony had been created as a place where some of the comrades (war wounded and invalids) could find health and tranquility in, as they put it, "an ambiance of fraternal affection and solidarity to raise their morale and give them courage after years of deprivation." They hoped that "mutual aid by friends would erase the inferiority complex which most of them had, due to their physical incapacity and the humiliating treatment they had lived through in official homes and hospitals.''

When I visited, there were 17 men in the pavilion. Four were over the age of sixty, two over seventy, and they suffered from a variety of illnesses—TB, pleurisy, stomach trouble, paralysis, asthma, Pott's disease, and psychiatric problems.

One offer to contribute $3,000 for the reservoir failed to materialize. Our new organization could not, with its very limited funds, finance this aid for Aymare. In 1969 the Colonie d'Aymare, overwhelmed by debts, had to be abandoned. It had been a noble experiment: the kind of mutual aid which the anarchists had practiced in rural Spain during the Republic.

Spain: Wasteland

We took a quick trip to Spain. I wrote:

My big impression was the poverty of the country, not of the people. We travelled through mile after mile of wasteland without a tree or a bit of green. But the North, San Sebastian to Vittoria, is green and fertile, and people ride on bicycles, and there are some cars. From there we climbed the mountains and came out on a high plateau which was mostly stretches of very straight roads between endless fields of rather thin wheat or else just wasteland filled with strange man-made-looking grey rocks.

It was harvest time and in every village the grain was being gathered. A man or woman sat in a chair, or stood on a piece of wood, tied behind a mule or a pair of oxen which went round and round in circles over the wheat (separating it from the chaff, I suppose). Then men and women with wooden pitchforks throw the wheat in the air (for separation and drying) and then the chaff is brushed away with brooms of twigs and the grain is piled for carting away in bags. We stopped at one place to take a picture of a proud old lady, all in black, sitting in her little chair and going round and round.

We had barely stopped the motor when all the children of the village were crowding around the car to look at it and us . . . .

Madrid is full of new buildings and ones in process . . . . an enormous city in the midst of a desert. Baedeker says that a long time ago the trees in this part of Spain were cut down because the Spaniards thought that the birds that nested in them were bad for the health! The greatest gift to the Spanish people, I would think, would be thousands of trees and winnowing machines.

Back in Paris I got in touch with Farrell, who was about to leave for Italy. I noted, "I certainly have all the contacts he has and many more, but he might be useful in forming a committee. On the other hand, I'm afraid he's much too involved with the Spanish Socialists alone and the factionalism among the Spaniards is *something*! Jim was very nice, even kissed me goodby." I also saw a friend of Farrell's, Bill Kemsley, who worked for MSA (Mutual Security Administration) in the labor training section, "a decent, honest sort of person, and clear-headed about the follies of American policy in Europe." (Later Kemsley was on our Board of Directors for a while when he was working at the U.N. in New York).

The boys returned with friends bound for New York and I went back to the South of France. I spent a day in Montauban with the wonderful Palacios family who ran the Spanish Republican Red Cross Dispensary, and . . . . we saw a few more Spanish needy together. In Toulouse Mme. Vitaller gave me a rather grim picture of Spanish Socialist politics: how they didn't help others, and kept for themselves funds meant to be shared. It was because of the Spanish Socialists, I gathered, that the Norwegian Socialists no longer supported the various Spanish Red Cross Dispensaries they previously helped. There had been eight, and now were only four. As far as I could make out, the dispensaries were nonpolitical and helped everybody without asking about their politics. Mme. Vitaller didn't like Communists; but if one asked for help, she gave it. The Norwegian Socialists, it seemed, gave money for scholarships for Spanish students the year before. It was intended for everybody but was to be administered by the Socialists. Only Socialists got scholarships.

I kept my promise to take Pedro Duran to Albi, to see the Toulouse Lautrec exhibit and the cathedral. On our way back a fete was going on in a small town and people were dancing in the middle of the main street. Nobody moved, so I stopped. A man came up to the side of the car and said "You'll just have to push them aside with the car," which I proceeded to do slowly, amid much laughter. In Albi Duran bought me a book on the Albigensian Crusades that I had admired in a bookstore window.

"HOLD THE OFFICE"

In September I wrote Dwight: "I think you had better keep hold of the office at 45 Astor Place until I get back. One of the things most needed by the Spaniards is *clothes*. They are horribly expensive here and the refugees who are in bad shape don't get enough to buy *anything* in the way of clothes, and have barely enough for food. An old man or an old woman over the age of sixty-five gets only $10 to $13 a month. Food is very high too, lodging is the only cheap item. So I figure the least I might be able to do would be to collect clothes to send, for which purpose the office would be perfect."

Before leaving Toulouse, Cabestany, to whom I had sent a saxophone through PPA, came to see me and insisted I go to his house and meet his wife and daughter and have coffee and talk. (Their daughter, Rose-Marie, became a professional pianist and I heard her perform beautifully at the Spanish Institute in New York around 1980.) I spent 3 days in Perpignan, mostly with the Olivés again, and spent part of one day with Gaspar Trafach, whose wife had been in the Resistance, acting as courier through the Pyrenees. She had been very ill with TB and had been helped with medicines by PPA. She died in May. Trafach was monologist, but I was sorry for him and felt I had to listen while he poured out everything, and listened to very little. I didn't see Casals, he was in Switzerland. I saw the local Service Sociale woman, Mlle. Py—bright, informed, and sympathetic.

I visited André Delecourt and her husband, Jean, in Lyon (they had written for *politics*). Back in Paris I met Antonio Trabal and José Jadraque, representatives of the Spanish veterans committee in exile, the Liga de Mutilados y Exilados (LM). I can still visualize them waiting for me in a bar on the Boulevard Raspail. It was a struggle to understand their mixture of Spanish and French as they asked me to help their 2,000 members. Trabal continued active for years with the Spanish veterans committee, working at UNESCO in Paris. Jadraque died in 1973.

Beside the Liga I visited the Federación Española de Deportados e Internados Politicos at 51 rue Boulainvilliers. I talked again to their Secretary General, José Ester Borras, who wanted to know if the new committee would be able to give his Federación a regular subsidy so that it could continue its work. (SRA did send them $50 a month for about 18 months when we started. Later we decided it was more important to help individuals than committees). I learned afterwards from his wife Odette that Ester, a militant of the CNT, had been active on many fronts during the Civil War. In France he belonged to the Resistance (Escape network "Pat"), and they helped him escape from the concentration camp of Vernet. Later he was arrested by the Nazis and sent to the KZ at Mauthausen, where he was active in the resistance inside the camp. Two Spaniards, José Bailina and Casimiro Climent, brought out with them the list of 7,211 Spaniards who had been there, only 2,398 survived—Ester among them. Ester was a Knight of the Legion of Honor, received the British King's Medal of Freedom and was awarded the American Medal of Freedom by Eisenhower at the same time as André Malraux. José's wife, Odette, a Frenchwoman, ran SRA's Paris office for 7 months in 1974 after the death of Suzanne Chatelet.

NOTE

1. He worked for Labor Press Services before the war and later at the U.S. Information Service in France and England and was a protégé of Norman Thomas.

PART II

6

What Is Needed?

*O*n October 18, when I returned from my 4 months in Europe I felt certain of two points. There was great need. But it would be impossible to get the Spanish groups to work together in France. The job of helping Spanish refugees would have to be done in the U.S.

I brought back with me 100 case histories given to the IRC by the Spanish veterans committee, the Liga de Mutilados (LM); the Socialist's Solidaridad Democratica Espanola (SDE); the anarcho-syndicalist's Solidaridad Internacional Antifascista (SIA); and the POUM's Solidaridad Socialista (SS). The LM had told me they had 2,000 members; the SDE claimed 800 sick members; and SIA sent us a long list of names and addresses to be checked in regard to need. (By the end of our first 6 months we had 561 cases.)

I also learned from Rodes that of the 500,000 Spaniards granted political asylum by the French Government between 1937 and 1939, there were still 200,000 at the end of WW II. Between 1945 and 1950, these exiles were being helped substantially by the Intergovernmental Committee for Refugees and then by the International Refugee Organization (IRO), which, when it ended its work in February 1950, had 7,490 *active* Spanish cases. (In 1951 it had 50,000 *applications* for aid.) Of their 2,427 hard-core Spanish cases there were

754 tuberculars
643 chronically ill
620 60 years old or more
240 war invalids
 96 women alone with children
 74 blind

These hard-core survivors needed our help. They had not only been through 3 years of Civil War in Spain, but another *6 years of misery* during WW II. Most of them had been in the grim French concentration camps of Vernet, Gurs, Noë, Argeles, or St. Cyprien. There were those who had fought with the French in WW II in France, Syria, Africa, and Norway. Others had been in the Maquis and were distinguished for their bravery; 10,000 Spanish exiles had been sent to the Nazi KZ at Mauthausen and other camps in Germany, where many had died. A few had returned from Russia via Spain. Some had come and were still coming from Spain after serving long prison sentences, because they had supported the Republic or were caught working in the Spanish underground. Some wives, coming to join their husbands, and others, fleeing persecution, traveled covertly over the Pyrenees. Mothers came with their children, who had suffered through the terrible bombardments in Spain and the miserable deprived years in camps throughout WW II.

About 10 percent of the exiles needed some sort of help because they were chronically ill, were aged, or widowed; and many had come to France already invalids, having lost limbs, eyes, and health during the fratricidal conflict.

During WW II, some of the Spaniards had to register with the Franco consulates in order to get identity cards. International protection was granted them only in July 1945 when a central office for Spanish refugees was set up. The Spaniards were "statutory" refugees and had travel documents in lieu of Nansen passports. In France they were under the legal and administrative protection of the Office Francais de Protection des Refugies et Apatrides (OFPRA), founded July 25, 1952, and which issued cards vouching for them as political refugees.

With the closing of IRO in February 1950, the Service Sociale d'Aide aux Emigrants (SSAE), an independent and nondenominational organization affiliated with the International Social Service, took over the job of assisting refugees in France with funds supplied by the government. During the war years, SSAE helped about 2,000 Spanish refugee cases per year. In 1951 80 percent of their cases were Spaniards. At that time they were giving the aged, ineligible for French pensions, $10 a month—inadequate for survival. The Spanish refugees, who were eligible (having worked in France continuously for 7 years), received $11 to $14 a month, also inadequate. (By 1983, French inflation had increased the old age pension to $263 a month, still inadequate, since the minimum living income was double that amount.) Beside the SSAE, the Quakers (American Friends Service Committee) had helped the Spanish exiles considerably after the war but were now no longer involved. The Unitarian Service Committee had an office in Toulouse helping them in that area. But there was no private organization devoted exclusively to their needs.

By 1952 there were still 160,000 Spanish political exiles in France—13 years after the end of the Civil War. There continued to be more Spanish refugees in France than any other national group of exiles. Many had migrated, mostly to Mexico and Latin America, and a few to various other countries. A number had died, and some had returned to Spain, willingly or by force. But by 1952 only a very few were going back, and those mostly to die. Those with life still before them chose to live it and to raise their children in free France.

THE FRENCH CONCENTRATION CAMPS

The 6 years of misery endured by Spanish refugees during WW II can only be grasped in the context of the French concentration camps. Here almost all the exiles whom we were later to help, had been held. Euphemistically, the camps were called reception, internment or lodging centers.

When Barcelona fell, the borders of France were opened on January 27, 1939 to civilians. Approximately 60,000 males, 170,000 women and children, and 10,000 wounded fled before the victorious Nationalist hordes of Franco. On February 5 approximately 270,000 soldiers of the Republican Army crossed the frontier at Cerbere, Le Perthus, Le Tour-de-Carol and Bourg Madame. The exodus continued until May. (The Mexican Legation and the Ministry of the Interior registered 527,843 individuals.)

After a few months, 100,000 had returned to Spain, by force or voluntarily. As Bartoli and Molins (1944) describe it in *Campos de Concentración 1939–194*. . . "some time around the month of May 1942, the Government of the senile Marshal of Vichy was able to announce to the world that more than 72,000 of these rebels had received burial in the lands of his domains." In November 1944 there were said to be 350,000 Spanish refugees still in France.

Before the end of the Spanish Civil War, France had already spent 88 million francs on aid to refugees after the fall of Irun and San Sebastian (September 1936), Bilbao (June 1937), Santander (August 1937), and Gijon (October 1937). When the new exodus occurred, France first refused to admit Spaniards. The frontier was guarded by a long line of Senegalese. At one point, it was opened, and then closed again. In *Pasion y Muerte. De los Espanoles en Francia,* Montseny (1969) records:

> I remember a horrible sight of a large group of wounded, who were driven back. The Senegalese with sticks in their hands beat them. The mass of humanity, howling and sobbing, fled beneath the blows. Those who fell to the ground were trampled on . . . A prophetic vision, sinister annunciation of what was to be in the very near future, the procedures of the Germans in the occupation of France and the treatment of the French in the concentration camps of Germany. (p. 23)

The new exiles were received in eight provisional camps, seven in the Pyrenees Orientales at Le Boulou, Prats de Mollo, Arles

9. *Gurs, one of the largest French concentration camps, euphemistically called reception, internment, or lodging centers.*

sur Tech, Saint Laurent de Cerdans, La Tour-de-Carol, Bourg-Madame, and Las Haras, and one in the Haute Garonne at Mazeres. Teresa and Manuel Palacios (speaking in French) told me about their stay, in and out of the camp at Le Boulou. His daughter, Carmen, was with them. Later they became very active in the work of our committee.

Teresa Palacios: "My name is Teresa Palacios and I came to France after the Spanish Civil War. We entered at Le Boulou and they put all of us refugees in a big square which was soon completely surrounded by Senegalese. No one could enter or leave. But my husband tricked a Senegalese and got out. And afterwards Manuel told him that he was going to enter, and he'd better remember him because he would be leaving again. The Senegalese didn't understand that Manuel had been inside and he let him enter the square and then he let all three of us leave.

"Afterwards, hiding ourselves of course, because there were a lot of policemen around, we went to a café. It was full of Frenchmen playing cards and having a good time, and we sat down. We had a little money and asked for a coffee. And that is how we started a very long stay of 21 days in a café, sitting at a table, sleeping in a sitting position the first few days.

"Then they ordered all cafés closed at night and that was the most painful time for us because we had to leave the café. All at once we could be arrested because, naturally, we couldn't sleep in the streets. We would have been picked up at once. The police, to be able to seize the refugees, closed down all the public toilets so that the exiles had to use the streets as a bathroom. The cafés had locked their toilets too. So at 3 in the morning we found ourselves completely alone in the street. But we had a pleasant surprise. The owner of the café came out with his wife and said: "It saddens us to see the three of you, come in and we'll hide you." So we went back to the café again, and it was marvelous after 8 days to be able to sleep lying down.

"Shortly after this, the police took over the café. And the owners, when they went to sleep at midnight, gave us the key so that we could open the door for the policemen, who slept above the café. And so, we, the refugees, who were persecuted by them, played porter to all the police! Those who came were not on duty and no one said anything to us. And so we stayed there 21 days.

"For all that time we had only one meal a day: one sardine, a little black coffee with some powdered milk, and a slice of cheese. In our small bag we had brought a silver fork and spoon and for these we were given 12 francs. For our wedding ring we were given 7 francs. With this money we were able to buy some cheese and pay for some coffee, because, after all, it was necessary to pay something to the café. We had to eat a small amount and drink a little in the morning so as to be able to keep going during the day.

"We were able to leave the café when we received a money order for 100 francs from Manuel's brother in Perpignan. Manuel was able to get it at the post office by showing his driver's license. In Spain there were no identification papers. Well, when we had the money to go to Perpignan, we weren't able to leave. But we had found a friend, a Frenchman, who told us: 'You must wait 2 or 3 days for the secret police to come from Paris.' Several days later this friend called us in and said: 'Our friends are here and you must sign a paper asking to go back to Spain.' Manuel told him: 'I can't sign a paper to return to Spain.' We distrusted everybody, even this friend. But in the end he convinced us by saying: 'You can believe that I am a real friend and that I won't trick you. You can sign, don't worry. And then you will see the result.'

"And that Sunday morning I was in the waiting room of the subprefect of Le Boulou. I saw people entering, leaving, entering, leaving. And after everyone had gone, our friend came and said to us: 'Look here, the signature of the Prefect.' And they had changed the 'reentry to Spain' to 'go to Bordeaux via Toulouse.' The Prefect had already signed so many other papers, he didn't look. And they made no difficulties for those who wanted to reenter Spain: they signed your passport immediately. Our friend the policeman was a Leftist, who dared to save Spaniards.

"When we got to Toulouse we went to the hotel and bar of the Opera on the square of the Capitol, where we found the proprietor, a friend who was a socialist. We slept there and the next day our friends took us to Hauterive in the Department of Lot and Garonne. And there we were in a kind of refuge where we passed the days together, only at night there were separate dormitories for men and women. So we were together and not separated."

Manuel: "When the Germans declared war in 1939, almost all the men in the refuge were officers. I was a major during our war. And we offered ourselves for the French army but they wouldn't accept us.[1] They left us in the refuge. And the last day of September they told us that everybody was going to work picking grapes and afterwards the concentration camps. And my brother in Perpignan phoned a friend here, in Montauban, and he sent a taxi to take us from Hauterive to Montauban. We left at 3 in the morning and arrived here at 7 a.m.

"We were taken to a bistro on the rue d'Albert, the red light district of Montauban. And the proprietor received us and told us: 'Here are three mattresses and you can sleep and if you are hungry, the bar is at your disposal. You can eat and drink all you want. I'm going now and I'll be back after 3.' And he left, and we slept. And since September 1939 we have been in Montauban."

This is how Manuel and Teresa left the provisional center of Le Boulou. But many of the refugees were not so lucky, and were sent to concentration camps, which were closed off by barbed wire and guarded by Senegalese with machine guns and by the French Mobile Guard and Spahis (foreign soldiers). Most of the women and children were sent to the interior of France, while the men and families were sent to the two largest camps, St. Cyprien (where there were 102,000 men by March 1940) and Argeles-sur-Mer (where there were another 100,000). At St. Cyprien, barracks were started 2 months after the camp opened. In Argeles there was no distribution of food at all for 3 days.

Pablo Casals (Corredor, 1957) recalls of Argeles and other camps which he often visited:

> These camps were frightful, not because of deliberate cruelty but simply because of the improvisation and confusion which prevailed when they were established. The unfortunate people who were shut up there lacked the most elementary commodities. I realized that my visits brought some consolation. . . . I tried to send small gifts to all those who asked me, and wrote little notes of encouragement. In those days I wrote thousands of letters and postcards (p. 215).

St. Cyprien and Argeles were by the Mediterranean where the refugees slept on the sand, with only the blankets they brought with them as protection from the rain and snow. A hospital, so called, was created after 20 or 25 days, and those who were very ill were sent to a boat called the *Sinai,* anchored at Port Vendres, or to the military hospital of St. Jean in Perpignan. It is no wonder that so many of these refugees today suffer from chronic diseases, often contracted in these miserable camps. From the *outside,* this is how it looked to Genet (in *The New Yorker,* March 11, 1939)

> What we saw was a maze, miles long, of dun-colored shapes which, when viewed close up, turned out to be white men—walking, standing, sitting on sand, sleeping on sand, breathing and eating sand as it blew on food and faces, men living by the thousand on a treeless beach, on the edge of a muddy, soiled sea.

From the *inside,* this is how it felt to Ramon Arquiaga, for 20 months a prisoner of the Spanish Fascists, who had crossed the frontier into France on February 11:

> We were sent directly to St. Cyprien. And there was nothing to eat, all on the sand, full of misery. We had walked to France without anything. They took us like wild beasts. A civilized country they say, but they spoke of the Spanish people as wild beasts. We spent 2 months in this camp. And the French Fifth Column came, Laroque's people, and went from camp to camp and barrack to barrack everywhere—it was we who had made the barracks because we were on the ground. And the Fascists said to us: "There are two paths to follow, go to Franco or go to the Legion." But we didn't want to go to either. Some people did go to the Legion, I don't know why, and 11,000 died in the Legion.

Of Argeles-sur-Mer Antonio Gomez writes:

> I shall never forget the fact that when one entered a camp, the human instinct disappeared almost completely. It was difficult to find anyone who was touched by the sufferings of another. Each one for himself, as if in a shipwreck. After being in the camp for a while, without hygiene or any sort of conveniences, we had become like bandits, dirty, unshaven, clothed in the oldest clothes and full of lice. Despite hunger, cold, and misery, I was surprised one Christmas. I don't know where they found the guitars or the desire to sing. But the songs that I had heard in my childhood were heard coming from various barracks, with singing, dancing, and hand-clapping. Another memory of the camp in that year of the floods—fearful of dying by drowning, the men's and women's camps got together and 9

months later the hospital at Perpignan had to put in an annex to the maternity ward, as the one they had was too small (result of the Spanish temperament)!

Besides Argeles and St. Cyprien, the other camps specifically created for the Spanish exiles were Barcares, P.O., which was the best equipped of the camps and had a little more than 20,000 men in it; Gurs, B.P. for the Basques and Internationals; Septfonds, T. et G., for technical and qualified workers; Bram, Aude, for intellectuals and old men; and Agde, Herault, part of it specifically for Catalans. There was also a disciplinary camp for about 400 men at Collioure, P.O., a horribly sadistic and cruel place, and two for women at Mont Louis and Reineros.

The most infamous of the French concentration camps was Le Vernet d'Arige, "a prison rather than a camp." Its loudspeaker proclaimed "Whoever goes within 2 yards of the barbed wire will be shot." It lay about 30 miles north of the Spanish border, 50 acres of mud when it rained; in good weather, rock and dust. This reception center was laid out early in 1939 to house Durruti's[2] 26th Anarchist Division, and for the men of the International Brigades who had fought in Spain. Later it was to hold over 3,000 inmates of 33 different nationalities, the largest number being Spaniards and the next Jews. Arthur Koestler and Gustav Regler, who have written about it, were among the many anti-Nazi intellectuals who passed through Vernet. Regler (1959) writes:

Vernet was an eerie cemetery. The huts stood like great coffins on the plain. Every morning the dead crept out of their graves to form up in rigid squares, a pathetic soldiery, and then, under the orders of uniformed men, went about the work of clearing paths, digging drains, stopping up ratholes, burning foul straw and cleaning their coffins . . . . But sometimes one of the dead, unable to endure the cemetery, would kill himself a second time. When we cut him down from the beam from which he hung, we had a feeling of picking a ripe fruit, and we felt something like envy when we laid him to rest in the real cemetery of the camp. . . . A man was by himself again (p. 334).

Koestler (1948) records:

> There were 200 men to a barrack, which measured 9 by 15 feet. Inside were two upper and two lower platforms with a passage between—50 men to a platform, five to a compartment; each man had 21 inches to sleep in. There were no windows, only shutters, no stove during the winter of '39, no lighting, blankets for half the inmates, no soap. The daily ration was 11 ounces of bread, unsugared coffee in the morning and a pint of "soup" at noon and at night, made up of chick peas, lentils, or vermicelli (often full of maggots and with no fat). In winter, road-building from 8 to 11 a.m. and 1 to 4 p.m. Beating up was a daily occurrence.

Soon after the Armistice was signed between Hitler and Vichy, the Gestapo paid its first visit to Vernet, looking for volunteers to work in Germany. Only a few went; but later they were forced to go. In late 1941 and early 1942 about 2,000 Spaniards were taken from Vernet to Africa to work on the Trans-Sahara Railroad (the "death train"). The Gestapo took over Le Vernet on June 9, 1944 and all but the wounded were sent to Buchenwald. Among them were many Spanish refugees. Vernet was closed June 30th, 1944, when the last five Jews were deported.

When I visited Le Vernet in 1967 only a few of the old barracks were left, and were being used by farmers. And there, in a field of corn and nettles, was the cemetery, surrounded by barbed wire. In the center was a monument to the dead, decorated with artificial flowers, from the comrades of those who had died. Some of the graves were empty; the Germans had come for their dead, and some of the Jews had been taken by their friends in Israel. Recently, a Spaniard's body had been taken to Toulouse for reburial. Wooden crosses without names stood among the weeds and there were many mounds with no marker at all. A man at a nearby gas station told me that the farmers are anxious to have all the bodies removed and placed in another garveyard. But it hasn't been done, because there were protests. The documentation on the dead is at Saverdun.

FORCED LABOR IN FRANCE:
"We prefer to die, it doesn't matter where, before bowing our heads to Franco."

Soon after the camps were established and barracks built, the French started to form the Groupement de Travailleurs Etrangers: (GTE), Foreign Labor Groups, to use the Spanish refugees. Pablo Casals described them as "a modern version of organized slavery." At first there were groups of 100 headed by a French captain of the Army Reserve, with a refugee as interpreter. Later, all immigrants between the ages of eighteen and fifty-five who had no jobs were sent to the groups and so were the *prestataires* (volunteers in the French Army). Then the GTEs were organized into groups of 250 men with two commanders, a French Captain and a Spanish one.

Eventually there were over 1,600 of these GTEs in France. They were used to fortify frontiers and later in agriculture, the mines, and forests. The Nazi Todt organization used them to work on the Atlantic Wall at Calais, Brest, Cherburg, and Bordeaux. In Bordeaux alone, 5,000 men were working as forced laborers, most of them Spaniards. The hours were 6 a.m. to 6 p.m. with 1 hour off at noon. There were day and night shifts. The pay in the GTEs was supposed to be 50 centimes a day. By the end of 1940 220,000 Spaniards were estimated to be doing forced labor in France.

Francisco Bardes Font was one of them. When I met him, he was seventy-three, living in a leaky òld shack in Perpignan, making a little money by selling junk. Since he was a congenial man, his neighbors invited him to spend a month in the mountains during the summer—"like the millionaires," he said to me. He often spent his winters in the hospital because of heart trouble and the damp and cold in his "home." But when I taped him, he still had the courage and spirit that carried him through his years as a forced laborer in France. Speaking in French, he commenced by describing his early life.

10. Francisco Bardes Font lived in Perpignan in 1967 in a leaky old shack and made a little money by selling junk.

Francisco Bardes Font: "I was born on November 11, 1895 in Castello de Ampurias in the Province of Gerona. I went to school until I was thirteen. Then I made my Communion like everybody, and went to work with my family. They were farm workers, and I took care of the cows and all that. But I always had books under my arm and I spent my days reading, reading, reading. I read everything and I was specially interested in foreign languages. But since there was no possibility for me to go to a proper school, I wanted to go to work. My father died in 1910 and I told my mother I wanted to go into the Navy. She didn't want it because one could drown in those boats. At last she agreed that I had to follow my ideas, and I joined the infantry regiment of St. Quentin in Figueras. As I was only fourteen I became a bugler, but when I came of age, I asked to become a soldier and I went to school.

"There were disturbances in Africa and one soldier was half dead with fright at having to go there. As I've always been adventurous, I asked him, 'Are you afraid? If you like, we'll find the colonel, and I'll go for you.' And he said: 'Oh, yes!' You see, I wanted to leave because exams were coming and I hadn't studied much. If I took the exams somewhere else it would be easier. So I took his place and left. My mother didn't want that either.

"I arrived in Morocco in March. The Lieutenant said 'Do you know how to write?' 'Yes, sir.' 'Sit down there.' I sat down and he dictated to me, about the battalion number one of the Catalonian Mountain Infantry to which he belonged. I started to write, and then he said, 'Stop a moment.' He took the page and said: 'Did you write that?' and I said, 'Yes, I think so, sir.' He said: 'Good, you stay here in the office with me.' Well, I stayed in the office at Melilla for a month.

"But I wasn't happy there. I wanted to see the country, you know. That's youth! He said: 'Well, you can leave but you'll regret it.' One fine day they gave me a gun, my equipment, and I was off to the mountains to a billeting in the direction of Rio de Oro. I was in a company that crossed the river of St. Fernando de Sevignola. Then I came back to Melilla to rest. Later I joined the native police, the Moroccan Guards, and I became a sergeant. We were in an engagement near Tangiers and I was wounded. Afterwards I changed companies and was under a captain who was the son of General Barrera.[3] I told him that he should check on the munitions and provisions. He told me, 'That's none of my business, don't bother me.' Later, some character sold all our munitions to the Moors and there was an investigation. I was accused. I had witnesses . . . but the other was son of the General. Sick with the African fever, I returned to my village in Spain as a common soldier.

"The Mayor of Castello de Ampurias found me and said, 'Listen, come and work in my office.' I did, and was there until Primo de Rivera [dictator, 1923-1930] kicked us all out. Later I worked at the exposition and then at the bus company in Barcelona. Well, I worked everywhere, I'm not ashamed to work, you understand. When the Republic came I went back to my village and the Mayor, Josep Borras de la Cuesta, a very intelligent man, asked for me. He said, 'Now we're going to reorganize all these people so that things work as they should.' We did a lot of good things: fixed up the streets and made sewers and installed central electricity. I handled the administration because most of the time we didn't have a secretary.

"When the war came and everyone went to the front, they said, 'You're a soldier, you must go to the front.' I said, 'I'll go when my turn comes, like the others.' Later the General Staff at Figueras said, 'It's not necessary for you to present yourself. You will take care of the Mayor's office and you will also take care of the Naval Base at Rosas as far as Palamos.' I bought the uniform of a Naval Officer as I belonged to the Navy at that time, and I stayed there until the end. At one on the night of February 6th, 1939, I crossed the frontier at Cerbere.

"I wanted to go to Perpignan because my wife was there. But the police stopped me and sent me to a concentration camp at Argeles-sur-Mer. And now my life as a prisoner started. There we were, 80,000 of us, women, men and soldiers on the sand with no shelter, without blankets, without anything at all. In February it snowed a lot, everything was frozen, and every day 20 or 30 died of the cold. There were a lot of wounded and there was no way to take care of them. We spent 5 days without eating and the fifth day trucks came loaded with bread. They threw the bread in and those who caught it were asphyxiated by the weight of those who jumped on them. After a few days they started to organize us into groups of 100 and they gave us bread, coffee, beans, margarine, and soap. But we had no pots for cooking. We managed as we could with tin cans.

"The month of March started colder than ever and there were no barracks. They said that the men over forty-five, who wanted to, could change camps. I signed up to go to the camp of Bram in the Aude. There at least we had barracks, didn't suffer from the cold, and were well fed. We were guarded by the police and the Mobile Guards. Sometimes we were sent out to the mountains to cut branches for making brooms.

"In September men were needed for the grape harvest. I signed up, thinking that at least we would have the grapes to eat, and I hoped that I would be able to go to Perpignan and find my wife. On the 15th I was taken with a contingent of 1,500 men. They gave us a can of sardines for five, put us in a box car for horses, and closed it up. At Bordeaux the doors were opened and we got out. There were 20 cars and when the police ordered us to get in again, we refused, for it was already 2 days that we had nothing to eat. The Police told the Prefecture about our rebellion and the Prefect came to the station with an interpreter and asked why we refused to get into the train. We told him, and after a few minutes, nurses from the Red Cross came with bread, paté, and bottles of cider. Everyone ate and drank and then we got on the train and were taken to Caen in Calvados, Normandy.

"When we arrived there, landowners were waiting who wanted workers to harvest sugar beets. They looked us over as if they were looking at cows and horses. I and ten others were taken by a Mrs. Bekaer to work on a farm at Aras-de-Manneville. We were well received by this woman. She was Belgian and her husband had been mobilized in the Belgian Army. I worked there until November when I went to work for Mrs. Arthur Casigneul in the village of Banneville-la-Campagne. She had a large house and big farm. They gave me eight horses. I had never in my life touched a horse, but one adapts oneself. They paid us 100 francs a month. It was nothing, but the food was good and our mistress was very nice to us.

"When war was declared and the Germans were nearing Paris, I said to my buddies, 'I'm not going to stay here, we must leave.' The mistress didn't want us to go but we were afraid of falling into the hands of the Germans. Sebastian Suganyes, Joaquin Cabanez, and I walked 32 days on foot before arriving at Marmande in Lot and Garonne. When we reached Couterne, the Germans were there. They saw us passing and asked us, 'What is this, are you Jews?' 'No, Spaniards! 'Ah, Spanish. Good comrades, good comrades.' They took us to a café and gave us something to drink. And I wanted to leave. There were several French soldiers with us, who had put on civilian clothes. We told them that they should let the Spaniards do the talking, otherwise we would be seized right away. We were able to leave.

"We went to Bordeaux, always on foot. We went to sleep in a barrack and a German officer, who spoke very good Spanish, told us, 'Beat it, as fast as you can. We are O.K., but behind us the Gestapo is coming and they have no mercy. But don't tell anyone that I warned you.' It was good advice and we escaped. We went to Marmande in the Free Zone and I hoped to go to Perpignan. We were at the Lodging Center for 4 or 5 days and I was working with a buddy, Anton Pastor, in the house of the Mayor of Mauvezin-sur-Gupie. Then an order came from the military command post of Marmande to pick up all Spaniards. The police came and took us to a military depot at the Reconstruction Works. For several days we were with trucks collecting clothes, guns, all the things thrown away by the army on the roads. After that we were ordered to leave for the National Powder Works at Sainte-Livrade. And there once again they formed the 83rd Company of Foreign Workers.

"This 83rd was sent to Annecy in the Haute Savoie to make strategic roads to go up to the Col Cherol. At 11 one night, we were ordered to evacuate. There was snow everywhere in the mountains; it was all white and we couldn't see. We lost our way, our suitcases, everything. We arrived in the morning, below at Doussard. Trucks took us to Albi sur Cheran, also in Savoie. I joined a group of 10 to repair the local roads with a road mender. We were there until May when we were ordered to leave again. The 516th Group attached to Lyon was reformed at St. Thibaud de Couz. We were here until 1943, working for the French as woodcutters and colliers. Afterwards the group was dissolved and we were attached to the Fifth Group at Voglans.

"On the 8th of June 1943, the special police came. They shut us up and tied us two by two, like criminals, to take us to the Germans at Lyon. At the station they asked us to sign documents saying that we were going to work voluntarily. We didn't want to and no one signed. That night they put us in cattle cars and gave us boiled potatoes to eat, without bread, without anything. We were 5 days going from Lyon to Brest, and during those 5 days they gave us nothing, not even water.

"When we arrived in Brest the Germans treated us to everything. There was a Portuguese-German from Brazil and he called us "Reds, sons of a bitch, Reds, Reds." Then they took us on a train to the Fort of Saint-Pierre-Quiberon. We arrived there at night and were told we must pay 600 francs for a mess-plate and a blanket. Those who didn't have the money did without. They put us in barracks in the moat of the Fort. Later, with bayonets on their guns, they brought us back to the submarine base at Brest. At the office they asked us our professions. As there was no equivalent for mayor's secretary I was put in the shovel-and-pickaxe brigade.

"We worked there every day of the week on night and day shifts. I was attached to a brigade run by an SS type named Blankenor. He wasn't happy unless he was doing harm. He hit people on the head to relieve his anger, or forced us to jump into the sea completely dressed and then made us work without letting us get dry. We were hungry and he threw moldy bread into the water and when we went to get it, he would pull it away so that we couldn't reach it. There were many Jews there and they were forced to work without food. We used to hide masses of raw potatoes so that they would have something to eat.

"When the Americans were approaching, we were shut up for 3 days. Then they launched a terrible bombing and the dead piled up. I had difficulty believing that a base like that, with a 54-foot-thick roof, could be destroyed by planes, as it was. It wasn't just waves of four or five planes, but of 50. One after the other they began to drop bombs. One could see nothing, not even the sun. The Germans ran in every direction, while we went into the shelters that we had just constructed, 33 yards under the mountain. But I and my friend, Villacamps, were pushed out of the shelter as bombs were falling everywhere.

"Then I said to my friend, 'We must escape. Let's see if we can find the Americans.' We brought some scissors and cut the wires and left at night. When we arrived at Landerneau, we saw a German car coming and we hid in the bushes. At that moment the wire of a mine was tripped and it exploded. But we were able to throw ourselves on the ground. The Germans arrived, shouting 'Terrorists, terrorists.' 'No, not terrorists, just workers.' Menacing us with machine guns, they took us to the barracks in Landerneau. There we were joined by four young men who were blindfolded, and the Germans sent us all back to the naval base in Brest.

"On the way, I asked these boys, 'What's going on?' They said, 'Don't say anything. We are in the Maquis and they caught us. It's all over for us!' They were Bretons. Well, we were taken to the base to a General who was with the Goering division of parachutists. And he said, 'Was ist das?' and the others said 'Terrorists, terrorists!' But just then a German named Theo passed by, who had worked in the canteen and knew me and Villacamps. He saluted the General and said 'Comrades, comrades, Spaniards.' The General said *'Heraus,'* and Theo took us, saying, 'Come quickly, and don't look back.' We heard shots, they were shooting the four little ones who had come with us. Theo said, 'If I hadn't arrived at the moment you would have gone with them. They took you for terrorists.' Well, he took us away and hid us. A good man.

"Later, while we were working, I and some pals diverted a train of equipment which fell into the sea. The Germans took us immediately and sent us by boat to the island of Guernsey as punishment. We worked there only at night. We were given one small meal a day until we were reduced to eating the dogs and cats. When the Red Cross came with food, the Germans took everything. Many of our comrades died of hunger.

"Then the Liberation came. We got into a boat again and when we arrived at Brest were taken to the Americans. They had officers who spoke Spanish and we explained our situation. I said, 'Listen, we were prisoners, we are civilians, we aren't the military. We were forced to work here and now you have come to liberate us.' It's funny, looking back on it. They made us leave the base and put us in another concentration camp!

"I thought, well, it starts off nicely! Then the French came and wanted us to stay with them. The others said, 'No, no—forward, forward.' They put us in trucks with the Germans and took us to Saint-Agonais, a camp where there were Russians, everybody, a whole mixture. From there they took us to Cherbourg, we got on a landing boat, and they sent us to England. Arriving at Southampton we were sent to Sheffield. There they put us in a partially bombed out factory and again we were surrounded by barbed wire. In our barracks there were Germans, Russians, Yugoslavs, Danes, Norwegians, Spaniards, Greeks—well, 17 nationalities in all. I went around with the Spaniards (I found myself with the same comrades who were with me in Savoia), the Hungarians and the Romanians. There was a Romanian who spoke a little Spanish and another spoke Italian, and like that we understood each other. I wrote a letter to the head of the camp asking why we were there but he didn't answer.

"Then we were moved to another camp in Lancashire. And again I wrote to the commander—and the same. Well, one day I said to myself, I must do something, and I started talking to an English soldier. I said, 'I want to know why I am here, I and my comrades?' And he said, 'Oh, as for that, I've been waiting for my retirement here for 30 years and I'm still here. You Spaniards want to go too fast. You must go slowly, put one foot forward and if it holds, then advance the other!'

"We changed camps again and they took us to Kirkham. There they put all the Spaniards together. One day a comrade told me, 'I've had enough, and I'm going to get my freedom somehow.' I said, 'You'll leave dressed like a prisoner and wherever you go the police will find you right away.' He said, 'I don't give a damn.' Well, he slept above me and that night I heard *brnnn*, glass breaking. I looked and he wasn't there. The soldiers came up right away and said, 'Who is that fellow who threw himself out the window?' They took him to the hospital at Preston and he lived for 3 days. A journalist came and asked for information and that fellow said, 'I am a Spaniard and I wanted to kill myself so that people would know we are here and want our freedom.' The next day some Generals came and they took us to a village near Preston. The commander told us, 'If you behave well, you will be all right here, otherwise you will be punished.' We said, 'We want to be free and treated decently.'

"At this time a friend of the Spaniards came from London to ask after us and was told there were no Spaniards, although there were 260. And we went on a hunger strike for 6 days. They asked, 'What do you want to do, die?' 'Yes, we prefer to die than to remain like this. Do what you like, but the responsibility will be on England and America.' We scared them. After we wrote to the French Consulate in London, they freed us and let us go everywhere. The French came and told us, 'We didn't know you were here in this situation. We'll arrange everything. Do you want to go to France, or do you prefer to stay here?' I said, 'I prefer to go to France.' So they came and took our photos for passports and on Christmas Day, 1945 we left. But as there was no transportation, we had to wait until February 5, 1946 to embark. I was in the 166th Prisoner of War Camp.

"When I arrived in Perpignan, my wife was in Spain and I never saw her again. I corresponded with her and when her father died I sent a letter of sympathy. But I didn't get an answer and it's now 8 or 10 years since I know anything about her.

"As long as Franco is there in Spain, we won't go back, nothing doing. If the regime changes, even if they put in a king, we will return. When we left Spain, we vowed never to return as long as Franco was there. We prefer to die, it doesn't matter where, before bowing our heads to Franco. Some have gone and are in prison and others have been killed, after the amnesty too. I prefer to die here, 40,000 times. We have an ideal, to do good and not evil. We want to transform humanity so that all the world can live in brotherhood. We want everyone to live decently while they are on this earth, working, eating and living well. We don't want more than that. I'm a Left Republican and my party is called Izquierda Catalan of Spain. My trade union is the Confederacion Nacional de Trabajo, the CNT. Those are the two organizations I belong to. But the Communist party? No, no, no. They profited at the expense of others. We went to the front to fight and they created disorders and incidents in the rear. The Communists promoted the disorders in May in Barcelona. There were many deaths, many deaths. If Durruti hadn't died at the front, and we had won the war, everything would have been different. But they took care to eliminate him."[4]

NOTES

1. Victor Serge remarks of the refugees in *Memoirs of a Revolutionary, 1901—1941*, Oxford University Press, 1963: "It would have been quite easy to accept them in ordinary life, settle them in districts with declining population, arrange for families to take in the children and youngsters—and even to recruit from their numbers one or two crack divisions for the defence of France, herself under threat of attack. None of these ideas occurred to anybody." p. 346
2. Buonaventura Durruti, militant of the CNT and FAI, killed on the Madrid front, November 20, 1936.
3. General Emilio Barrera was one of the signers of the treaty with Mussolini to aid the rebels. He was shot by the Republicans at Guadalajara at the beginning of the Spanish Civil War.
4. There were many theories about Durruti's death: killed by the enemy, by the Communists, by his own people, or in an accident by his own gun.

7

Setting up SRA

*T*he story of Francisco Bardes Font is a sharp example of the fate of many Spanish refugees in those 6 miserable years from the end of the Spanish Civil War in March 1939 until VE Day, May 8, 1945. He and all those comrades stood in need of our help.

Our first leaflet, *Proposals for a committee to Aid Spanish Refugees in France,* listed 7 basic needs:

1. Used clothing, specially for men
2. Regular monthly subsidies for the Republican Red Cross Dispensaries in Montauban and Toulouse
3. Help for 90 people in hospitals
4. Aid for 754 tuberculars
5. Special help, such as sewing machines, hearing aids, work tools, artificial limbs
6. Bedding—100 people were in need of this in Perpignan alone
7. A clearing house for information

These proposals, drawn up by Dwight and me, were sent out on December 10, 1952 with an appeal in my name on the letterhead of PPA. They went to friends who had contributed before asking them to give something for Christmas for the Spanish refugees. I explained that a committee was being organized and that James T. Farrell, the novelist, had agreed to be chairman. We collected $600 for Christmas and another $525 came in before our incorporation papers were received.

On December 14, Margaret De Silver, a friend from the old days, who was to become our Treasurer, took me to have lunch with Louise Crane at the Hotel Seville. Louise was about to start publishing *Iberica* magazine, and her close friend, Victoria Kent, who had been Director General of Prisons for the Spanish Republican Government and was now their representative-in-exile in New York, was to be editor. We discussed our mutual interests and Louise promised to help us. Our first meeting was in her home at 820 Fifth Avenue and her first contribution in April 1953 was $500. She helped us every year thereafter, and over 31 years contributed a total of $106,775. I often called on her in a financial crisis; she always generously responded. Her mother and brother between them gave $114,950 during those 31 years. Louise's *Iberica,* came out monthly from 1953–1974.

Margaret De Silver, who became SRA's Treasurer, sent a contribution every month from the beginning until her death in 1962 at the age of seventy-two. She had helped us with money for *politics* during the forties. She was a founder and the treasurer of the New World Resettlement Fund, whose Chairman had been Oswald Garrison Villard and Executive Secretary, America Gonzalez. During the forties they had helped Spanish refugee families in France to resettle in Ecuador. Margaret's first husband, Albert De Silver, was a founder of the American Civil Liberties Union. He died in an accident. Her second husband, Carlo Tresca, an Italian anarchist, who fought both Fascists and Communists, was murdered on Fifth Avenue and 15th Street one evening in 1943.

At a memorial meeting for Margaret at the Community Church, Norman Thomas said of her: "She was one of the forthright people who don't ask, 'What is life?' but give meaning to it; one whose goodness made the world better; a dear friend whom we have loved and lost, but not from memory."

In December 1952 I also wrote to Mary McCarthy, George Woodcock, Dorothy Day, Norman Thomas, A.J. Muste, Jesus de Galindez, Jaume Miravittles, Arthur Schlesinger, Jr., and Waldo Frank. I asked them to be sponsors of a committee to be called Spanish Refugee Aid; it "will have James T. Farrell as Chairman, Margaret De Silver as Treasurer, and I will be the Executive. We will have offices in the old *politics* office and I expect the overhead will be very low."

They all agreed to lend their names. By our first meeting on February 24, 1953, we had 44 prominent sponsors. (See appendix 1 for list of all our sponsors during 31 years) Farrell was responsible for our seven trade unionists. There were six Spaniards, whom I had contacted, and five prominent Europeans (Albert Camus, Christopher Isherwood, and Mrs. George Orwell, as well as the English anarchists Sir Herbert Read and George Woodcock).

We also had five religious sponsors, two musicians, nine Americans in arts and letters, four involved in politics, and six miscellaneous sympathizers with the cause. Best of all, Pablo Casals had agreed to become our Honorary Chairman.

PABLO CASALS

Although, as I have noted, Casals was in Switzerland at the time I tried to see him when I was in Perpignan in 1952, I had better luck in 1954. A friend gave me these instructions: "Go in the morning at 12 or at 5 p.m. to see Mme. Capdevilla. She is beautiful and proud and full of emotion. You can talk with her about anything that's in your heart and she has great understanding. . . . she was Casals' first pupil and she is taking zealous care of the great man . . . Walk in the big iron gate, go into the front door of the little house on the left and walk up the little stairs and knock on the glass. If this isn't one of the big moments of your life, I'll eat my hat." It was, indeed, a thrilling experience and very moving when he played some Bach for me and my son, Michael ("he groans when he plays and closes his eyes—but wonderful").

In the meantime he had agreed in February 1953 to become our Honorary Chairman, and to sign a letter appealing for funds. He was very appreciative of what we had been able to do so far. From the beginning we decided to put aside $50 a month for him to distribute personally among the many exiles who came to see him or wrote to him. He was deeply concerned about the fate of his fellow exiles.

Pablo, Pau Casals, "Le Maitre," as he was variously called, was born on December 29, 1876 in Vendrell, Spain. He was married on April 4, 1914 in New Rochelle, New York to the American singer, Susan Metcalfe. After 14 years together they separated and in the spring of 1957 divorced. During the many years in Prades his friend, Sra. Frasquita Capdevila, shared his exile. She was the widow of Casals's friend, Sr. Capdevila, who had been treasurer of the Orquesta Pau Casals in Barcelona. When he died in 1920 he made Casals promise to take care of Frasquita, who suffered from Parkinson's disease. She had lived with him ever since, till her death in January 1955. She was buried next to Casals's mother in the Vendrell cemetery. The only time that Casals returned to Spain was for her funeral. Casals married his pupil, Marta Montanez, on August 5, 1957.

During the Spanish Civil War Casals gave numerous benefit concerts abroad to raise money for the Republic. In 1938 he broadcast an appeal: "Do not commit the crime of letting the Spanish Republic be murdered. If you allow Hitler to win in Spain, you will be the next victims of his madness. The war will spread to all Europe, to the whole world. Come to the aid of our people!"

Soon after the end of the Spanish Civil War, in the autumn of 1939 Casals settled in Prades, and vowed never to return to Spain until Franco was gone. He immediately set to work to help his compatriots in the French detention camps. With Catalan friends and exiles he bought food and clothing to distribute. As we have noted, he personally visited many camps and wrote thousands of letters and cards to comfort and encourage the Spanish exiles.

11. Pablo Casals (right) arriving a the Perpignan airport in 1965.

In 1940 Casals was invited to become President of the Spanish Republican Government-in-Exile, but declined. In 1945 he broke off a concert tour in England to protest the policy of the democracies toward Franco. For many years thereafter he made no public musical appearances until the famous Prades Festival started in 1950, when he justified his appearance there because these concerts were in honor of Bach.

Throughout the years I made many proposals to Casals for special help. In May 1953, at the suggestion of the cellist Bernard Greenhouse and the moviemaker Robert Snyder, I asked if Casals might make a record of Catalan songs with a statement about Spanish refugees. He did not reply. On March 29, 1956, we suggested an eightieth birthday celebration at Carnegie Hall. Again I talked to Greenhouse and Herbert Barrett, the manager of the Bach Aria Group. They talked to William Scheide; all were enthusiastic. We wanted Casals to conduct. He wrote: "I wish I could say yes to your suggestion to conduct or taking part in it. I *cannot.* You know my strong reasons—although these have nothing to do with my love for America and the American people."

In 1958 when Casals came to the U.S. to plead for peace at the U.N., and where he played Bach's Sonata for Cello and Piano, #2 in D major, with Horszowski and finished his plea by playing his Catalan *Song of the Birds,* I once again urged him to do something specifically for SRA, to no avail.

In May 1961 he wrote me regarding his Oratorio *El Pessebre* (The Manger): "If I see a possibility of doing something on behalf of the Spanish Refugees, I will certainly do it, but things will be much better if I arrange them personally. There are many things involved and one must be careful of details which can be of great importance; there are the musical matters, and organization, etc. Unfortunately there are also political implications which, if not treated carefully can ruin our good intentions. So please let me see if something can be done; you can be sure that no one has more interest and more willingness to help our refugees than myself." Again, in November 1961 he wrote, "Be assured that as soon as I see a propitious occasion I will see to the arrangement of this concert." But despite his "good intentions," that "propitious occasion" never arose.

In January 1962, Louise Crane, one of our most devoted "angels," wrote me: "It has been most disturbing to me and to many other American contributors to Spanish Refugee Aid, that your Honorary Chairman, Sr. Casals, has not yet given a concert in this country for the benefit of the Spanish refugees. To my knowledge, in addition to his appearance and sponsorship of the Casals Festival in Puerto Rico, Sr. Casals has made three appearances in recent years; first at the United Nations, secondly at the home of Mr. David Rockefeller, a benefit for the Israel-American Cultural Society, and now recently at the White

House.[1] Yet he has given no concert for the benefit of the Spanish refugees." She offered a donation of $10,000 to underwrite one for SRA. "Not only would the Spanish refugees be materially and morally aided by such a concert, but the attendant publicity would be of inestimable value in calling attention to their plight." The U.S. Committee for refugees offered to sponsor the concert but Casals turned them down and didn't respond to Louise Crane's offer.

In Prades during the 1940s Casals composed his oratorio *El Pessebre,* his "message of peace." In May 1961 he told us that if it were performed in the U.S. he would consider making the occasion a benefit for SRA. It was performed for the first time in San Francisco in April 1962 with Casals conducting, and again at Carnegie Hall on June 22. In the next 10 years it was performed almost 70 times all over the world but never as a benefit for SRA. In 1962 the Pablo Casals Foundation was formed to receive the profits of the performances of *El Pessebre.* The first donation of $5,000 was sent to SRA. But that was hardly the same as having a concert just for us. In 1970 Casals gave a benefit performance at Columbia and when I asked for a similar benefit for SRA, Marta Casals, who since 1963 attended to all the "Maitre's" correspondence, suggested something for the fall. But nothing came of that.

This wily "Catalonian peasant," as someone called him, caused me many frustrations and much disillusionment. But even if Casals would not give a benefit for SRA, I could not forget that this was the man who gave up appearing in public for many years and remained in exile all the rest of his life, refusing to accept the Franco regime. I knew he really cared about the fate of his fellow exiles. At every concert where he played the cello, "his weapon," he played *El Cant dels Ocells* ("The Song of the Birds"), a medieval Catalan folk melody which he called "the theme of the Spanish exiles," and which conveyed "what was closest to my heart, freedom for my people." For many years this man insisted on answering all the letters and appeals for aid from his fellow exiles, saying "Every letter means something human. When a person takes pen and paper and writes to me, he has an idea, a hope connected with me, and at the very least I must respond to this, from common humanity.'' As our Honorary Chairman, he helped us get established in our early years and subsequently provided both spiritual and financial support. After he died at ninety-six on October 22, 1973, his widow, Marta Casals, continued to make appeals for SRA and sent us contributions.

On March 5th, 1953, Spanish Refugee Aid (SRA) became a membership corporation and our papers, drawn up by our lawyer, Ernest Fleischman, were signed by James T. Farrell, Mary McCarthy, Arthur Schlesinger, Jr., George N. Shuster, and Norman Thomas. We were granted tax exemption from the U.S. Treasury Department in December 1954. Our first office was "the old office," at 45 Astor Place, the Bible House, where *Partisan Review, politics,* and *politics Packages Abroad* had had offices. We paid $18.75 a month (by 1983 our rent at 80 East 11 Street, where we had moved in 1954 had risen to $550 plus electricity).

Over its lifetime, SRA had a Board of Directors of 9 to 20 members and 40 individuals served on the Board from 1953—1983. (see Appensix) I became Executive Secretary (later Director and Chairman) at a salary of $25 a week. When I retired I was making $160. Margaret De Silver was our Treasurer until her death in 1962, when she was followed by her son, Harrison De Silver. James T. Farrell was our Chairman from 1953–1958. He was followed by Mary McCarthy (1958–1960), Hannah Arendt (1960–1967), and Dwight Macdonald (from 1967 until his death in December 1982). I was Chairman from 1982–1984.

Our first of 80 board meetings in the home of Louise Crane was the only meeting I missed in 32 years. I had German measles; Dwight reported for me. Dwight said that we had $771.72 on hand, we owed $150 for clothing bought from Nancy's cleaner (clothes cleaned but not called for) and we agreed to buy $150 worth more. We voted a budget of $50,000 for the year, we had 600 cases to help and funds were to be distributed in France by Mme. Albert Camus and Pablo Casals.

Two more Board meetings followed in March and April, where we decided to ask to be on approval of the State Department

Advisory Committee on Voluntary Foreign Aid (we later voted not to participate, believing it would not be useful to us); and arranged for our lawyer to prepare by-laws. We also voted to send $100 a month to the Montauban and Toulouse Spanish Republican Red Cross Dispensaries.

SRA AND THE COMMUNISTS

The question of the Communists and Spanish Refugee Aid arose even before our first Board meeting. Arthur Schlesinger, Jr., one of our founders, wrote me in February 1952 that the committee's appeal "should be, in my judgment, humanitarian and not political; i.e., there would be nothing in it incompatible with support for a military agreement with France. . . . As for the Communist issue, I would get around that by making the committee so unmistakably anti-Communist in its composition that the issue would not easily arise." However, the question did arise, and in all sorts of ways.

Our incorporation papers stated as our purpose "to improve the individual and social conditions and alleviate the human suffering and distress of Spanish Republican, Anti-Communist Refugees." Our tax exemption papers said that "The purpose of this organization is to give aid to Spanish refugees who presently reside in France. These refugees are non-Communist and, because of their 14 years of exile. . . . . " Our by-laws also made reference to non-Communist refugees.

Our first general circular stated that "At least 90 percent of the Spanish refugees are strong anti-Communists, with vivid memories of Communist treachery and terror during the Civil War. The tiny pro-Communist minority is cared for by the well-heeled Communist movement, but the great non-Communist majority has been shamefully neglected by the free world. Spanish Refugee Aid has been set up to help this majority." We felt that because so many of the committees to aid Spain and the Republicans during and after the Spanish Civil War had been Communist-oriented that we had to make it very clear where we stood. For almost 10 years we kept this statement in our circulars, although in 1959 a number of people objected. But our Board voted to characterize the Communists as we had from the beginning.

In 1960 and 1961 we printed in our general circular a long quotation from our Honorary Chairman, Pablo Casals, headed "Are They Communists?" In 1963, however, we cut the statement so that it read, "Politically, they were Socialists or Anarcho-Syndicalists, members of one of the two great working class movements of pre-Franco Spain. The Spanish refugees have always been ardent anti-Communists as well as anti-Fascists."

The first attack on SRA came from the Right through the Medway Plan Foundation. This was a grass roots, person-to-person outfit run by William Montgomery Bennett, a retired economist, who had helped found the organization in 1948. In 1953 they claimed to have secured the "adoption" of 3,000 aged, ill, or permanently disabled refugees and to have raised $3,000,000 for them. I heard about this foundation from Charles Sternberg of the International Rescue Committee and I decided it could be very helpful to SRA. They were working along the lines used by *politics* Packages Abroad, and their aim was a combination of material aid and moral support. They also claimed to be working for a peaceful world. So I wrote to Bennett in Woodbury, Connecticut where he lived, confined to a wheelchair because of arthritis and spinal neuritis. I suggested that Dwight and I visit him, which we did in early February of 1953. Afterwards he wrote "You made a good case for that group and I want to help you as much as possible."

Actually we sent Bennett the stories of 204 cases (449 individuals) until we were denounced by the Comité Medway in France on January 9th, 1954. The gist of the accusations was that "The group of Spanish refugees here are mostly commies or worse—anarchists. . . . that under the tuition of the Republican Government in Paris they are preparing to return to Spain as raiders. . . . that they are trained to destroy or maim all U.S. activities in Spain and they hate the U.S. . . . they are also being trained to be the assault troops for the great day when Communism takes over France. . . . *Every one of these Spaniards is under surveillance of the French state police. . . .*'' They also wrote that ''Casals is or was a communist'' and that M. Camus has already been identified with commie setups in France.''

I answered this letter, writing Mr. Bennett that ''My husband and I both remarked after we visited you last fall that you had a good deal of the anarchist in you. It showed both in the way, as an individual, you had taken the responsibility of helping other individuals and in your unwillingness to have your project regimented under the State Department.''

I sent a copy of my letter to Camus, who replied at great length, and noted: ''The immense majority of the Spanish refugees in France are anti-Communists.'' He said that he would be glad to meet with the Medway Comité in Paris; and ''If one is called a Communist for not resigning oneself to see the Blue Division defending the ideas of the democratic camp, then we are all Communists,'' and he defended the anarchists, who had fought ''our common enemies and were at our side in the movements of resistance against Hitler's army.'' He found the report of the Medway Plan Foundation hilarious, but their ignorance made him impatient.

Casals wrote me that Bennett's letter was full of ''incredible stupidities, and your reply remarkable for its energy and logic.''

In January 1954 the Comité Medway in France retracted its denunciation and Mr. Bennett had to admit that ''my face is red. The long delay in receiving the report had determined me to go forward with you on our own. I shall now advise our French friends of that determination.'' Understandably, however, relations had cooled and in March 1954 Bennett accused me of breaking my promise not to send SRA appeals to his people. I told him that I would never break my word and pointed out that some names could have been on other lists which we had used for appeals. But the connection had been broken and Bennett did not ask us for any more cases. In April 1954 he wrote me that he would no longer help because his French committee would not back down. William Bennett died in March 1956 and the Medway Plan Foundation came to an end.

After the Medway debacle, an attack came from different quarters. On May 20th, 1955, the *Daily Worker* printed a letter from Pablo Casals stating that he "sends this urgent letter to the *Daily Worker*" which starts out "Dear Friends." On May 25 in a letter to the New York Post, James T. Farrell, SRA's Chairman, pointed out that the *Daily Worker* did not say that this was a form letter sent to 14,000 individuals and that they did not give our address. He added, "Casals is in no way responsible for the use to which the *Daily Worker* put our form letter and our organization has nothing to do with the Communist Party here or abroad and wants no aid from it."

I wrote to Casals telling him about the *Daily Worker*'s story and Farrell's press release. I added, "It appears to me that the intent of the Communist Party was to smear us and you as Communists. They may have been attempting to confuse their readers, as the CP front Spanish organization is called Spanish Refugee Appeal. They were most certainly not trying to help us!"

Minor problems concerning the CP and SRA came up in March 1958 when the French police called on Suzanne Chatelet at her home in Perpignan where she conducted the work of SRA. They wanted to find out if there were Communists in the Ligue des Mutiles (LM), the Spanish Republican Veterans organization, which we were helping regularly. The Spanish Communist party had been outlawed in France and the police were trying to find out about its members. I knew personally that the directors of the LM were members of the CNT and not Communists. They helped all those who were injured during the Civil War and currently needed help.

That same month I heard from Bill Kemsley of the ICFTU in New York that he had received a phone call from the ICFTU in Brussels asking if we were a Trotskyite organization. The DGB in Germany had heard that Nancy Macdonald and Suzanne Chatelet were Trotskyites and that 90 percent of our funds were going to the Party and 10 percent to the refugees. Among others, Peter Blachstein, a Socialist Deputy in the Reichstag wrote a strong letter of protest and said that he supported our activities. No doubt this was a CP attempt to smear our work.

On March 14, 1961, I wrote to Dwight in London, where he was working for *Encounter* magazine, that a Committee for a Democratic Spain "is now headed by Waldo Frank and assisted by Freda Kirchwey, Otto Nathan, and Del Vayo. Their main program is to get amnesty for the political prisoners in Spain. I imagine they are tied in with a big conference which is to take place in Paris on March 25 consisting of groups from many countries also asking for amnesty. . . . It seems to me that these are front organizations for the CP and here we are back again in the thirties, except it's not quite the same. Or perhaps it is and I don't remember. One is for the things they are shouting about but if one takes part, one will get hopelessly compromised with people who don't really care for the things they are fighting for."

In the meantime Dwight wrote me and asked if he should become a sponsor of this committee. "I'm sure you know all about it, will trust your judgment as to whether it's a Commie front or not. . . . I'd say the tests wd. be if other parties among the Spanish exiles are cooperating; also, of course, the content of the material the committee has put out." He added "I trust, by the way, that SRA hasn't done anything so foolish as asking Waldo Frank to resign because he's mixed up with the Commie fronts. Test should be if he tries to take over SRA or to manipulate it in Commie direction—otherwise, it's his own business if he wants to make an ass of himself."

I advised Dwight not to become a sponsor, and told him I had asked our board member Gabriel Javsicas to "go around and see this man Colloms. G. thinks he is not a Commie but is obviously being used by them. And Colloms seems to have represented the U.S. in Paris! When Gabriel asked him why the UGT and CNT didn't take part in the Paris Conference, 'he said that they were of no account'!" Finally I wrote to Dwight on April 26 "I am enclosing a clipping that appeared in the Spanish Socialist paper re that Conference. . . . The CNT also repudiated the Conference and so did the Basque Government-in-Exile."

Our second crisis over the CP question began in late 1961 and concerned Waldo Frank and the Castro regime in Cuba. Waldo had been one of SRA's sponsors since we started. He had contacted General Lazaro Cardenas for us in March 1953 and wrote us that the General accepted *con agrado* the Honorary Chairmanship of SRA. When the Civil War ended in Spain in 1939, Cardenas was President of Mexico and saved thousands of Spanish as well as other refugees by granting them visas.

In October 1961 our Board of Directors voted unanimously to drop General Cardenas as our Honorary Chairman. He had never answered our letters or shown any interest in our activities. We wanted to invite the Spanish statesman and scholar, Salvador de Madariaga, to join Pablo Casals as Honorary Chairman. But he had made clear to me when I visited him in Oxford during the summer that he would not serve with Cardenas, who was closely allied with the Communists in Mexico. Although the question of Cardenas's politics was raised at our meeting, it was decided on practical grounds rather than political ones to drop him.

At the same meeting we tabled the question of dropping Waldo Frank as sponsor. Nor, after a heated discussion, was a vote taken on whether to help Spanish Communist refugees. Our Chairman, Hannah Arendt, pointed out that our by-laws stated that we help non-Communist refugees but they did not state the converse of this proposition. (Note: SRA continued to help all refugees who were in need and never asked them about their politics.)

On February 27, 1962 we learned that Waldo Frank had written a book about Cuba and Castro which appeared to have been paid for by the Cuban Government. We decided to try and authenticate this information and ask Frank for an explanation. If he admitted it, we would ask him to resign. On February 14, 1963, Ruth Berenson Muhlen, one of our Board members, resigned because Frank was still a sponsor. She indicated that our yearly donation from the International Rescue Committee might be withheld because of this. (It was not). A special meeting was to be called to discuss the whole question, when Dwight, who had been ill, could attend.

Soon after this we received a letter for Casals from the Libertarian Movement of Cubans in Exile, dated February 15, 1963. They wrote that they could not give aid to SRA because Waldo Frank, our sponsor, "supports the tyrannic regime which today oppresses and exploits the people of Cuba.'' He not only ''writes in favor of Cuba's Communism, a regime as cruel as Franco's, but he has publicly acknowledged he has received the amount of $5,000 for writing a book in favor of Castro's Cuba . . . You have refused to perform in countries that helped enslave Spaniards. We, following your example, refuse to support an organization that houses individuals that help to enslave Cubans.'' Marta Casals responded to this that the opinion of her husband was that Frank be dropped as sponsor if ''it is true that Mr. Frank is pro-Castro and pro Castro's regime in Cuba.''

At a special meeting of our Board on March 12, 1963, it was voted to drop Waldo Frank from our list of sponsors because we had received protests from various sources and ''his presence had become an embarrassment to SRA and that it impairs the operation of our committee.'' We notified Casals, and also Muhlen, who returned to our Board by November 1963. (She resigned again when SRA considered forming a separate committee to aid political prisoners of Franco in Spain.) When I wrote to Madariaga about dropping Waldo Frank as a sponsor, he replied, ''I am not surprised at what is happening with W.F.. He is an excellent man but wayward and unsteady.''

Our last controversy on the CP issue was triggered one day in 1978 when our Board member, Gabriel Javsicas, said to me, ''I wouldn't be found in the same gutter with that woman Lillian Hellman.'' I rashly replied, ''But you've been on the same committee with her for 8 years.'' Dwight had suggested Lillian's name as sponsor in May 1969 after he had persuaded her to sign his petition sent to Moscow from 30 U.S. writers protesting the charge and methods in the Sinyevsky and Daniel trial. He believed Hellman had given up Stalinism and that ''joining our list of sponsors would be good for her and us.'' Gabriel was at our meeting on May 13 when Hellman's name was proposed as sponsor and voted for unanimously; he was at our Board meeting in October when I informed the Board that she had accepted, and raised no objections. Later he said that, knowing nothing about her at that time, he had trusted Dwight's judgment; or perhaps his hearing aid wasn't functioning.

Now, almost 9 years later, Gabriel asked the Board to drop her as sponsor and told us that he had a dossier showing that she was still a Stalinist. Accepting his word, the Board of SRA voted to drop her in April 1978.

Dwight had not been at this meeting, nor seen the dossier, and he asked that the question be reopened. Dwight and I now read the dossier, in which we found no evidence of current Stalinism. The Board reinstated her. Gabriel resigned, and persuaded both James T. Farrell and Mary McCarthy (two of our founders) to join him. Farrell died shortly after, before there was a chance for us to persuade him to reconsider. But Dwight did convince Mary to continue as a sponsor, pointing out to her that SRA's work was not as censor and if Lillian had continued an apologia for hard-line Stalinism in her book, *Scoundrel Time,* he too would have favored dropping her; but she had not.

Gabriel Javsicas joined the Board of SRA in April 1953, proposed by our Chairman James T. Farrell. They were old friends, and Gabriel claimed to have "discovered" Farrell, helping him find his first publisher. Javsicas was born on January 13, 1906 in Gargzdai, Lithuania (Russia). He graduated with honors at the London School of Economics in 1928 and did postgraduate work for 2 years at Columbia University. He lived in France from 1930–1939 and, having married an American, moved to the U.S. in 1939. He made a living buying and selling mahogany (his father's business) and by shrewd trading in foreign currency.

During the Spanish Civil War he was an economic adviser to the anarcho-syndicalist trade union, the CNT in Barcelona. Since meeting Emma Goldman in his London boardinghouse in the twenties, he had called himself an anarchist. In February 1964, when a CNT man stopped by at the Oriente Hotel in Barcelona to see him, the Spanish police rounded them up with two more men of the CNT. As a result he spent 3 weeks in the Modelo prison. He was charged under Chapter 2, Title II of the Spanish Criminal Code, for relations and contacts with "subversive" elements aiming to overthrow the Spanish government. His friends and colleagues at SRA protested vigorously and he was released unconditionally on February 27.

Gabriel was a thickset man, a lively raconteur, bon vivant, and a marvelous cook. He once spent 2 days in my pond-side place in Cape Cod, cooking a *poulet au vapeur* with truffles. Board meetings often took place in his apartment on 15th Street, where he served us delicious patés and fine wines and liquor after we had finished with the serious business of SRA.

Dwight characterized him as "very ignorant, and a professional Communist-dreader for years." For example, Gabriel called Lillian Hellman's Committee for Social Justice a CP front and transmission belt to Moscow, and continued to do so in the face of conclusive evidence to the contrary. Actually it was founded by lib-labs to help cases which the American Civil Liberties Union couldn't handle.

Gabriel's interests, though assorted, were circumscribed: food, Sacco & Vanzetti, the CNT in Spain, the CP, and mahogany. On the last subject he was expert from his many trips to Ghana and Virginia, the shipping points for his wood.

Gabriel was a stubborn and one-track man. Once he had decided that Lillian Hellman must go, he could not accept the vote of the Board to keep her. He suggested that I write all our sponsors asking them whether they wanted to remain if Lillian Hellman was one. When I refused, he said he would do it himself, and also write to all our big contributors suggesting that they might want to cut off their support.

Gabriel pledged that he himself would continue to send us money for his "adoptees." Instead, he sued SRA for $160 in Small Claims Court for receiving his contributions under false pretenses in the interval between Lillian's termination and reinstatement. He lost the suit by nonappearance, and we heard nothing from other sponsors or contributors, although another of his threats was a class action suit on behalf of all our contributors.

This was a sad, crazy ending to a long friendship. Mary McCarthy urged him in the name of his own anarchist principles to desist in his attack on SRA. (She herself would be sued by Lillian Hellman for $2 1/4 million for "defaming" her on Dick Cavett's show on Channel 13, having called Lillian "a dishonest writer"—"even her *ands* and *thes* were lies.") The Board of SRA urged Gabriel to return and forget his extreme anti-Stalinist stand: the only sufferers would be the refugees. But he was adamant up to his death, which occurred in March 1982, from a heart attack.

NOTE

1. Casals tried to persuade President Kennedy to condition future aid to Spain on "an agreement for the reestablishment of freedom and human dignity in that country." He also wrote protesting to Truman about Marshall Plan funds being sent to Franco's Spain and to Nixon about U.S. military support of the Franco regime.

8

Fund-Raising

An old line of Dwight's was, "if you can't give us your old money, give us your old clothes!"

SRA's goal for its first year was to collect $25,000. In 32 years we raised over $5 million. We managed to raise in 1953–1954 $19,000 in cash and almost another $4,000 in clothing and "goods in kind"—hearing aids, typewriters, and other useful equipment.

Much of the money was given by individuals in small amounts. We first mailed out 5,500 appeals signed by Casals. Renée Peterson, who had been a fund-raiser for the International Rescue Committee, suggested that we mail 500 from Prades, France. We did this, with no notable response. She also explained how to exchange lists with other organizations whose donors might be interested in our cause (Spanish, musical, libertarian, humanitarian), and how to approach foundations and give benefits. Besides appeals sent in the name of Casals (and later of his widow, Marta Casals Istomin), we sent them from our Honorary Chairpersons, Salvador de Madariaga and Alexander Calder. One year, letters were sent in the name of Albert Camus.

SALVADOR DE MADARIAGA
(JULY 23, 1886–DECEMBER 14, 1978)

Salvador de Madariaga became a sponsor of SRA in 1953 and, with Pablo Casals, our Honorary Chairman in 1961. He was born July 23, 1886, in La Coruña, Spain, one of 11 children. Madariaga headed the disarmament section of the Secretariat of the League of Nations from 1921–1928. He was Professor of Spanish literature at Oxford from 1928–1931 and author of many books and articles, including a history of Spain and studies of Hernan Cortes, Christopher Columbus, and Simon Bolivar. He was a Deputy to the Republican Cortes in 1931 and Ambassador in the U.S. and France from 1932–1934. He left Spain in 1936 and only

12. *Salvador de Madariaga in his garden at Old Headington, Oxford, in 1967.*

returned in April 1976 after the death of Franco. He settled in Oxford soon after the beginning of the Spanish Civil War and it was there that I first met him at 3 St. Andrew's Road, Old Headington, in 1961.

In October 1969 Madariaga wrote me: "You will be amused(?) or indignant(?) to know that one of Franco's scribblers has published an article in Spain in which Casals and I, together with a number of Spanish public men abroad are presented as gangsters." SRA was delighted to have this "gangster" on our side. He was always an active chairman, who wrote about and for us— in 1964 an article for *SHOW* magazine about the refugees, a twenty-fifth anniversary article; and for *Réalités* in November 1976 about Spain today and its relations with Russia and the U.S. In 1957 his SRA appeal went, in England, to *The Times, The Guardian, The Daily Telegraph, The Observer, The Sunday Times* and *The Spectator*; in the U.S., to the *New York Post, The Nation,* the *Catholic Worker,* and *The Progressive.*

Madariaga not only wrote for us but contributed generously. In November 1961 he sent us $714 from his Mariano de Cavia prize; in 1970, $500 to celebrate his marriage to Emily Rauman, his literary collaborator for 40 years. In 1971, and again in 1972, he sent $1,000 for 8 scholarships for the children of our exiles, and an extra $100 to celebrate the one hundredth birthday of a refugee, Sra. Maria de la Paz. In 1973 he received the German Charlemagne Award for "special merit in the service of a united Europe" (he was very active in the European Movement and the College of Europe in Bruges).

I met Salvador and Emily a number of times in Oxford, and had lunch and tea with them, discussing the problems and needs of SRA. Once in 1962 I met him at the solemn Reform Club in Pall Mall, where I found him snoozing in an enormous black leather armchair. He told me "I have been tethered short by my heart, which is beginning to find that too many things are happening too much at the same time." In 1972 he wrote me that he and Mimi were leaving England for good—"I can face no more Northern winters: I cannot go to my country because of its political winter." They settled in Locarno, Switzerland, and Emily remained there after his death at the age of ninety-two in December 1978. (His first wife had died at the home of one of his daughters in London.)

A few months before he died, Madariaga resigned as our Honorary Chairman because of age-related problems and also because he felt that help should come from Spain now that Franco was dead. He wrote, "It is unseemly that a free people should continue to rely on foreign charity when it is free to organize its own aids and helps." Before his death he wrote me, "Emily asks to be joined to me in our esteem and admiration for your work and in the expression of the friendship it has caused and maintained between us." It meant much to me when Emily wrote me afterwards calling me a "*Quijotesa,* who, lance in her hand, fights with indomitable courage those Spanish windmills, now standing for Fascism and now for democracy."

ALBERT CAMUS (NOVEMBER 7, 1913–JANUARY 4, 1960)

To understand Albert Camus's feeling for the Spanish refugees one must remember that his mother was Spanish and his close friend, the actress Maria Casares, was daughter of Casares Quiroga, Minister of Defense of the Spanish Republic. Maria was 13 when the Spanish Civil War started and worked as a volunteer in a hospital in Madrid until her father moved her and her mother to France.

Camus made a trip to the U.S. in March 1946, organized by the French Government. He was detained by Immigration, who asked him if he had ever been a Communist or had friends who were, and to name them. He refused to answer, but was finally allowed to enter. He spoke at Columbia and at Vassar. Dwight and I heard him, and then met him at a gathering in the home of Mary Jayne Gold. As he had at Columbia, he spoke about making no distinction between conqueror and conquered. We are all responsible, he said.

In February 1949 the Spanish Government-in-Exile gave Camus their Order of Liberation. In August 1949 he organized an appeal published in the CNT's *Solidaridad Obrera,* to help Spanish Republican refugees. The appeal was sponsored by the Federación de Deportados and signed by Gide, Mauriac, Sartre, Char, Silone, Carlo Levi, Bourdet, André Breton, Orwell, and Casals. I heard nothing more about this appeal. In 1951 Camus spoke at the Casa de Cataluna; in 1952, at the Salle Wagram (where Madariaga also spoke); in the same year he joined Maurice Joyeux of *Le Libertaire* at a meeting for the Spaniards. In 1955 a commemoration of the three hundred fiftieth anniversary of the publication of *Don Quixote* was organized by *Solidaridad Obrera,* with Camus and Madariaga as sponsors; on October 30, 1956, at a meeting organized in honor of Salvador de Madariaga's seventieth birthday, Camus gave a *"discours très espagnol dans su defense d'un liberalisme qui refusait de se laisser intimider par les zelateurs du totalitarism."*

When SRA was starting in 1953 Camus became a sponsor and Francine Camus, his wife, was to have been our representative in Paris. Unfortunately, she became ill and was unable to assume this work. Miriam Chiaromonte, who had also offered to help, was likewise unable when her husband Nicola decided to move back to Rome.

Dwight and I met Camus a second time when he visited the U.S. again and there was discussion of starting an international magazine in English, French, Spanish, and Italian. Nicola Chiaromonte, Enrique Gironella, Camus, and Dwight exchanged ideas and Camus was to have sent a draft of his own, but did not follow through on this.

I remained in touch with Francine for a number of years after the death of Camus in 1960 and until her own death in 1980.

COMMITTEES AT HOME AND ABROAD

IRC

The International Rescue Committee played a special role in the life of SRA. They gave us some of the names from their lists when we started. But the next year they refused to let us use more, because they were planning to help Spanish refugees again themselves! Nevertheless, they helped in many other ways. Their accountant Werner Wille set up our books for us and instructed me in keeping them, always ready to explain and help. At the end of each year he did our books and the reports for the Internal Revenue Service and for the State Charities Commission when we registered with them. By 1959 we felt rich enough to offer him $35 a year for his services! (In our thirty-second year we paid $1,000 to our CPA.) Werner did our books for us until he died in June 1971.

Werner was born in Germany and received his law degree at the University of Berlin. He was one of the few lawyers who defended opponents of the Hitler regime in political trials. A member of the "new Beginning" resistance group, he fled to France in 1938, was on the Nazis' non-Jewish opponents list, to be surrendered "on demand." He came to the United States in 1941. After the war he was invited back to Germany to resume his law practice, but decided to continue his work for refugees in the U.S.

The IRC also shipped clothing abroad for us without charge. In 1954 and 1955 they gave us 81,000 pounds of U.S. Government surplus butter, milk, cheese, and eggs for our Spaniards, and 1800 packages of food for Christmas 1954. These were U.S. Foreign Overseas Administration surplus supplies. In Montauban alone, 1,000 families were helped. In Toulouse, 90 people a day, three times a week, jammed rue Thionville outside our tiny office to get their package. Later on, IRC gave us $1,000 a year, then $1,500, and afterwards $2,000 towards helping refugees designated by SRA. Charles Sternberg, for whom I worked when I was at IRC, and who later became its Executive Director, was always available when I had any kind of problem. When SRA decided that we must cut down on overhead and start phasing out, Sternberg helped us become a division of the IRC where we could continue the work still needed with some 300 exiles depending on us.

Switzerland

Aide aux Refugies Espagnols (ARE) was founded in Geneva in 1956 by Henry and Frieda Jacoby (German refugees whom I knew while they were in America) and their friends, Dan and Elizabeth Gallin. The Secretary was Jeanne-Marie Perrenoud, schoolteacher, and its President was Rinaldo Borsa, until his death in January 1975. Borsa, a militant Socialist since 1919, was watchmaker, teacher, and statistician at the UN, combined, in the words of his wife, Juliette, "the best in the traditions of the humanists, libertarians, and universalists, which were also those of the Spanish Republic." ARE's sponsors included 12 Socialists, of whom three were co-op people, three trade unionists, one deputy of the Parliament, the general secretary of the party, as well as five liberals, including one Protestant minister, and one Leftist Catholic professor. Founded specifically to help SRA, they sent us gifts of money and clothing for 28 years, ranging from $1,200 to $2,500 a year.

In 1958, to raise more money in Switzerland, ARE tried to get the approval of Entraide Ouvriere Suisse (EDS). Their official, Jules Humbert-Droz, also a sponsor of ARE, responded that SRA's work would have to be approved by the Spanish Socialists in Toulouse before EOS could grant approval. I wrote to Pascual Tomas, Secretary General of the Spanish Socialists in France, who replied that he had no information from Switzerland. Humbert-Droz then wrote to Carlos Martinez Parera, another key Spanish Socialist, who replied: "There is no problem as far as the Spanish refugees are concerned, all of them having become integrated into the French economy thanks to the magnificent social security laws in France, and old clothes are certainly not needed. The only thing that is needed is money for vocational training of youth." Llopis, another Spanish Socialist leader proposed *estudier tranquillement ce qu'on pourrait faire*"!

In November 1958 Dan Gallin relayed to me that Llopis and Parera had told Humbert-Droz "to stay away from SRA because it was helping only Trotskyists and POUMists and because it spends a large part of its money on administrative expenses (salaries, trips, etc.)''

In actuality, SRA had been working with Solidaridad Democratic Española (SDE), the Solidarity committee of the Spanish Socialists for 5½ years and had helped many of their comrades. An SDE report of 1951 informed us that they had 20,000 members of whom 4,000 were in some sort of need and 800 ill.

I wrote to Julian Gorkin asking if he would ''try to find out from M. Llopis what is behind this kind of treatment, and ask him to please stop undermining our reputation and start giving us their support. I know that they want us to go on helping their comrades and so don't want to stop, but it is depressing and disillusioning when we are doing our very best for them to receive slanderous treatment in return, and this from Socialists. In any case we don't want the 'little man' to suffer because those at the top are acting ignobly.''

By March 1959 the Spanish Socialists backed down and agreed that our help to them was valuable. But it had been rough going. By March 1968 the Spanish Socialists publicly acknowledged in an article in a French periodical the good work of SRA. But they omitted praise for the work in Montauban (probably because Manuel Palacios, in disagreement with their politics, had left the Spanish Socialist party).

Germany

In Germany, Peter Blachstein, a Socialist Deputy in The Reichstag, and Rose Froelich, widow of Paul Froelich (see PPA), founded the Deutsche Komitee zur Hilfe fur Spanische democratische Fluchtlinger to help SRA. They sent money regularly for 30 years and also provided clothing, scholarships, ''adoptions'' (at one time they had 22), hearing aids, five magnificent Telefunken radios (''music raises our low morale and oppressed hearts,'' wrote one recipient), typewriters, and an electric wheelchair. They also gave money to the Socialists in Spain. Rose Froelich sent a personal contribution to SRA every year, even in her nineties. In 1968 when Peter Blachstein was appointed West German Ambassador to Belgrade, Heinz Ruhnau, a member of the Executive Committee of the German Socialist Party and also Minister of the Interior in Hamburg, took over the job and ran the German committee until it closed down in 1984. Blachstein died in 1977.

England and Chloe Vulliamy

On my second trip to Europe in 1954 I came to London twice to try to set up an English branch of SRA. The poet Myfanwy Stephens (Rodnight), who had been in touch with me through *politics* magazine, introduced me to John McNair, Secretary of the Independent Labor Party (ILP), and its representative in Barcelona during the Spanish Civil War. When George Orwell went to Spain, as correspondent for the ILP's *New Leader,* he carried a letter of introduction from H.N. Brailsford to McNair. Later, Orwell's first wife, Eileen, volunteered and became McNair's secretary. McNair was a self-taught man and dedicated Socialist who had spent 25 years in France in the leather trade and was fluent in French and Spanish. He and the Orwells fled Spain together after the POUM, sister-party of the ILP, was suppressed on June 15, 1937 and most of its leaders were in Stalinist prisons. They felt lucky to get out alive.

Now on my visit to England, 17 years later, McNair and Sonia Orwell (George's widow) promised to bring together a group of possible sponsors for an SRA branch in England. When I returned to London in the fall, I learned that H.N. Brailsford, Michael Foot, Fenner Brockway and A.J.P. Taylor had agreed to be sponsors. But no individual had been found to organize an English committee for us. McNair was too busy, Myfanwy too crippled by polio to take on the job. At the suggestion of the anarchist writer George Woodcock, I also met Vernon Richards, who had written an excellent book about the anarchists called *Lessons of the Spanish Revolution and the Spanish Civil War* and was one of the editors of *Freedom,* the English anarchist paper. He was too busy to take on an English SRA. But he did take me out for a magnificent Spanish paella at the Majorca, whose maitre d'Hotel was a friend and a member of the CNT. I also tried, unsuccessfully, to interest Stephen Spender in our projected English Committee. Many years later, in 1976, he did become a sponsor of SRA at the suggestion of Joseph Buttinger.

Although Myfanwy could not form an SRA branch in England, she put me in touch with the Oxford Committee for Famine Relief (OXFAM) in 1956. They sent 50 pounds sterling to our office in Toulouse and promised a steady flow of clothing. They sent four bales of blankets in 1958, a ton of clothing in 1957 and again in 1959. In July 1961 they invited me to address their staff in Oxford on our programs. In 1962 they sent almost $5,000, and thereafter a stream of money, food, clothes, and toys, until 1970.

When the International Reufgee Organization (IRO) was ending its work in 1951, they had 754 Spanish cases suffering from TB. By 1956, 42 percent of SRA's cases had some form of lung disease. They were people like Nemesio Z., who had not much left of his lungs after contracting silicosis in the mines of Morocco; Antonio Alcaraz, imprisoned in Spain for 10 years, in need of nutritious diet for his stabilized TB; and tubercular Francisco S., in his sixties, living in a barn with no heat for 3 freezing winters. They and many others needed money for food, heat, and clothing. For 2 years OXFAM matched our $6,000 as a special help for this disabled group.

In England, beside OXFAM, there was Aid to European Refugees (AER), which started in 1954 by giving us $1,000 for new sweaters and urging their contributors to knit more. They adopted 10 of our very old refugees and sent funds for them every 3 months for 19 years. They also gave special gifts for orthopedic shoes, repairs for a cellar apartment, scholarships, and money for the Foyer Pablo Casals. Two other committees in England that helped us regularly were Help the Aged and Wings of Friendship.

In 1967 I met Chloe Vulliamy, an Englishwoman who had sent us a contribution and came to London to tell me about her experiences with Basque children during and after the Spanish Civil War. There were 3,800 sent to England in May 1937 who were helped by the National Joint Committee for Spanish Relief. By the middle of 1939, 3,000 were repatriated.

At the time that I met her, Chloe was living in Hempton, a small village in England near Banbury. She was a short, compact woman, with graying hair pulled back severely in a bun, but humorous and full of vitality. She and her sister Poppy went to Spain for the first time in 1934. This was the period of the abortive revolution in the Asturias.

Chloe Vulliamy: "We loved Spain, and the Spaniards, and we both of us intended to go back, and more or less settle there. The idea was to run mobile village libraries or something like that, to help on with the very backward education. But then the Civil War came and it was impossible. My sister Poppy and I both volunteered. But I had really not the qualifications they wanted at all. I couldn't either type or drive a car and my sister's lame; and possibly for that reason they didn't think she was suitable. Anyway, later she was with the International Commission at the end of the war, and she was in Barcelona a lot during the war. The Commission was largely, though not entircly, Quaker relief service that took bread lorries in, and met the defeated army coming out—and then helped in the camps when they got into France.

"In the meantime I had 100 refugee children that I was looking after. They came from Bilbao, at the time of the blockade. Remember, there was a 6-week blockade of Bilbao, and everybody got very excited about it. The British Government agreed to take first 2,000 and then 4,000 children, unaccompanied by adults, except for a few teachers and helpers.

"I wanted to do something. I put an advertisement in my local paper and was absolutely dumbfounded to be offered six large houses by just local people. It was the first time that anything like this had happened and we made every conceivable mistake. I don't know why we thought they would be Catholics, and got a priest to welcome them, who was Spanish. I remember my sister bringing them up the drive and saying: 'I picked you all nice little Reds.'

"Anyway, having got over the first difficulties, we settled down to it and I was with refugee groups of one sort or another for 10 years, until the very last children's home. . . . The children came over in 1937. The adults came at the last minute when Spain was just about to collapse, a last boatload of 400. And there were a number, singly or in small groups, guaranteed by English individuals, who came separately.

"The children came on a boat called the *Arana*. I think we chartered it. There was a quite influential committee called the National Joint Committee for Spanish Relief which had been working through the war. It had a number of M.P.s on it and they persuaded the rest to invite these children and took financial responsibility for them. They formed a subcommittee called the British Committee for Spanish Refugees which undertook to look after the adults. For a time I was joint secretary of the British Committee, in between doing children's work.

"There were 90-odd homes, varying widely in size. My first was one of the largest—for 100, which was really too many. Afterwards, we decided that 40 was a maximum that you could do properly. But some of them were quite tiny with a dozen children, run by a small local committee. They were all over England. Mine was near where I lived, just outside Ipswich. The final one, where I was at the end of the period, was at Carshalton, just out of London, near Croyden.

"Of course, conditions varied greatly. We started at the height of luxury with a 30-bedroom mansion and got into trouble because some of the children were madly destructive at the outset, and we were demoted and moved into an abandoned roadhouse. A few of the adults arrived with their pockets full of bombs. My sister took on the bad boys, the ones nobody else would have, whom even the Salvation Army turned down, the ones that would have originated the stories you heard about knives. They were the big ones, who really were hardly children and needed different treatment. And she had a wonderful Anarchist cook, who was very good with them and made a great success of it. Lord Faringdon let her, more or less, camp in his park and was very nice to them all. And you know, all the boys adored her and outwardly behaved quite well.

Meanwhile, many of the children went back. The Bilbao scare was soon over and physically the conditions were quite possible, and some of them came so young, it would have been mad to keep them out away from their families if you didn't have to. So there were only a few hundreds of the older ones left by the outbreak of the War. They stayed and settled down, and I was with them until the last home closed, during the War. They were only supposed to be up to fifteen when they came in 1937, but by the looks of them, some were nearer eighteen. Because boys wanting to escape their military service were never made to go back if they didn't want to.

"At the beginning we were not allowed to send the children to local schools. They were not allowed to be a charge on the rates. But when they had been here a couple of years, we prevailed on the Government to change that, and we sent them to the ordinary local schools, where of course the young ones forgot their Spanish and became completely English-speaking. They all became fluent and had a normal education. Very often, if they showed any special ability, we were able to get sympathizers to help.

"They were not quite near enough the Pyrenees to speak Basque. Bilbao isn't a Basque-speaking town. It's only in Guipuzcoa that there's anybody who speaks it. They danced their traditional dances and that was a great fund-raising thing. There's a wonderful series of boys' Sword Dances, (*espada*), which are immensely effective. We worked them out from what the few adults could remember, and the occasional song that one or another of the children could piece together. We made all their clothes and got together a concert troupe and they went around performing and collecting money and it was very successful. There are still a couple of *chistu* players, which is their local instrument. The *chistu* is a long pipe, peculiar to that part of Spain. The bagpipe is an instrument farther along to the west in Galicia.

"After the last home was closed, quite late in the war, about 1944, I rather lost track of them, apart from my individual friends. They were all growing up, and we found homes, adoptions, for the few who weren't quite ready for jobs; the others were already independent. One became a quite well-known ballet dancer, several of them are artists, some got routine jobs; but they all did very well."

In 1961 Chloe made a trip to Spain for an English Amnesty

committee, to distribute money to some 25 families of Franco's prisoners. She was picked up by the police and spent four nights in the Central Police Station in Cordoba. From there she was sent to Madrid and expelled from the country.

When I met her in 1967 she was still deeply concerned about the Spanish Republicans. She offered to visit some of our refugees in isolated regions in France, and did this faithfully from 1967–1973. She contributed her time, and we paid her expenses. One year she visited two of the exiles in Andorra and another year she saw 16 of our Spanish friends in the miserable "Home" in Tribomont, Belgium. In 1972 she went to see 19 isolated refugees in central France and in 1973 she saw others in Grenoble, Nice, Toulon, and Hyeres.

Chloe also translated some of my Spanish tapes into English. She travelled with her sister Poppy, and on her trips collected art objects for the Ashmoleon Museum in Oxford. She was also Secretary of the Michael Karolyi Memorial Foundation which ran an artists' colony in Vence in the South of France, similar to our Yaddo and the MacDowell Colony. Chloe died in the late 1970s.

Sweden

Another very effective European committee was *Individuell Manniskohjalp* (IM) in Sweden. It became involved in 1963 and continued to help us for almost 20 years. One of their social workers, Siv Follin, whose salary and expenses were paid by IM, came to France for 6 months every year. She brought and distributed money and clothing, and made regular visits to Spanish exiles in Paris, Marseilles, Montpellier, Perpignan, and surrounding areas. In 1968 she visited 87 families in and around Marseilles. IM rented an office next to ours in Paris for their clothes and files.

In 1964 IM proposed to open a Foyer in Perpignan, similar to our Foyer Pablo Casals in Montauban. The UN High Commissioner for Refugees did not answer their inquiry on this project, possibly because Perpignan is so close to the border of Spain; so this idea had to be abandoned.

In 1965 IM gave us $2,310 to pay for 8 scholarships; $4,800 was given directly to our refugees. An electric wheelchair went to a legless veteran of the Spanish Civil War. Christmas packages were given to 45 refugees, hospitalized Spaniards in Perpignan were visited and given money, and three refugees were given 6-week vacations in Vrigstad, Sweden. One, Alexandre M., a seventy-six-year-old engineer, wrote from Vrigstad: "My life here has been full of excursions, lectures, parties, walks in the forests and by the lakes—everything is magnificent in this country."

That same year IM invited me to pay them a visit in Sweden. Siv Follin took me to Vrigstad where our refugees had vacationed; we saw their office in Lund; I met and was entertained by the Tibetan girls they were training in native skills and arts. Siv and I dashed through Copenhagen and Stockholm. Most vivid were my memories of the midnight sun, the friendliness and kindness of my hosts, and the four nights I spent on sleepers (the Swedish ones incredibly narrow) from Perpignan to Paris, Copenhagen, Stockholm, Paris.

The aid from Sweden was varied, and met needs such as: a stove, $200 to fix a leaky roof, a transistor radio, new underwear and clothing, books for a hospital circulating library, money for heating, Christmas packages. Quite often SRA shared with IM the cost of helping to pay debts, repairs, or dental work. Official aid from IM ended in November 1981; but Siv continued to keep in touch with many refugee friends and to visit from time to time on her own.

FOUNDATIONS, TRADE UNIONS, BEQUESTS

Our first Foundation money came from Mrs. Maud A. Murray, Trustee of the Helen G. Murray Fund, which gave us a total of $14,000 from 1954–1957. Three other Foundations gave us almost $159,000: the Howard Bayne Fund, $38,350 from 1961–1982; the Ingram Merrill Foundation, $60,740 from 1963–1982, and the New Land Founation, $59,860 from 1968–1983. We never learned who the Murrays were, or why the were interested. But we had personal contacts with individuals in the other three Foundations, Daphne Shih, James Merrill and John Myers, and Joseph and Muriel Buttinger.

Since almost all our refugees were workers and many had been active trade unionists in Spain, belonging to the UGT or the CNT, we tried to interest American trade unions. The most generous and regular contributors were the United Automobile Workers, the American Federation of Teachers, and some of the ILGWU unions. A local of the Amalgamated Clothing Workers "adopted" a couple and helped them every month for 9 years. Other unions occasionally gave small amounts.

From 1971-1982 we received over $40,000 in bequests ranging from $100 to $10,000. Isabel Robertson, who had "adopted" several refugees for a number of years, left SRA $10,000; Mrs. Marjory Harkness bequeathed $5,000 in 1974 so that her adoptees would continue to receive $50 a month in Spain where they had returned to live. Annemarie Bergman, a Jewish refugee from Germany, who helped 6 refugees and corresponded with them, gave us money to help them before she died. (As a token of friendship, she sent me her silver tea strainer.)

OFFICE VISITS, ADVERTISEMENTS, PUBLICITY

Some contributors brought cash to the office. A sailor, Ernest Anderson, came in from time to time with $100 and left us $3,706 in his will. I heard that Brendan Behan had a special feeling for old people, and wrote him about ours. He dropped by, peeled off 20 $10 bills, and offered us old clothes. Mrs. William Korn of the Mayer Family Fund came in and asked us all sorts of questions. Evidently she was satisfied, she and her family contributed regularly thereafter.

We tried advertisements (paid, and a few free), but they rarely paid for themselves. During our 32 years we scarcely ever received any important publicity, although the old *Herald Tribune* ran an article about our memorial meeting for the 25th Anniversary of the Fall of the Spanish Republic. This was thanks to a friend, Ruth Biemiller, a staff reporter, and her article appeared in the Sunday magazine section on May 31, 1964. Eleanor Roosevelt wrote two columns about us in the *New York Post* on March 2, 1954, and again on March 16, 1960. *The New York*

Times ran an editorial about SRA on December 20, 1959, and I wrote two Op-Ed articles published January 30, 1976 ("Spanish Refugees: Waiting") and June 21, 1980 ("Spaniards in France").

BENEFITS

Benefits were another source of income for Spanish Refugee Aid. Although many were not very profitable, we had one almost every year, as public relations activities. They were often fun—sometimes disasters, as when at a 10th anniversary dance, a drunken guest broke a picture window which we had to replace out of our small profits.

Our first benefit on July 12th, 1953, was given by a friend, Joan Colebrook, in a restaurant she was running in Wellfleet on Cape Cod. There were no expenses and we made $183 by selling tickets to our friends for $2 apiece. I organized our second benefit in Provincetown in September 1955. We showed Bob Snyder's movie of Casals playing Bach's First Suite for unaccompanied cello at the Colonial Inn. I had to have posters and tickets made, get notices in the local papers, and sell tickets. I wrote my aunt that "It 's a job I don't enjoy but I felt I must do it. We hope to sell 225 tickets and I'm getting various friends to assist." We netted $275.

On a small scale, this was how our benefits were organized— announcements, tickets, friends. We showed movies, gave parties, had a musical evening, art sales, viewings of private art collections, speeches. In New York, a benefit first night of *To Die in Madrid* netted us $1,555; Arrabal's movie, *Viva la Muerte* produced only $426.

Most frustrating were the viewings. In 1961 we made $500 when our contributors came to see Ben Heller's private art collection. In the 1970s his *Blue Poles* by Jackson Pollock was sold to the Australian Government for $2.2 million. In 1965 Mr. and Mrs. Victor W. Ganz permitted us to hold a viewing of their Picasso collection. Surrounded by priceless paintings and graphics, we struggled to make $850 for our refugees.

Most profitable were our art sales. One on December 4, 1975, netted us $8,076; 4 netted a total of $21,000. We had artists, painters, sculptors, photographers, who contributed as often as four times. Some gave special editions, made for us by James Brooks, Elaine de Kooning, Antonio Frasconi, Joan Miro, Robert Motherwell, Constantine Nivola, Rafael Soyer, Saul Steinberg, and Esteban Vicente.

ALEXANDER CALDER

Alexander Calder (Sandy) was a very special contributor. In contrast to our dealings with Pablo Casals, the "shrewd peasant," those with Sandy were always open and direct. He was the most generous and modest of men. His scribbled notes were always to the point. "Have you received some gouaches from me or have you not? My memory is loose." When we asked him in 1964 if he could contact Miro for us, he wrote that although he knew him well, "I feel loath to ask him to donate anything for it's a rather delicate, or rather indelicate, situation." He suggested that we write to Fernand Gerassi and Rufino Tamayo for contributions.

In December 1954 Calder sent SRA $100, his first contribution. We had found his name on a list from the American Committee for Cultural Freedom. Calder's interest in Spain dated back to the thirties, when, after his marriage to Louisa James (the grand-nice of Henry), they went in 1931 to Majorca for a vacation. In 1932 they went to Barcelona to see the Gaudis and to watch the sardanas being danced. Later they visited Miro at Montroig. In 1936, Agnes Rindge, my art professor, gave Calder his first one-man show at the Vassar College Art Gallery. He gave her a mobile, *Agnes' Circle,* which she donated to the Gallery in 1963. In 1937 Calder donated a "mercury fountain" for the Spanish (Republican) Pavillion at the Paris World's Fair. The Pavillion had been designed by Jose Luis Sert. Miro had donated a large painting and Picasso's *Guernica* was hung there.

Calder's first artistic contribution to SRA was a small stabile, *Yellow on Red and Blue,* which he donated for our Homage to

Albert Camus benefit at the Stuttman Gallery in 1960. It sold for $600. In 1962 he answered our invitation: "I would be very much pleased to be made a sponsor of Spanish Refugee Aid. I enclose $50 check. Cordially yours and I thank you."

In 1965, Margot Karp, of our office staff, got the idea that we ask Calder for some lithographs. He agreed immediately. "I could do 5 or 6 lithos for you, 100 prints of each, signed (by me). And I think you could sell them for $60 or $75 (those at the Guggenheim were very cheap, $50—but I was just starting on my career)." He added, "If you have a chance, call us—Tel. 14 in Saché and come to see us here."

Since I was in France that summer of 1965 with my son Nick and his wife Elspeth, and we had rented a car, we phoned and set out for Saché (Indre et Loire) in a torrential rainstorm. I learned later that Balzac did much of his writing in Saché, and Rodin, with his mistress, Camille Claudel, spent the summer of 1893 there. When we arrived in this village we had great difficulty in finding "Monsieur Cal-der," who was said to live near a mill.

Finally we reached him very late in the day—a busy one for Calder, with photographers and reporters. He hugged us when we arrived and we all sat down at a long table in an enormous living room, where dried onions and fruits hung from a low ceiling. A big bottle of red wine was passed around. Sandy drank and slept and said a few friendly words about SRA and was off again. Louisa Calder was there to carry on the practical world of her dreamy husband, and we had a rather heated argument with her about Communism. Finally Sandy took us into his studio to show us sketches for lithographs of the type he was planning to do for us. Both Calders made us feel very welcome and at home. The artistic eye was everywhere, even to the toilet paper holder which was a small mobile.

This was how we received our first 400 lithos. They continued to come from Calder to SRA for the next 10 years, always in the friendliest manner. "Dear Nancy, You should have the lithographs by now—60 of each of 5 drawings. I hope you like them. Although I would do it for you anyway, I think I may as well profit from the tax deduction.'' ''If you would like some more lithos, let me hear. I may have been lazy, for a moment. Sandy.'' ''Dear Nancy, I will be very glad to be an honorary Chairman. What do I have to do; other than supply my annual prints? I am very happy to do that. Saludos!'' ''I am sorry you lacked those 'wonderful Calders.' If such a condition recurs please *call it to my attention* and I will get to work. I am rather vague about all I have to do—because there are so many requests but I always want to do some things for you. Affectionately, Sandy''. . . . ''We will be in Paris the 15 May, and at the Hotel Madison. You might come to breakfast at the Cafe St. Claude (next door)—but ring us first. Ciao! Sandy.'' (I didn't make it for breakfast. That is my least mobile time of day.) Once SRA invited Calder and Louisa for cocktails. He sat like a Buddha on my sofa while our Board members came to speak to him, one by one. It was an odd gathering, not spontaneous, like our written relations with him.

Calder gave us a total of 2,705 lithographs (32 sets). The prices ranged from $60 to $800 apiece, and they netted SRA over $500,000. For Christmas 1973 we were able to give an extra $25 to each one of our then current refugees and the $500,000 over 10 years meant much needed extra help for our Spaniards during that period. After his death in May 1977, Louisa Calder sent SRA $2,000 at Christmas and became an Honorary Chairman together with Marta Casals Istomin.

CONTRIBUTORS: 25¢ TO $1,000

Most of our funds, however, came from individual contributors. At one time we had 13,000 and they gave us sums varying from 25¢ to $1,000. The average donation was $10, with inflation, became $25. Spanish exiles in the U.S. and Mexico gave regularly, some for 20 years. In 1981 we had 25 pledgers, who gave from $5 to $45 a month.

We had strange donors like the Sinister Wisdom Books and illustrious ones like Willy Brandt, who had been a war correspondant for a Swedish newspaper in Spain and who in 1972 gave us

$900 for three scholarships for children of the exiles; and Albert Einstein, who contributed small amounts several times. Many, like Einstein, had been refugees themselves. Mrs. M., a German anti-Nazi, who was helped after World War II through PPA wrote, "We shall never forget the help coming from Mr. F. in the hardest times." She and her daughter, a student in Berlin, sent packages to two Spanish refugees. Erna L., who contributed often, was a German refugee in Montauban during WW II and was saved from deportation by the Mayor. Some had ancestors who had been refugees: "I am a descendant of a refugee of the Inquisition, Moses Maimonides." "My paternal ancestor was a refugee from Montauban after the Revocation of the Edict of Nantes."

Contributions were made in memory of men who, like Brandt, had been correspondents in Spain during the Civil War—Alexander Uhl, Jay Allen, and Camillo Cianfarra. Other correspondents contributed, such as Martha Gellhorn and Leland Stowe, who sent $50, writing "The gallant battle for freedom and democracy branded my soul more deeply than any of the battles which I reported from war zones."

Many gave in memory of International Brigade members who died in Spain: "Your cause is close to my heart, my younger brother lost his life while fighting with the Loyalists for La Republica Española." "I am a Lincoln Vet and just returned from Spain (my first visit since the war) with my son of twenty-one. Being able to go back (after Franco) for me was a very emotional experience and I hope our refugee friends can somehow be able to do the same."

Some people who had had personal contact: Esther K. wrote, "Forty years ago I helped the American Friends Service Committee feed the children in Murcia. I learned to know and admire those in their Government in Valencia and it is in their memory that I am sending the enclosed check." "My Dad (and his friends) during the 1930s collected enough money to purchase an ambulance for the Loyalists." A German Jewish refugee contributor had been in the camp of Septfonds, France, "where I met these unfortunate Spanish refugees, the sight of whom I'll never forget." A veteran of the 29th division of the POUM wanted to write to someone in his division. "We were a mixed bag from everywhere and my Company Commander was George Orwell." Robert and Emma P. were superintendents of a Basque children's home near London for 3 months in 1938—"an entrancing experience." They themselves were refugees from Austria and came to the U.S. in 1938.

Others gave for more general theoretical principles like the United Auto Workers Union which sent $1,500, calling SRA's work "a significant expression of solidarity with the Spanish people that deserves encouragement, especially from the American Labor movement." A friend who received restitution from the German Government sent $500. Dr. B. gave a scholarship for several years in memory of her father, a Jewish attorney, who fought in the Dutch resistance and was killed in prison by the Nazis. The George and Minna Ledebour Foundation (he was a Socialist member of the Reichstag before Hitler) gave us money for "militant comrades who have fought for the cause of Socialists and are in need." *Masonic Inspiration* gave because "Many Masons or relatives of Masons have been murdered by Franco's agents". . . . A gift of $25 came in memory of the Spanish scholar Don Tomas Navarro Tomas, who contributed his work almost until his death at ninety and was a "great example of dignity and loyalty to the ideals of the Spanish Republic."

At one time Spanish Refugee Aid had as many as 13,000 contributors. I am specially grateful to one of them, Liberal Press, which did printing for *Partisan Review, politics,* and finally SRA. Every year they sent a small contribution. But best of all, they let us pay our printing bills whenever we could, and never reminded us. First there was Joe Cannata; then his brother George and his nephew Pat, and finally Moe Hirsch. They were real friends to us and our refugees.

9

The People Who Worked with SRA

NEW YORK STAFF: ASTOR PLACE/80 EAST 11

All our fund-raising was organized and carried through by the 22 people who worked for SRA during its 31 years. For a benefit some of our board members also helped. Our American staff also handled the more than 5,500 case histories received in New York. Each refugee (or family) had a number, a file, and a card with their life story, recording when and how we helped. Further information was added based on visits by our European workers and from letters sent to us directly by the refugee.

At first our office was in the old Bible House, across from Cooper Union on Astor Place. Then we moved to 80 East 11 Street, where we started in a very small office and moved twice to larger quarters in the same building. During our 31 years, SRA had 21 paid workers (see Appendix) and a few volunteers. Sometimes there were six of us but more often two or three—all part-time workers. Most of us knew French. Some were proficient in Spanish, like Betty, who was married to a Mexican poet; Carmen Guillen, who was an exile from Spain in Germany and

151

came to us via Myfanwy Rodnight in England; and Meg, who came from New Mexico and had travelled in Spain.

I was quite fluent in French because as a child I had a Swiss governess. My Spanish, despite my struggle to learn in my spare time, was rudimentary. But I managed to read most of the letters we received in Spanish, since they were quite similar. Otherwise I sent them to our volunteer translators, Marie Englert and Olaf Domnauer, or they were translated in the office by Meg, Betty, or Carmen when available. Much of my time was taken up with reading case histories and deciding whom to help and how. I corresponded with our staff in France and with many of our contributors, big and small.

My first assistant was Hilda Rodman, my ex-sister-in-law, a wonderfully efficient volunteer who worked for SRA regularly from 1953–1955, and also contributed financially. Jeanne McMahon, who was studying for a degree in philosophy at New York University under Sidney Hook, was our first paid worker (beside myself) and she worked at SRA until early 1956 when she married and went to live abroad for 2 years. We then had all sorts of workers including musicians, writers, a painter, housewives, mothers, students, and a film maker. My friend Marty Hall, who had helped me get names at IRC when we were first beginning to organize, came sporadically as a volunteer. She served on our Board of Directors for many years and when we planned benefits was one of the most active participants.

During our 31 years we had two people whose main work was fund-raising, Frances O'Brien and Ruth Leopold. Sonya Leobold, Margot Karp, Betty Aridjis, and Margaret Childers worked primarily on adoptions. Jane Potter was the office manager while I was in Europe or vacationing on Cape Cod. Meg Randall, who knew many young artists, organized the 1960 art benefit Homage to Albert Camus, of 129 painters and sculptors. Many unknown at the time became famous later; others were already famous. We netted $7,000.

All of the people who worked for SRA were part-time. They came at their convenience. Everyone knew what had to be done and work passed from one person to another easily. The office was an informal place. Evie came with her cello, Lee brought her dog, Sally arrived on her bicycle and Nick sometimes came with my grandchildren, Ethan and Zack (who often attended our benefits and enlivened our fund-raising events.) Sometimes our office was overwhelmed with barrels of clothing. When it got to be too much, Hy Palansky, always good-humored, in a hurry, and full of energy, came and hauled the clothes away to Numar Standard on Grand Street, where they were baled to be forwarded to France (the IRC got special rates for shipping clothes and included us in their shipments.) Hy also met me at the boat (the SS France, the Liberté, and the Queen Elizabeth) when I returned from work in Europe. He knew all the customs men and he sent me through their hands rapidly. Hy often met boats with refugees coming to IRC and he took it upon himself to meet me too.

As early as 1957, when he was twelve, my son Nick came to the office and did useful odd jobs for SRA. He was paid small sums from Petty Cash. From 1970–1983 Nick worked regularly, but part-time, for Spanish Refugee Aid. He was our very efficient fund-raiser beginning in 1976. He also did our accounting, wrote appeals, and reports, and kept me from giving away our money too fast. In 1962 we had a debt of $8,000 and again $7,000 in 1968. I loaned SRA $6,000 of my savings in 1970 (I was repaid and so was Dwight for the $2,000 he loaned in 1962). By 1973 we were out of the red and had a big surplus in April 1982, thanks to Nick's good planning. In 1965 Nick made a 16mm black and white film for SRA called *Land of Exile*. It ran for 20 minutes and was silent with captions. When SRA became a division of IRC in 1984, Nick left and now is back in the field of moviemaking, as well as teaching and writing about them.

When Spanish Refugee Aid closed down and became a division of the International Rescue Committee, Margaret Childers took over the job of carrying on our work. It's not clear to me how she manages to do all my work and Nick's as well as hers, with only one part-time assistant. But she does it, and with all the personal touches that were the trademark of SRA. I keep up correspondence with a few exiles like Pilar Armentia, Petra Barinaga, Olga Femenia, Antonio Gomez, Eusebia Moreno, and Juan

Porcel (my adoptee) because they have become my friends. I also keep in touch with our former and current workers in France, Faustina, Francois, Ramon, Teresa, and also Antoinette Caparros and Maria Batet who run SRA's office in Toulouse. When I was there in May 1985 I phoned Mercedes Vive and was glad to hear that she goes to Barcelona for Christmas with Jacques's family and that they visit her often. And she is keeping up Vive's garden which he cultivated with such pride and care until his death in 1982.

SUZANNE CHATELET AND FRANCOIS OLIVÉ

When SRA began raising funds in April 1953, we planned to open a central office in Paris. As we have noted, Miriam Chiaromonte, who was to have run it had to move to Rome, and Francine Camus, who would have taken the job, became ill. Cleta Mayer, the wife of the French Deputy, Daniel Mayer, worked for us during the summer of 1953, but Farrell, our Chairman, felt she wasn't the person for the job, nor did he approve of Mlle de Blonay, Louise Crane's suggestion. We then turned to Suzanne Chatelet and until March 1960 she headed the work in France from Perpignan. At that time, she and Francois Olivé, who did SRA's bookkeeping, moved to Paris where SRA's work continued until 1976.

During PPA days Suzanne had handled several problems for us very efficiently. We reached her through Francois, a Spanish refugee, who, in Spain, a member of the POUM, had been the organizer of a trade union in his town, Tarrasa. He had modestly asked PPA for a pair of pajamas and a fountain pen, and had put us in touch with a number of other needy refugees. When I met them in 1952, Suzanne was working as a masseuse and Francois had a job as accountant in a cork factory. He had a wife in Spain, who didn't want to come to France and Suzanne had been separated for a long time from her French husband. Because divorce was impossible in Catholic Spain, many Spanish refugees lived *en concubinage,* as they called it. Suzanne and Francois met

13. Suzanne Chatelet and François Olivé in Paris, 1965. They were witnesses to the marriage of my son, Nick, and Elspeth, on June 12 at the Mairie of St. Sulpice.

in Paris, where he, after the end of the Civil War was being housed and hidden by Gaston Roux, a French painter, and his wife, Pauline. (I met them later when they were living with Christine Magriel at Arcangues.) Suzanne lived in the same building and it turned out that all the tenants were hiding "their Spaniard"—even from each other! Francois became ill and Suzanne was asked to come and nurse him. They fell in love and when Paris was occupied by the Germans, they went to live in Perpignan.

Perpignan is the city I have come to like best in France. The refugees love it too. It is near their country, and since this area was once part of Catalonia, the culture is partly Catalan. Catalan is spoken frequently, Catalan materials and espadrilles are sold in the stores, the Catalan sardanas are played and danced. In the summer of 1976 I went to a Catalan music festival held in the Palace of the Kings of Mallorca. There were many Spanish refugees in this region because it is near the border and near Argeles and St. Cyprien where so many spent their first miserable years in French "reception camps" after the Spanish Civil War.

The old part of the city is a maze of narrow streets with low, ancient buildings where many of the refugees have lived since 1939. The rents were low and accommodations often primitive—bathrooms were rare, and "stand-up" toilets in the halls or courtyards were usual. Now there are some medium-priced apartment buildings (HLM—Habitations Loyers Modérés) in the outskirts. But the refugees often preferred to stay in their old neighborhoods, where they were known and where they had lived for years, even though conditions were poor.

In Perpignan, among the first refugees who came to ask for SRA's help were Antonio Gomez Baños whose taped story appears later, and Francisco Bardes Font. Suzanne wrote of Gomez, "He was an aviator during the Spanish Civil War and lost both his legs. I went down to the street to talk to him becaue he cannot leave his wheelchair. He says he has written to ask you for an ultraviolet ray lamp. Let me know if you think we should help with this?"

Suzanne worked for SRA for almost 21 years. In Perpignan her door at 12 Avenue de Gaulle was open at all hours to any refugee. She often gave her own clothing to Spanish exiles who had none. In May 1955, Angel R. wrote to her "A few lines probably badly expressed, sufficed for you to come immediately to the aid of one who was shouting in silence but in desperation. Thank you for everything, Mme. Chatelet, healer of ills and heartener of those who are disheartened in life's struggle. My admiration for the morale which you express so simply but with so much affection in your letters, which I read with total absorption and complete satisfaction." In May 1956, Suzanne wrote me, "Last week I was visited by an old woman and a young girl of nineteen. Here is their story. The father, a farm worker, came to France at the end of the Civil War. His wife and two children stayed near Toledo and worked on the land. Now the wife is blind, and came to France with the children. The young girl cannot read or write and was in rags. I gave her the last coat I had here and some of my own things. It makes one sad to see such misery."

Our main office was moved from Perpignan to Paris in March 1960. Suzanne felt that there would be many advantages in our being in the capital city where most of the French Government agencies and service organizations were located. Refugee problems such as work papers, pensions, and retirement into old people's homes, could be handled much better. The French office of the UN High Commissioner for Refugees (UNHCR) and the French Office for the Protection of Refugees and Stateless (OFPRA), with whom all political refugees were registered, were also in Paris. Suzanne worked closely with them, as well as with the French Social Service organization (Service Sociale d'Aide aux Emigrants—SSAE), which recommended cases to us and handled problems we could not. Julio Just, the Minister of the Interior of the Spanish Republican Government-in-Exile, also sent us many cases, and refugees whose friends had been helped came to us for aid.

A contributor wrote us about our Paris office: "I found Mme. Chatelet in a basement, more a cellar than a basement, but clean, whitewashed, with shelves, a table and one chair. Just enough for an efficient operation, with no frills. This underlined to me the difference between SRA and other aid organizations, and I felt with a pang of immediacy that what you, Mme. Chatelet, and others are doing, is my concern, our concern; that aid is not given to "clients" (what a horrid word welfare organizations have come to use, but how fitting for them) but to our own, who have fought and suffered." The only "frill" in our cellar was an Alladin lamp for the frequent Parisian electrical strikes.

Suzanne had no frills, either. She was an outspoken woman, stubborn about ideas and repetitious in speech. She strode rather than walked and was thick-set. But the effect was lightened by her lively eyes, her lusty Gallic humor, and her wrathful denunciations of injustice. She was an excellent cook, stirring with one hand while she gestured with the other, and she always made me and her many friends at home in her apartment on the Avenuce de l'Opera (a series of rooms in the apartment of a friend) and later at the rue Truffaut.

Suzanne died suddenly on November 10, 1973 of a heart attack. I flew from New York to be at her funeral, and to search for a replacement. Many of our refugees came to the Paris office in tears when they heard about her death. Others wrote: "We will miss her valued strength in continuing our work." "I was used to her letters and thought of her as my mother." "We will miss her as a friend, a woman of great wit and humanity, whose presence we will feel with us always." " . . . this great woman, who dedicated part of her life to the cause of the refugees. Her devotion was without limits." About herself, Suzanne had written long ago: "I would like to be able to move mountains and make everyone in the world happy. One has the spirit of Don Quixote and would like to be as powerful as God the Father. I am full of longing to better the lot of others."

Besides Francois Olivé, who continued to keep our books, Odette Ester worked for SRA for 7 months. Then Ramon Alvarez ran the office until 1976 when he returned to live in Spain and to work for the CNT. Finally Mathilde Droulin, our French representative in France after the death of her old friend, Suzanne, kept the office open until June 1978. By that time there were only a very few needy Spanish refugees in the area.

ANNE MARIE BERTA AND JACQUES VIVE

When SRA started receiving contributions, we gave the Dispensary of the Spanish Republican Red Cross in Toulouse $100 a month so that Anne Marie Vitaller (neé Berta) could continue to work there for the great number of needy Spanish refugees in and around this city. In June 1957 we opened our own office at 13 rue Thionville, where Anne Marie lived—in a tiny, sunless, medieval apartment, surrounded by our clothes and clients. She wrote us "I was poisoned by the fumes and never had a moment to myself."

When she received West German Government restitution for her activities during the occupation, she and her father bought a small house in the outskirts of Toulouse at Cugnaux. There was a garden with a fig tree, flowers, and vegetables, and a shed where M. Berta kept his *escargots*, which he found, fattened, and sold.

Anne Marie had been born in Figueras, Spain, in 1908. When she was five, she came with her parents to live in France and studied there until she received her Brevet; so she was fluent in French and Spanish. When I met her, she had been separated for years from her husband, Vicente Vitaller, who had passed his exile in Venezuela. Her daughter, Lydia, and her grandson, Philippe, live in Paris.

14. *Anne Marie Berta and her father in their garden at Cugnaux, a suburb of Toulouse.*

Mme. Berta was a lively, gay person, despite her poor health and a bad limp, the result of childhood osteomylitis. Good-hearted and enthusiastic, if often unsystematic and erratic, she was devoted to the Spanish Republican cause. She acted as intermediary at the hospitals, preventoriums, and French Government agencies, where she was well received. She did a good deal of visiting for us in Hospitals and Old People's Homes, as well as to many exiles in and around Bordeaux and Toulouse. In November 1963 she visited 45 refugees in Bordeaux and in February 1964, 148 Spaniards in 16 hospitals and Homes. She reported to us about the last that "almost all of them need clothes as they are miserably dressed. In Lectoure the food is very bad and insufficient. They ask for supplements of sardines, butter, jam, chocolate, and cookies from time to time. Life is very sad. After years of struggle and exile they feel so abandoned."

Fernando C. wrote: "A few days ago your representative from Toulouse, Mme. Berta, paid me a very pleasant visit. We talked in Spanish because she is a Catalan and I told her about my projects for the future. When I leave this Sanatorium in May, she promises to help me get settled with my sister near the border and very near my very dear family from whom I have been separated since the beginning of the Spanish Civil War in 1936! She is also sending me a coat and a pair of shoes. This visit was a great comfort to me and I feel easy now that I have the protection of Spanish Refugee Aid and for one who is seventy-eight you can imagine how that is."

To commemorate the founding of the Spanish Republic in April 1933, Anne Marie organized a Fiesta de Fraternidad for children of the Spanish solidarity committees on April 17, 1960: 400 children came with 300 parents. Berta spoke; there were marionettes, fairy tales were told, a ventriloquist and clowns performed, and toys were distributed which had been donated by OXFAM and the German Social Democrats. Each child received cocoa, candies, an orange, and cake.

In addition to visits and follow up on cases, SRA in Toulouse bought and distributed food packages, and gave out new and used clothing, sent from the U.S., England, Switzerland, and Germany. In the spring of 1975, 222 packages of rice, noodles, sugar, oil, milk, sardines, and soap, were distributed. Jacques Vive, who had taken me to see the Colony of Aymar in 1952 and was the secretary of SIA, came to work for us in 1961 and with his companion, Mercedes, who volunteered to help, handled the distribution of clothes and food.

In Spain Vive had lost his right arm in an accident. When the Civil War broke out he was teaching in a village school. In France he worked for a while as a shepherd, which he loved, and he was very fond of gardening. When he retired in 1975, having been granted indemnification by the West Germans for his internment in the concentration camp of Nöe during the Nazi occupation of France, he was able to buy a small house with a garden on the outskirts of Toulouse. He and Mercedes lived there year round, largely on the vegetables and fruits of their garden. Vive had six

15. *Jacques and Mercedes Vive (photograph by Nick Macdonald).*

grown sons in Spain, and many grandchildren, and they often came for visits. When he retired, Maria Batet, another Spanish refugee, who had been working for SIA, took his place. Antoinette Caparros, bilingual in French and Spanish, came to do the visiting when Anne Marie Berta was no longer able. With the closing of the Foyer Pablo Casals in June 1983, Toulouse became SRA's only office in France.

16. Antoinette Caparros (left), Nancy, and Maria Batet (right) saying good-bye in May 1985.

TERESA AND MANUEL PALACIOS AND THE FOYER PABLO CASALS

I had visited the Spanish Republican Red Cross Dispensary in Montauban on my first visit in 1952. In April 1953 SRA started supporting it with $100 a month. In May 1959 Teresa Palacios reported: "The Dispensary is open every day from 3 to 5 p.m. except for holidays. Here Manuel and I give advice and moral support, which is so much needed by the many refugees in the Department of Tarn & Garonne. We take all necessary measures for getting pensions, free medical assistance and other benefits, and are in close touch with the Relief Department of the Mayor's office and the Prefecture. We translate Spanish documents into French, interpret, help obtain Identity Cards, Residence permits, and change of domicile permits, required by the police

17. Teresa and Manuel Palacios at the Foyer Pablo Casals, which opened in October 1961.

from political refugees. We arrange for hospitalization, and burials for those who have no family in France. Every week we visit the Spanish refugees in the Hospital (12 this month) and once a month give each of them 1.200 francs from the funds of SRA. We also visit many sick and old people outside the hospital. We have helped 214 families with clothes and blankets, we gave 2,000 francs apiece to 55 old people over the age of 60 for coal and wood. We look into requests for help and recommend those who need and deserve it, to your New York office. Before closing I should like to ask for something which the old people need desperately for next winter—woolen underclothes. I am present when these people undress and I know that this request is more than justified."

In October 1961 SRA had raised enough money to open the Foyer Pablo Casals, named after our Honorary Chairman. We started by helping 99 people over the age of sixty with monthly food packages. Our peak year was 1970, with 319 individuals on its rolls. Some 1,140 Spanish refugee families lived in and around the small, old, provincial city of Montauban in south-central France, where many refugees were sent after the fall of the Spanish Republic. The old people were living on pensions of $15 a month, half the *minimum vitale*. Winter months were especially hard for them; rents were low, but houses were damp and often designated uninhabitable. They lacked money for sufficient food and clothing. SRA wanted to found a Foyer where "These old people may meet, keep warm, enjoy a few comforts and pleasures, visit, and esape from the solitude and misery which is so often their lot."

Manuel and Teresa Palacios found an old garage at 45 rue de la Banque. They helped remodel it into a Foyer, which a large living room with chairs, tables, books, a TV, radio phonograph and records, and decorated with paintings donated by Spanish refugees; a lavatory with modern toilets for men and women (a luxury in Montauban); a small kitchen with refrigerator; an office for the work of the Foyer and SRA, a dressing room, a large clothing and sewing room, a separate ample storeroom for clothes and food supplies and a small garden. Twelve organizations and foundations gave $15,000 (including the French Committee for World Refugee Year, which gave $6,122 for installing heating, plumbing, and electricity, as well as donating a TV and refrigerator). Individuals gave $10,000 towards expenses for the first year.

We gave an inauguration party on July 27, 1961. Pablo Casals could not be there and sent his friend, Andreu Claret, who spoke for him. I attended, and so did all our field workers. Among the 200 guests were many old Spanish refugees, as well as Spanish and French officials from Montauban and Toulouse. We served refreshments and several short speeches were made.

Teresa and Manuel both came from Madrid and had worked during the Civil War in a Republican Government office there, and later in Valencia. Manuel was a quiet, conscientious man, with a strong sense of humor, who worked hard to help his countrymen, first as a Socialist, then as the Director of the Spanish Republican Red Cross in Montauban and finally for SRA. He died in 1971. Teresa, in her sixties, was a pretty, blond woman, short, plump, and energetic. She talked fast, and was enormously efficient as well as being warm-hearted and kind. People came to her with their problems and she always knew how to help and console them.

When the Palacioses came to France, they went to Montauban in September 1939. Teresa: "We had only a little money and we found a very, very big house in the country. It cost a lot, but 14 of our friends came to live with us. In Montauban there were round-ups to put Spaniards in concentration camps but they hardly ever came to the country. There was a policeman, who was a leftist, and when there was going to be a raid, he would warn us: 'Tonight the men must go, eh?' They went to the farms near by and the women stayed—it was only the men they took in Montauban. At that time the Prefect was Mr. Bocoiran, a man of the left, a good type, who helped a lot. There were many people in Montauban who were radicals and socialists and that is why many Spaniards, Jews, everybody, came there. [Among my friends, Hannah Arendt, Louis Coser, Henry Jacoby, Norbert Muhlen, and Hans Sahl, all had fond memories of their stay in

Montauban.] The Prefect made all possible concessions and protected us. Many disabled refugees were taken to Caussade (near Montauban) on entering France and the hospital in Montauban was full of disabled people too. And because they were protected there, they stayed.''

Manuel told me about his work for the Resistance: ''At the time of the Occupation, all the parties were dissolved. And we got together with some Socialists and were the men who reconstructed the whole Spanish Socialist Party in exile; eight men only, four from Montauban and four from Toulouse. The former met practically every day, because we worked in the Resistance with a man, who was editor of *La Depêche,* M. Irenée Bonnafous. It was very hard to find a place to meet. . . . Next to where we live here, there was this Hotel du Commerce that was taken by the Gestapo. All day and all night they were on guard on all the sidewalks.

''And I said to my comrades: 'These Germans, I don't know if they are very stupid or very childish, but it is very easy to trick them. And I think if we meet at my place it would never occur to them that we could hold a meeting next door to them. That would never enter the brain of a German.' And we met here, at a small table that we made out of a packing case. We were in the Resistance but we only passed along information from one place to another, all the way to Bertaux's network in Toulouse. M. Bertaux was a real personality, whose name was given to the network which worked in Toulouse. And we were the contacts here. But there were no engagements with weapons, simply work of this kind: to send bits of information from one place to the other, but no fighting.''

At the Foyer, from 1961 to 1978, in 16 years and 4 months we gave out 47,176 food packages and quantities of new and old clothing. Mme. Palacios wrote, ''Nobody realizes the importance of the Foyer. We are a 'wailing wall' for the Spanish refugees, who always come to it with every kind of problem, trouble, illness, or joy.'' She often stressed the importance of giving comfort and told me about the visit from Juan Curos, whose daughter had just died in Spain. He told her that he couldn't cry; and when Teresa talked to him and put her arms around him, then he cried, and felt relieved.

In February 1978 we stopped distributing food, which Mme. Palacios felt was no longer needed, but rather cash and new clothing. In 1982 Teresa applied for her pension as a former Civil Servant of the Republican Government during the Spanish Civil War. After endless red tape and working 9 months in Spain, she was successful. While she was away, her stepdaughter Carmen substituted for her. The Foyer remained our office until we closed down in June 1983. We gave the furnishings of the Foyer to some of the refugees, to our workers, and for the office in Toulouse.

ORGANIZATIONS IN FRANCE

During 32 years Spanish Refugee Aid had over 5,500 cases on its roles. Where did they come from? As was mentioned earlier, the first 100 were given to me during my trip abroad in 1952 by the Solidarity committees of the Socialists (SDE) and Anarcho-syndicalists (SIA), and the veterans committee of the Republicans, the Liga de Mutilados (LM). These three organizations continued to supply us with names for many years.

The Liga de Mutilados had a special relationship with SRA. Enrique Guillamon was Executive Secretary of the Liga de Mutilados until his death in 1979. Then headquarters were moved from Bordeaux to Toulouse, where Marcelino Boticario assumed charge of the archives. I visited the Liga regularly in Bordeaux and again in Toulouse. It had been founded during the Spanish Civil War and at the end of the war in 1939 it became the Liga de Mutilados en Exilio.

When I went to Paris in 1952 I met Antonio Trabal, who had been a member of their executive committee since 1946. Whenever I came to Paris during the next 33 years I conferred with Trabal, and he remained a valued friend. During my last visit he picked me up at the airport in his car and took me on a whirlwind tour of Paris. Several days later he took me to lunch at UNESCO where he had worked since 1956.

18. "To our friend, Nancy, with our affection and friendship, from Antonio Trabal" (with his wife and one of six grandchildren, August 1985).

Antonio Trabal Bisbal was born in 1920 at San Feliu de Llobregat (Barcelona) and his father was mayor during part of the Civil War. His parents worked in the textile industry and were sufficiently well off to send him, until age fifteen, to a private school run by a cooperative movement. Antonio's family was traditionally anarcho-syndicalist and during his teens he was active in the Libertarian Youth movement. He joined the Army of the Republic early in 1938, was wounded at Segre in May, and trepanned.

He and his family came as refugees to France in February 1939. Antonio was in the internment camp of Argeles and later Bram. He worked with his father at Cajarc (Lot) where they were both in the 508th Company of Foreign Workers. From July 1942 until the end of the war he joined a group of resistants organized by the Spaniards of the CNT, which acted as liaison between the city and the maquis. After the war he worked with his wife in an enterprise making espadrilles. In 1956 he got the job at UNESCO where he remained until his retirement in 1980 and where he continued to work from time to time. He and his wife have three children and six grandchildren and his father is in his nineties.

Not only did the Liga recommend cases to us, but SRA was able to give the LM $46,415 during 28 years, most of this being a yearly subsidy from Louise Crane for administrative expenses. The rest came from the Pablo Casals Foundation. Their major support came from Mexico via Indalecio Prieto from 1952–1977 and amounted to a total of 1,400,000 NF (about $175,000 at the 1985 rate of exchange). This was used for regular subsidies to the neediest among their members (the wounded and widows), and for special aids. The money was part of the interest on capital deposited in Mexico by the Spanish Republican Government, administered by the Mexican Government.

The Liga also received about $50,000 from José Calviño Osores from 1949–1977. I first met Calviño in Paris in September 1954. He was an engineer, and associated with the Ministry of Finance of the Spanish Republican Government. In 1954 he was still collecting money due to the Republic for deposits made for armaments ordered but not delivered during the Civil War. He distributed these funds to the Liga and other Spanish organizations; most went to help those fighting against the Franco regime.

He returned to Spain in 1963 and I visited him in Madrid in 1978. He was then eighty-three and still interested in the LM. I hoped he could be helpful in pushing for the payment of invalid pensions by the Spanish Government. But he felt he was too old to do more than distribute help. At that time he was giving the Liga de Mutilados in Madrid 50,000 pesetas (about $300) a month.

Other organizations such as the Service Social d'Aide aux

Emigrants (SSAE) in Paris, Bordeaux, and Perpignan, recommended many people to us. When we lacked funds, we, in turn, asked them for help with special needs. Some cases were recommended by mayors of small towns and villages in France. Some refugees came to us through their friends. The Basque Government-in-Exile in Paris (50 rue Singer) told us about their people, and even the French representative of the UN High Commissioner for Refugees in Paris, Mme. Taviani, told us about needy Spaniards. The Minister of the Interior of the Spanish Government-in-Exile, Julio Just, sent on to us all the Spaniards who came to them for aid. Formed in Paris in 1939, their office was at 35 Avenue Foch. They had an embassy in Mexico City until March 18, 1977 when 38 years of diplomatic relations were terminated. Mexico recognized King Juan Carlos's Government on March 25. At that time, Jose Maldonado was President of the Government-in-Exile and Fernando Valera was Prime Minister. Julio Just, who had been Minister of Public Works in 1936 in the Largo Caballero Government in Republican Spain, was Vice President of the Government-in-Exile at the time of his death at the age of eighty in October 1976. He was buried in Port Vendres, France.

One of my favorite solidarity committees was the Federation Española de Enfermos Cronicos e Invalidos (FEECI), whose representative I had met in Montauban during my first visit in 1952. This was a small organization of 300 members, headed by Mariano Puente, whose story shortly follows. Puente, who was educated in Scotland, sent me the names of the refugees belonging to the FEECI, who needed SRA's help, and wrote: "In our lists, most of us are TBs and aged people, and our cases are the most delicate of them all, because most of our adherents are those who nobody wants, for the simple reason that they are Mister Nobodys. But they are the real fighters, those who struggle in fight to death saying nothing, the humble death of the unknown heroes."

After much friendly correspondence I met Mariano Puente when I drove to Belhade in the Landes in 1961. He was waiting for me by the side of the road outside this little village, so that I wouldn't get lost. He lived in the woods, in a rundown, primitive country house with his French wife, Argentina, and his young nephew and niece, Carlos and Marisol. Their father had died in Spain and their mother had abandoned them. Mariano and Argentina both had lung trouble and he also suffered from stomach ulcers.

They had a small vegetable garden, and some chickens, turkeys, and rabbits, which helped eke out their tiny pensions. Their water came from a well and there was an open-air, stand-up privy in the woods. Every time I came to Europe after that, I visited them for one or two nights at Belhade (and later at Le Brous, another tiny hamlet in the Landes). We talked and walked and visited the neighbors or some of the members of the FEECI.

In his Scotch-English, he relates his story in his own words.

MARIANO PUENTE:
"*. . . a laborer and a warrior.*"

"I look, as I am, an old Castilian. It seems as if I have come out of a picture to relate things of the past. I am not nice-looking, toothless, it gives my nose a disproportional measure. But is me, just as I am, skeptic and energetic, two contrasts that have followed me all my life. I don't think is a consequence of any deception, no, is a inheritance from my ancestors. That is what I think I represent, a laborer and a warrior. That is what they were, laborers in the hard clay soil of Castile and warriors of the faith. They were humble and great.

"I think I see them now as they were, dressed in black velvet, with the same severeness that you can see in my closed mouth and straight regard. The same severeness that I have employed in all my doings. The last is this one of Belhade, where I know I have made something nice of what was a wild place; and this beautiful family that we brought up here. I know this is not nice speaking of oneself in such proudness, is pretentious and uncorrect, but I can't help it, is the man in the photo that is saying what he was and what he is, and pardon him for his frankness.

In 1967 and 1968, in his Scotch-English, Puente told me his story about the taking of Puigcerda by the Communists:

19. Mariano Puente—describes himself.

"My name is Mariano Puente, militant of the CNT[1] in Spain. I was born in Burgos in 1900 on the seventh of December. My father was from Santa Cruz del Tozo and my mother was from Elas. They met in Vitoria and got married there and went to Burgos. My father established himself as a blacksmith and my mother was a seamstress. I had a big brother, Carlos, the father of Carlitos and Mari Sol. He died in 1955 and we brought the children here in 1956.

"At the age of one I lost my mother and at the age of three, my father. My brother, Carlos, being the oldest, took me to one of my uncles in a town called Villadiego, where I lived till the age of seven or eight. And then I was taken to Burgos to live with the family and was educated there till the age of twelve and six months. My brother went away to Bilbao and caught a ship and became a seaman.

20. Marisol, Argentina, Mariano and Carlos Puente, at Balhade in 1967, "where I know I have made something nice of what was a wild place."

"This brother, Carlos, took me to Glasgow, Scotland, to go to school, and he paid for everything. I was there from 1913 till 1916. He came to see me every 2 months. When he took me back to Spain, I was already sixteen years old and he employed me as an interpreter of Spanish and English in a seamen's boarding-house in Bilbao. We used to receive people from torpedoed boats, take them to the hospital if they were wounded or sick, and then find them employment. I was in that house till 1920 or 1919 when I went away to Barcelona, where I lived a few years. Then I came back to see my family again and I crossed the Pyrenees and came to France. I found a Norwegian ship in Bayonne on which I became a seaman, a seaboy. And then I've been living as a seaman for 7 or 8 years."

Where did you go?

Puente: "I went to the States. I was there only a few years. I went to South America for four or 5 years, I don't remember well. Then I went back to Spain. I was selling novels, house to house, in Barcelona and they took me to the Carcel Modelo prison because they thought I was a propagandist. It was during the repression of the CNT by Martinez Anido and Arlegui[2]. I wasn't in the CNT yet. I was in prison 3 months when they found that I should have been in the Army. They took me to the Army and 3 months later I ran away and crossed the Pyrenees once more.

"In France I worked as a seaman again. In 1925, I think, I came back to Bordeaux from South America and started to work. I learned the trade of boilermaker, but in one of the last crises of work that we had in Bordeaux, I lost my job. I was already married to a Frenchwoman and she wasn't working either. Then I thought I could sell Spanish fruit, and it would be an easy thing. This was about 1933 and I started with one of my friends. We bought a box of Spanish oranges to sell in the streets, three oranges for a franc. I remember that. In 1936 I really earned very well my life with 4 hours of work.

"When the Revolution started I went to Spain, because I considered it was time for the Spanish people to get rid of the military caste that has been dominating Spain for several hundred years. I went there also as an idealist. We have a climate and we have a temperament, we Spaniards, that we could be one of the happiest people in the world. I wanted my country to realize that state of life. And so, when I heard of the revolt of the Army against the Spanish Republic on the nineteenth of July,[3] I went to see my friends. And every one of us thought it was our duty to go and do whatever we could to save Spain from the new oppression. So I abandoned everything, leaving my wife and home, and with my friends went to Spain.

"From Bordeaux we went directly to Puigcerda,[4] where there was a group of comrades of the CNT with whom we were in contact before the revolution. We had a friend who had a very old truck and he ventured to take 10 of us. But he didn't even know the road. So at night (we only rolled at night), he entered a small road that took us directly to a river. It was lucky we didn't fall in! You see, it's typical. We had with us also some old guns from the War of 1914–1918. We only had about three or four of them and there were 10 of us.

"We arrived at Puigcerda about 5 o'clock in the morning. We were all tired but we were very content, very gay, because we were back again in Spain, to do something that we had never done before, and we considered it as a duty. In Puigcerda we were received as brothers. I remember those young men and old men, all those who were from the CNT and that have suffered so many repressions. They were so full of hate against those that you could call their former masters. And we saw how brotherly they received us.

"We wanted to go to the front, but they said: 'You can't go to the front. We need you here. This is a very strategic place on the frontier and we need you to defend it. Because if the Fascists come through here and get the frontier, well, they will have the connection with their partisans in France and we wouldn't be able to stop them.'

"You know, the Pyrenees are very long mountains, not very high. In Puigcerda it's only about 4,300 feet high. But it's a very nice place and it's very easy to smuggle arms or anything. So we said: 'We'll stay with you.' So we stayed with them and organized the militia with the people of the town [Each one of the Popular Front parties organized its own militia at the beginning of the Civil War.]. And later others came from other parts of France and they also stayed with us.

"We in Puigcerda, we made the revolution. We did what we thought and felt as libertarians we should do. We equalized the condition of life of every citizen. We gave each family the same amount of money weekly, so that they could all live in the same conditions. Those that were able to do something better for themselves were allowed to keep it. But economic equality was realized in Puigcerda. We had very, very good men, not very intelligent but men of good faith, such as Antonio Martin. We named him governor of Puigcerda, only to have a responsible man to indicate to us what was our duty.''

When the CNT took over the town, what happened to the landowners?

Puente: "Well, we took all the properties of the big proprietors of Puigcerda, but we left all the small proprietors with their cows and their land. And we municipalized the rest of it. As we had a milk factory in Puigcerda, those from the factory were organized. And we had a cooperative where we used to collect all the agricultural products that we distributed to the townspeople with their cards. At the beginning we had no cards. But later we were obliged to have rationing on account of the rarity of some articles.

"The big proprietors fled. Some of them were caught and killed because they had had a very bad conduct before the revolution with the working class, especially with those of the CNT. Each time there was a strike or something like it, our comrades were taken to the police station and were beaten by those people. So those from the CNT that remembered took them and they disappeared.

"We had in Puigcerda a few chalets, villas of very rich people, who used to come for winter sports, because a small town close by called Alp is a very snowy place and they used to go skiing there. We took all those villas and we placed children there in colonies.

"Puigcerda was a town that was very well organized according to the libertarian principles of equality for everybody. The only two privileged groups that we had were children and old men and women. We gave them everything they needed. I remember going with Antonio Martin to the hospitals and giving the old people cigarettes, cigars, and everything we took from the smugglers that used to come over even during the revolution. We had a nice colony of children. Even refugees from Malaga [Malaga fell to the Nationalists on February 8, 1937] came to Puigcerda, where we gave them all we could.

"The town is big, at that time about 3,000 people. Some of them were radicals, especially the agricultural workers because it's an agricultural town. And there were very few Socialists—very, very few. In Catalonia we didn't have many Socialists. But there were some, two or three I think, and they all had a place in our town committees. There were no Communists at all, but to give them a chance, we admitted the Communists from Barcelona; we had two or three of them. But they were such a small minority that they couldn't do anything.

"When the Communists tried to get Puigcerda the first time, they sent a train full of Carabineros.[5] It was before the May Days in Barcelona.[6] I remember well, I was the delegate of the administration at the station as interpreter because I spoke English, French, and Spanish. At the same time I was the delegate of the CNT. I remember that Antonio Martin told me that if they wanted to go up to the town that I should tell the officer to come along with two or three men of his group with me. We could have gone, but not all the Carabineros—they could have made trouble.

"So when the train arrived—I remember well—all the Carabineros descended, maybe three or four hundred. I think it was a trainful. I went to see the officer and told him what Antonio Martin had told me, that if he wanted to go up to the town he should go with me and two or three of his men, but we wouldn't allow all the Carabineros to come at the same time. We knew that they were coming, because they had telephoned from Barcelona that they were coming with the intention of taking Puigcerda.

"This man didn't even want to listen to me. He said: 'I came here and I have an order from the Government and I don't have to receive any order from you. So I told him: 'If you want to come and speak with us after you have spoken with your committee, you may be able to enter or no. It's according to the intentions you have. We are a peaceful town. We have never made any trouble for anybody and we are doing our duty on this frontier. Until now, nobody has complained about it. And if you come to take the town brutally, we'll have to defend ourselves.'

"When the officer saw that we had very good positions to defend ourselves, he said, 'All right, I'll go.' And he went up to the town with two of my comrades and two or three of his. They stayed about an hour and came back, and returned to Barcelona. I think they didn't consider themselves strong enough, because they thought we had more arms than we really had. We had arms, but we could hold out only for a few hours because we didn't have enough ammunition. But they got afraid, or maybe they though they could take it without noise.

"In Catalonia (I can't blame all the Catalans for it), there are a sort of Catalan Nationalists. And they are against any other countrymen that are not Catalans. But the revolution had reduced them. They couldn't work because the CNT in Catalonia was the most important organization. It was like that before the war, and even more during the war. And they organized what we could call the crime of Bellver, that I'm going to tell you about.

"I don't think there is any town in the world that could have all the necessities for all the people of the town. We had potatoes but we had no meat for the citizens. We had two delegates for food supplies, Basañes and his friend, sons of Puigcerda, who were always travelling in the outskirts, specially to Bellver, to try and get the meat for us. Bellver is a town that is about 10 or 12 miles from Puigcerda, and the butcher of the town was a Catalan Nationalist and Communist, as were most of the small proprietors and shop owners.

"The butcher of Bellver was well known by the farmers of the other towns because that was his job, also before the revolution. The revolution having taken nearly all the profit he used to make from his business, he didn't see Basañes and all his friends as comrades, working for the benefit of the people, but competitors who forced him to keep his prices down. That was the begining of the tragedy.

"I remember that we had already had some trouble before. Sr. Tarradellas[7] from the Generalitat,[8] with two other members, came to Puigcerda to see what was happening. We had a public meeting and the butcher of Bellver and some of his friends came—also Basañes and I think Antonio Martin—altogether 40 or 50 people. Sr. Tarradellas and his friends presided. The butcher of Bellver complained about the interference of Basagañes and his friend in their search for meat and the prices we paid to get the meat necessary for the town. I remember answering him, sayng that we were in a revolution and we weren't going to reestablish conditions which we considered had brought us to the revolution. I remember that Sr. Tarradellas approved discreetly with his head. We didn't come to an agreement.

"Our delegates continued going to the towns looking for meat and one day at the entrance of the bridge of Bellver they were received with pistol shots. They came back to Puigcerda and told us about it. We let it go for the first time, but we had to get meat for the town. A few days later they went back and again they were received with gunfire. They came back and we called a meeting of all the militants of the CNT and the militia. And we had the libertarian youth of Seo de Urgel, a nearby town, to give us a hand. At that meeting we decided to enter Bellver."

Antonio Martin:
   "The man who went first everywere."

"Bellver is on the top of a mountain and it is very difficult to get inside. Se we prepared to enter from two sides at the same time, armed of course, because they received our delegates with pistols. Those who came from Seo de Urgel came from the West and those from Puigcerda came from the East. When we were approaching Bellver, they fired against us. I was in the car with Antonio Martin and we heard a shot. We had with us one of the delegates of the libertarian youth from Seo de Urgel whose name was Fortuny; a very good and intelligent young man. And when we heard the shooting, Antonio Martin came out of the car and, as soon as he got out, he received a bullet in his left hand and he turned his back and received another one. . . . . [too overcome with emotion to go on] . . . .

"He turned his back suddenly to enter the car again but he got another bullet in the kidney and fell. Our friend, Fortuny, with his gun, went to the bridge and hid behind one of the big stones and fired, but he also got caught. I found myself with these two men, one killed and Antonio Martin wounded. And the chauffeur of the car went away with the car and I was alone with Martin.

"I don't know how I got him under the bridge. I wasn't able to carry him and I tied my belt to him to try and drag him under the bridge. But I don't know how it happened, I don't remember well now. We were under the bridge and there I waited hours and hours for somebody to come to get him to the hospital, to get a doctor, to do something for Antonio Martin. The militia came and took him to the Puigcerda hospital. I stood there to see if we could enter Bellver to stop that firing against us. But we didn't enter Bellver; we came back to Puigcerda.

"And poor Antonio Martin died the same night. He was one of the best men I have ever known in the libertarian movement, a man who didn't even know how to write but with the ability I would have liked to see in many diplomats. He had treated with the French authorities many times, always with that laugh that he used to have, and that *savoir faire*, and he always got everything he wanted. A man who represents the Spanish people. They have knowledge petrified in themselves, because they have seen so much, they have suffered so much.

"Who was this man criticized by his enemies? He was a very ordinary man, with intelligence, courage, and character. He could read, but wrote with difficulty. It was hard, and I think still is, for most Spaniards born in the country. He was born in a small town in Estremadura. From there he went to Barcelona and then to France, near Paris, where he worked as a bricklayer. He was expelled from France for social activities and came to Puigcerda a few years before the revolution.

"He was medium-sized, with very thick black hair, brilliant black eyes, and a long laughing mouth, broad shoulders, long arms and no belly. He had one stiff leg from an accident which I think he had in France. He was married to a Frenchwoman and they had a daughter. He tried to bring them to Puigcerda during the revolution but they never came. He was a very active militant of the CNT in Spain and France and well known in the town of Puigcerda. That is why he couldn't work in his trade and was forced to be a smuggler. Smuggling on the frontiers is a common thing in every country, not only by workers without work but by important businessmen for the profits they make from this trade.

"As soon as the revolution started in Barcelona on 19 July 1936, Antonio Martin and Basagañes and other militants of the CNT, with a few pistols and a lot of courage, took Puigcerda and neutralized all the forces of the town, specially the Carabineros who had real strength. They took the telephone exchange and other important buildings such as the town hall and prison and they organized controls all over the town and its surroundings. As Puigcerda was the most important town in the Cerdana, all the others followed suit and created municipalities, formed by the Esquerra [the Catalan party led by Luis Companys] of Catalonia and the CNT. There were no Socialists or Communists. The CNT in Puigcerda also took control of the frontier pass and the railroad. They never took control of the barracks of the Carabineros, but they guarded against them. As soon as they were in control of the town, they sent a delegate to Perpignan, France, where there were groups of militants of the CNT and anarchists, and they sent telegrams and letters to all the groups in France. That is how I knew about it and came to help them.

"Antonio Martin was what other groups would call the leader of the CNT in Puigcerda. He was the first to come out in the street with his pistol and he was the man who went first everywhere, like a lion, without fear. He faced all the dangers and responsibilities in the first moments and later. That is why he was named Governor. In the first days the lower classes had been so badly treated by the rich and the authorities that you couldn't stop the revenge. Things happened that happen in all revolutions. But to blame Antonio Martin for what happened in Puigcerda is done in bad faith.

"I remember, once, Antonio Martin and I went to Barcelona as delegates to a meeting. When we came back next morning, we were informed that the militiamen took revenge against twenty citizens of the town that were marked as Fascists. They had been shot. I don't know if the lot were really Fascists but some of them were and had taken part in the beating of militants of the CNT. Martin said of it: 'I didn't know anything about this till I came back from Barcelona but I take the responsibility for it, since I am in charge. But I don't approve and I promise it won't happen again when I am here or when I am away.'

"Antonio Martin had no bad habits; he didn't smoke or drink. He was what is called a sober man, but he was tolerant of others and not a fanatic. He was always dressed as a simple militiaman in blue overalls, with a leather belt across his chest to hold his pistol. His boots were the ones he had before the revolution. He wore a ring with a fake diamond on his land hand—his chauffeur had one too—and a watch in the pocket of his overalls—no other luxuries. He ate where he worked in the Governor's house, a simple bourgeois home in a street named 19 July after the first day of the revolution. He worked there from early in the morning until very late at night. Every day at midday he walked around the town and spoke to the people, simply as the man he used to be. When anyone had a complaint, he promised to do what he could, and he did. He was paid like all of us, 30 pesetas a week, which he gave to the landlady of the house where he lived. He did his duty with the responsibility of a man in a difficult position. There were weekly meetings of the militants of Puigcerda and those who came from France, where he answered questions. Also there was a monthly public meeting in the town theater, where after telling what had been done during the month, he asked the public for questions, suggestions, and complaints. He answered and promised to do the possible.

"Of course he was criticized by the Communists but not publicly (although they were invited with the others to participate at the monthly public meetings). The revolution in Puigcerda consisted in municipalizing the land that was not used directly by families, the houses that were not lived in by the owner, the hotels and restaurants, the coffeehouses, the workshops, and the factories, like the canned milk factory, the sawmill, the textile factory. All these working places were collectivized directly by the workers and they were responsible to their unions. Nothing was left to chance. Everyone was guaranteed a means of living according to the size of his family. Even those who had been punished by the revolution, the families of the men at the front and those who had money in banks, were allowed to take out weekly that same amount allowed to other families. The municipality took charge of everything to do with the health of the people; the hospitals, doctors, pharmacies, dentists. We created a big cooperative for all sorts of food. The tailors were municipalized and when anyone needed a suit, he received a ticket for it, and the municipality paid for it as well as for other personal effects.''

Why did the Communist Party criticize Antonio Martin?

Puente: ''I think it was because the CNT held the frontier and didn't let anybody else participate in the control, except for the Carabineros who were there before the revolution. Also because they thought that the CNT got arms through the frontier from France and that it was a frontier for all the needs of the CNT, without CP control. The Communist Party and the Catalan separatists portrayed Puigcerda as a horrible town and treated Antonio Martin like a criminal, saying a lot of things that never happened. They even used his physical defect to call him 'The Cripple of Malaga,' a sarcastic name to compare him to an unscrupulous bandit.

''With these calumnies they made a lot of bad feeling, in the official centers, in the CNT, and even among our CNT militants in the town, so that in his last days, even he was disgusted. He knew that he had to fight against an invisible enemy; he had nobody to catch, nobody to face. He was so disgusted that at the last meeting of the militants he resigned from his job as governor. He did it at a public meeting in one of the moviehouses. I was at his side as I had been every time that he was criticized, and I opposed his resignation. But he resigned. The Communists had won. He wanted to go to the front, but with his stiff leg he couldn't do it.

''He stayed in Puigcerda as a simple militant until the happenings at Bellver, only a few days later. And there he found his glorious death, facing those who had criticized him so much, the

Communists and Catalanists, defending the revolution for which he had lived and to which he had given all he had. There also he was the first. When the shooting started, he told the chauffeur to stop, against my will. He was too heroic; he had so much courage. As soon as he stepped on the bridge, he was shot, he fell, this is how he died. They took him to the hospital and he lived a few more hours. Doctor Pomar did everything he could because he knew that he was a good man, a man devoted to the people and the revolution.

"Before the death of Martin, members of the Regional Committee of the CNT of Catalonia came to Puigcerda to tell us that the Central Government wanted to take control of Puigcerda and the frontier. Of course we had no faith in the Carabineros, knowing that the Communists were the ones who commanded those forces. I remember that Antonio Martin said to them that we would never abandon the frontier to the Communists or the Fascists. But after his death they returned and insisted. We made them responsible for it because we couldn't do anything else, we had to obey the organization to which we belonged, the CNT.

"Some time later the Carabineros entered Puigcerda at night, several trucks full of them, and little by little they took all the strategic positions of the town, even all the corners of the streets. They came from Barcelona from the barracks but I think they were gathered from the center of Spain because they weren't Catalans—they were Castilians and Andalusians. In Puigcerda we were a minority, we were only about 20 to over a thousand of them, armed with pistols and rifles and bombs. And five of my friends got killed by the Communists in what we called the crime of the sawmill.

"The night before, we members of the CNT in the town had a meeting in my home. It lasted late, past midnight, and we decided to abandon all our positions on the frontier and start to work in the places we had decided one for each one of us. I think it was this decision that precipitated the *coup d'etat* of the Carabineros. I should say that our militants used to guard the frontier with one Carabinero from the beginning of the revolution, the two of them doing the same duty together.

"The repression started at 5 o'clock in the morning, a few minutes after dawn, just at that moment when these five comrades were killed. When I came out of my home between 7 and 8, to go to my new job at the sawmill, I saw Carabineros, rifles in hand, watching on both sides of the street. It looked strange to me but I continued to go to the station and the little road to the sawmill. The town square was full of Carabineros and townspeople. I went on to the lookout. Puigcerda is on the top of a mountain and at the end of the valley is the railroad that goes to a town called Latour-de-Carol, and on the other side to Barcelona. And at the lookout I could see the station and hear the shooting. I asked where the firing was and was answered: 'At the sawmill.' I went to the coffeeshop where most of the comrades used to go and found Doctor Pomar, and I asked what had happened. He said, 'I don't know, I don't know.' And a few minutes later I was arrested.

"Later I was told that the Carabineros surrounded the sawmill very early in morning and waited, I think, until the five comrades entered to work. I say, I think, because if the comrades had seen the Carabineros coming they would have fled to the frontier that is not far, or hidden in the mountains. But they were surrounded by the Communists, who fired against them with rifles and bombs. What have they done with the bodies? I don't know. Why have they done it? I am sure they were scared of us, the militants of the CNT. They thought we had money, arms, and ammunition. But they didn't need to kill them; they could have arrested them as they did me—for anything, even if it wasn't true, as they do usually. But it was the easiest way to get rid of them. That was the crime of the sawmill, committed by the Communists—a political and vulgar crime."

And the Communists kept control of Puigcerda?

Puente: "They had Puigcerda but they never conquered the people. This was the end of Puigcerda. The year was 1937, soon after the uprising of the Communists in Barcelona. The Communists wanted to control the town and they took it and controlled it until the last moment. It's a pity, it's a pity, that we were so kind to them. They were so cruel to us. Oh, I could tell you more about it but it gets me sentimental feelings that I don't want to have, because they are no good for me now. I don't want to forget it but I don't want to think on it very often because it hurts me too much. Our National Committee was so compromised with the Spanish Government[9] that they couldn't stop things like that. Because of the arms that Russia sent, the Communists presented themselves as the saviors of the Spanish people.

"When I was detained by the police, I was sent to the police station. The station is where we had the Government in Puigcerda, where Antonio Martin used to be. I remember well, three policemen were waiting for me there. They started to question me. I wasn't scared. I asked them, 'What has happened? What have you done? What do you want? 'It is for you to answer,' they told me. And I remember that one of the policemen fired his pistol and the bullet passed close to me.

"And this is how it ended. They put me in the church of a convent which they had transformed into a jail. We were about a hundred of us. I was there 3 or 4 days and without telling me why I was detained. Then Dr. Pomar intervened and said I was very sick and they took me to the hospital. I was there about a week. I remember that I couldn't eat; I was so affected with everything that happened and I didn't want to live. [Pauses, overcome] I remember when the two Civil Guards took me in the train from the hospital to the prison of Gerona. They handcuffed me so strong on my wrists that they bled. They accused me of a crime against a man that I have never seen in all my life, and they asked for 16 years of jail. I have never killed a person. I don't like that sort of cold-killing people. If a man is on the front and he has to kill those who are before him, because he has no other way to do it, well, I'll do as the other men do. But kill a man coldly? I will never do it. I haven't the spirit of a killer. I'm not a killer. The repression of the CNT was everywhere in Spain. And *they* called themselves from the CNT.

"I want to say that my wife was with me in Spain. She came a few weeks after me to Puigcerda. We lived there, as any other matrimony, me doing my job and she doing the house, as she has always done. She suffered from the life that I had to live during the revolution. At night I came home at 2 or 3 in the morning, because we had reunions and we were trying to do things in the town. And when I was taken to prison—well, she went to tell the police; why did they take me to prison?—that I have never done anything to anyone. And they didn't even answer. The only thing they said to her was: 'Don't worry about it.'

"And when the National Guards came to the train for Gerona, she came to the station. She saw how I was handcuffed so strong and bleeding, and she really got revolted. I have to say that the Director of the prison has been very kind and permitted my wife to come every day to bring me some food, because I was sick and usually ate only some meat and milk that she could get for me. She has been a very faithful person to me, my wife, specially in those hard moments when I was in jail. It was very difficult for her to make a living but she worked and she came every day to me. Is something that I will never forget.

"I was in jail 8 months and my wife got me a lawyer from the CNT. The comrades of the CNT in Gerona investigated and saw that I didn't even know the man I had been accused of killing. They got me out of jail provisionally. And from there I went to Barcelona, where I got a job as archivist for the CNT defense section that I organized with the comrades. I stayed there to the end of the war."

How did you leave Spain when the war ended?

Puente: "The night before the Fascists entered Barcelona, we left on top of a truck, my wife and I and another one of the committee who worked with me. One morning, we tried to cross the frontier through the mountains, but it was impossible. Then we found a shepherd who showed us the road that passed directly from Rabos to Port Vendres. There we got separated, women were taken to one side, men to the other. We stayed about 48 hours in Port Vendres and from there they took us to Perpignan and the camp of Le Haras. I was there about a week. Then they said all the aged and sick people should be taken to a village where they were prepared for us. They took us to Bram, where they were building a camp, but nothing was built. There was only wood, and we built the first barracks for the refugees of Bram. I stayed there 9 months. Then I came out to work, building hangars in the military airport of Chateauroux. In 1940 the invasion of France came. I went to Bordeaux and started to work and I worked during the occupation. In 1944 I fell sick—my lungs. The French Red Cross took me to a Sanatorium in Limoges, where I stayed nearly a year, I think. Then I came out to Bordeaux and I've been sick all the time since.''

Can you tell me why you don't go back to Spain?

Puente: "I don't go back to Spain because my temperament and my character may be able to support some things once, twice, a hundred, maybe a thousand times, but once I'll crack. I won't support no more. Then there will be the end of it. I would lose everything, I would lose my life. And I'd rather die in peace in France if I had to die. But my family tells me to go over there. They are workers, they have a good situation. But I wouldn't go back. I'm scared, very scared of myself. Yes.''

Mariano Puente died of a brain tumor on July 22, 1974, a few days after my last visit to him. I kept in touch with Carlos and Marisol. She married a Spaniard, Ramon Munoz, and their child, Isabelle, was born in March 1975. When I was in Bordeaux in July 1976 with my friend, Virginia, Carlos, who worked as a mechanic there, came to pick us up in his car and we spent the day with Argentina and Marisol and her family in Le Brous. Marisol and her husband both worked and they too had a car. They all kept in close touch with "tia" Argentina, who was getting old, and was lonely. She died in 1980.

NOTES

1. Confederacion Nacional del Trabajo (National Confederation of Labor). Syndicalist organization, started in 1910, with Anarchist tendencies.
2. General Martinez Anido's *pistoleros* assassinated hundreds of militants of the CNT in Barcelona in 1921. Among them was Salvador Segui, secretary of the CNT. At that time Anido was Civil Governor of Barcelona. Later he was the first Minister of the Interior under Primo de Rivera and Minister of Public Order in Franco's first cabinet. Miguel Arlegui was Lieutenant Colonel in the reactionary Guardia Civil and later Director of Security in Madrid.
3. 1936, the beginning of the Spanish Civil War when the military uprising against the Spanish Republican Government took place.
4. Puigcerda is on the border of Spain in the Pyrenees, east of Andorra.
5. They first came to Puigcerda on April 17, 1937. Acting on the orders of the Finance Minister, Juan Negrin, they began to reoccupy the frontier which had been controlled by the Anarchists since the beginning of the Spanish Civil War.
6. See chapter 2.
7. Josep Tarradellas, Finance Minister in the Catalan Government, was an exile in France for 38 years. He returned to Spain in October 1977 and became President of the Catalan Government, the Generalitat.
8. Official name of the Catalan Government, which at that time was granted certain local rights by the Central Government, as it has again today.
9. They were compromised because there were four CNT members in the Central Government, contrary to the principles of the CNT to take no part in bourgeois politics or governments.

10

SRA's Programs

A particularly human way that we had found to show solidarity and friendship after WW II was through Politics Packages Abroad (PPA), when our readers "adopted" individuals and families. I applied this program for SRA. Both givers and recipients were delighted with this person-to-person connection. "I cannot remember ever having had so much satisfaction out of helping others," one donor wrote us. Another wrote, "We do not give this help out of pity but as a natural expression of solidarity." Two German anti-Nazis who had been helped by PPA now became donors. Jose wrote his adopter, "I wish you could read in my heart what is so difficult to say in words. What a comfort it is to have a friend, far away, who thinks of helping. I will never forget it."

In Simone Pétremont's biography of the French philosopher, Simone Weil, I was delighted to read that she had adopted a Spanish refugee, Antonio, after the Civil War and they corresponded. Weil wrote him: "Don't worry that I am depriving myself for you. It gives me pleasure to send you something from time to time and what gives pleasure cannot be a privation. . . . I wish money were like water and that it would flow by itself where there was too little.''

In its first year SRA arranged for 70 "adoptions,'' but aid was sporadic. Later, help was organized on a regular basis. Money was sent to us monthly, quarterly, or yearly, and was distributed quarterly by our offices in France. We had the most adoptions, 476, in our 21st year (1973–4). People gave from $1 to $50 a month, averaging $10. Many sent clothing and gifts, corresponded with and visited their adoptee in France. A few completely changed the lives of those they helped.

Fulgencio Sanchez was one whose life was changed dramatically. He had volunteered to defend the Spanish Republic when he was seventeen. He had been wounded in the head so that he could scarcely open his mouth. When he was "adopted'' by some Spanish exiles in the U.S. he was thirty-four and living in an old-people's home ''surrounded by hopeless human wrecks, completely isolated, without any affection'' and without hope.

His adopters determined that the first thing ''is above all to make him feel that he is not alone.'' So they sent him $20 a month, clothing, books, and letters. Within 2 years they had arranged for him to leave the home and to enter a technical training school for electricians in Limoges. ''The merit of getting out of the Home and into the school is wholly his, he was so marvelous about not getting discouraged.'' After passing a 6-month course, Fulgencio set up his own shop and his adopters gave him $140 to get tools and said they would continue to send him $20 a month until he was self-supporting. After 6 years the adopters reported that Fulgencio even owned a secondhand car. They had visited him in his attic room and seen ''his rather terrible ice-cold basement shop'' but ''he is independent and no longer a miserable young man lost in an old people's home.''

Jesus Yuste was the refugee I adopted because he had Parkinson's disease and I knew what it was like because both my mother and my grandmother had had it. He was living in Morocco, where he had been recommended to SRA by the representative of the UN High Commissioner for Refugees. Soon after adopting Yuste I learned of a brain surgeon in Sweden, Dr. Lars Leksell, who was successfully operating on Parkinson patients. I wrote to him and he agreed to operate on Yuste without charge. The trip to Sweden was paid for by the UNHCR's office in Morocco, the International Rescue Committee, and the Swedish Committee, Individuell Manniskohjalp. The operation was successful, and the Swedish Government took care of retraining Yuste for a job, finding him work, and teaching him Swedish. Yuste is now well and he keeps in touch with me. Occasionally he goes to Spain to see his sister and her family. When I was in Barcelona in June 1977, I visited his sister, her daughter, son-in-law, and three grandchildren, and they brought out a bottle of champagne to celebrate the occasion. I had hoped to meet Yuste there but he had put off his trip until September. He plans to stay in Sweden where his future is assured.

Most of the adoptions were not dramatic like these two; but many friendships were formed, adoptees visited, morale lifted and daily needs provided for. The adoptees reciprocated in whatever way they could—by knitting, embroidering, correcting Spanish, sending postage stamps for collections, and expressing their affection. One of my own adoptees, Juan Porcel, wrote:

> Spain for me and many others has meant the disintegration of families, misery, illness. To speak about it is a nightmare, a horror. I came to France when I was twenty-eight, and here I am at sixty-four, having lived here for 36 years without my family, my country, and sometimes obliged to bear the insults of those who don't know what it is to live at the mercy of others. All these are the calamities which have been a part of living through a revolution. . . . I hope you will forgive me for writing all this but I must. In any case, the fact that you write me and give me your friendship, is like the plank that the sailor in distress finds in the middle of a storm. Thank you.''

My first visit to Juan Porcel Zamorano in the summer of 1974 (I went again in 1976) I wrote about. "My friend, Virginia, and I took a long bus trip out from Bordeaux to Pessac and then an even longer walk to the Hospice at Haute Leveque. We were limping when we arrived and then had some difficulty in finding the three Spaniards whom SRA helps in this vast Home. Finally we located them. They had been waiting but didn't imagine we would arrive on foot so had not connected us with their expected visitors. We sat and talked in Porcel's room on the ground floor (not unpleasant). The Hospice is surrounded with very tall trees and some woods. Porcel was voluble. He lost the use of one eye because of an unsuccessful cataract operation. He should have an operation on the other one but is afraid and says he'll put it off until he can't see anything. When we were ready to leave, he offered us his 'velomotor' to drive back on. He said we could leave it somewhere and he could pick it up. We declined!''

Porcel is a charming man, who is quite lonely. He begged me to keep in touch. He was born in 1911 at Bujalance near Cordoba. His parents died; one sister spent years in Franco's prisons, and his brother-in-law, who was in the Republican air force, was shot by the Francoists in 1939. Juan's wife died in Spain and the only time he saw his son was in 1938 when he was a few months old. He heard that his son is married and has two daughters but they are not in touch. Juan fought in the Basque Army and came to France in February 1939. From then until 1941 he was in French internment camps and then in work company #88. Later he worked in factories as a laborer until he fell ill in 1947 and after 4 years in hospital was declared incurable. He had been in the Hospice at Pessac for years. In February 1983, at the Mayor's Office in Bordeaux, Juan married Pierrette Gregoire, who was living in the same Hospice. They both write me regularly and send me odd postcards as they know I have a collection. I have helped Juan for almost 10 years with small gifts.

Another adoptee, Quintin Sarmiento del Collado, was born in October 1902 in Santander. His father died when he was 12. Quintin had been a chauffeur mechanic in Spain. His mother died during the Spanish Civil War and he was wounded in the lungs. I had been attracted by Quintin's beautiful flowing handwriting and had written him some letters when I went to see him at the Sanatorium of La Meynardie in 1967. He had had TB since 1951 and suffered from nervous depressions.

21. *My adoptees Pierrette and Juan Porcel. "Spain for me and many others has meant the disintegration of families, misery, illness. To speak about it is a nightmare and horror."*

When his TB was stabilized, he moved to the Retraite La Garenne at Souppes sur Loing. All the Spanish refugees there disliked it and most eventually left. As far as SRA could fathom, the Director, a Socialist, was unsympathetic and bureaucratic. Quintin disliked La Garenne too, so we arranged to have him moved to the Maison de Retraite at Hyeres on the Mediterranean near Marseille. I visited him at Souppes and also at Hyeres. Teresa Palacios visited him too, and wrote him often to try to raise his spirits. He died of heart disease in 1981. He was my adoptee for 14 years.

Purificacion Acon (Pura), the widow of Victoriano, was born in February 1884 in Villaroya de la Sierra. I adopted her in 1970 and continued until she died in 1975 at the age of eighty-one. Her husband fought at the front during the Spanish Civil War and he called himself a rifleman. Pura had friends with children whom she adored, but she had none of her own. Mme. Acon was a lacemaker and made me a beautiful handkerchief bordered with her intricate lace, made on a cushion with many bobbins that she tossed back and forth in creating her skilled work. In her last years she was too rheumatic to continue. Whenever I came to Montauban, she came to see me, a lovable, spirited woman, always dressed in black with a brimmed hat (I never saw her without it). She talked very fast in Spanish and told me about her problems and, understanding very little, I could only nod sympathetically. Later on, Teresa translated.

I adopted Francisco Fuentes for 10 years. He was very ill with Parkinson's and lived on the top floor of a dreadful tenement on the Quais of Bordeaux. He lived with a woman who took care of stray dogs, and when I visited I was greeted with a barrage of barking. Francisco always insisted on accompanying me down the steep stone steps when I left and I was terrified that he would fall, being quite unsteady in his heavy black boots. He died in January 1981.

These were the adoptees I was most involved with. I helped six others for shorter periods. Three were in Spain: one was blind, another was the sister of a sculptor who was in prison, and the third was the widow of a Republican Civil War invalid. The other three were Rosario Jimenez, Pedro Madonal, and Pedro A, who lives in Paris and whom I am still helping anonymously. Rosario, whom I helped for a year, has 3 grown children who now can give her the extra help she needs. I was attracted to Pedro because of his name, since I was often called Nancy Madonaldo. I met him once in Bordeaux, where he appeared to be living in a brothel, and we had a funny visit. He didn't invite me in, but seated me on a chair in the doorway of the building, while he stood awkwardly on the other side, as a troop of women passed between us! Since he didn't really need regular help, this adoption ceased.

SCHOLARSHIPS

Felisa Bengoechea was thirteen at the end of the Spanish Civil War. Her father, who lost his right arm during the war, could not afford to send her to school in France. When I met her in 1962, she was thirty-five and wanted to be a singer, but her voice was not sufficiently remarkable. She told me that her second choice was nursing. SRA arranged for a 2-year correspondence course in preparation for nurses training school, paid for by the *Arbeiterwohlfahrt* in Germany. Felisa wrote me, "Here is my dream, realized as if by magic. I know that I shall have to work very hard to pass the entrance exams but will do my best to succeed. I am really happy and don't know how to thank you."

SRA continued to help her, and in her first year of nursing school she placed second among 42 students. At forty, Felisa passed her exams with a citation and became a Registered Trained Nurse. At fifty-seven she owned a car and a house (where she took care of her parents and aunt), and married a fellow exile. She retired after many years of hard work. When I visited Montauban, Felisa took me and Teresa Palacios around in her car to see refugees in the outskirts. She drove with such animation I had to remind myself that her job in the hospital at Montauban was in *reanimation.*

Most of the c. 250 students we helped during 23 years were younger than Felisa. But quite a few, like her, had fathers who were invalids of the Spanish war or were chronically ill. Or they had widowed mothers and had been forced to go to work instead of learning a trade or studying for a profession. We helped them with scholarships varying from one to 10 years.

In 1966 SRA sent out an appeal in the names of Hannah Arendt, Daniel Bell, Richard Hofstadter, Hans Morgenthau, Reinhold Niebuhr and David Riesman, for a scholarship fund to honor Salvador de Madariaga on his eightieth birthday. Madariaga, SRA's Honorary Chairman, was also Honorary President of the College of Europe, to which, at his request, we gave a $1,000 scholarship, for a law student from Oviedo, Manuel Benigno Garcia Alvarez. SRA was also able to give another 66 scholarships during that year.

In 23 years we helped students to become teachers, nurses, secretaries, accountants, mechanics, cabinetmakers, engineers, civil servants, and farmers; with a sprinkling of agronomists, lawyers, architects, musicians, psychologists, laboratory workers, butchers, house painters, computer programmers, doctors, horticulturists, and even a policeman; one blind girl became a telephone operator.

HOSPITALS AND HOMES (H & H)

When SRA first began to disburse aid, we knew of 90 men (and a few women) in hospitals and old people's homes. By 1968 there were 456, and by 1984 only 106 were left. Most had died, some having gone back to Spain to die. At first we helped these refugees with as little as $5 a year. At the end we were able to help them all regularly, and many had been "adopted." These refugees were sometimes the only Spaniard in the institution where they lived (78 out of 438 in 1956). Others were in groups, from 74 at Hyeres, to three or more in Mirande, Vic Fezensac, Lectoure, Auch, Bordeaux, Revel, Castelnaudary, Cahors, Isle en Dodon, Carcassonne, and Lezignan.

Although all of these refugees received pocket money—10 percent of the French Government pension; (90 percent went to the place where they lived), the extra cash we were able to give and the visits we were able to make brought, as one wrote, "joy and smiles." For some, our money meant cheese for days, for others mounds of fruit, cookies, or wine. For those on diets it meant being able to buy the foods the Hospital did not supply. The money was also used for clothing, shaves, cigarettes, and stamps.

Mme. Berta, who had just visited 18 hospitals and homes in February 1963, wrote: "Some of these places are quite pleasant and the superintendents are kind and interested in the needs of the Spaniards. Others, often located next to the cemetery, are gloomy, old, and prison-like. A ninety-year-old said to me with tears in his eyes: 'This is the first time I received something as a refugee, after all these years of suffering!' ".

Antonio S. wrote us in 1966: "I have arrived in the Old People's Home without drum or trumpets and I shall have to have a saintly character to get used to this place. They feed and clean you here but *no more,* haircuts are free but no shaves. I hope you can send me something as it's hard to have to pick up cigarette butts discreetly and not be able to write to friends."

Mariano Puente of the FEECI wrote me in his eloquent broken English: "I wish you could find 'adopters' for all those in hospitals. It gives them such psychological shock, when they see that someone thinks on them. They feel so lonely, so closed by the hospital walls, turning round them with no more hope for anything. These small helps that you get for them are really fresh air of pure life, that they breathe when they come."

In 1969 one of our veterans wrote: "Here holidays are not celebrated. On Christmas Eve we had noodles and tea. On New Year's day we had sausages and salad. But thanks to the solidarity of all of you, we bought sardines, jam, and wine and we celebrated our own holiday. We send a fraternal embrace and we hope that in 1969 we will be able to return to a free and democratic Spain." When Suzanne visited Francisco T. in Chartres, she wrote us "He is so alone, and never has visitors. He cried with emotion when he saw me."

I made a special effort to see refugees in hospitals and old people's homes when I came to France. These visits were hard to make because of the sad surroundings and bleak future for these exiles. But I'll never forget those two refugees in the Sanatorium of La Meynardie, a beautiful but isolated place. Ramon was almost blind and tubercular, Quintin had had lung trouble for years. Visits were rare (Quintin's sister had visited him 2 years before my visit). When I left, they clung to me like abandoned children.

My visit to Paulina Flores in the Misericorde in Perpignan was unforgettable. She was sitting on her bed in an enormous, empty, dreary room full of empty beds, and when I explained who I was, she started to cry and all she could say was *estoy contenta, estoy muy contenta.*

Francisco Pinos, in the hospital of La Grave in Toulouse, I had met and taped in 1967 (see chapter 11) when he was living in his closet in a Quai on the river Garonne. He was brought to the hospital after trying to commit suicide by slashing his wrists. He had lost a leg, and much weight since I last saw him, and it was difficult to find words of comfort. His remaining leg was disabled because of torture by the Gestapo. He died in 1980. When I visited the Old People's Home in Chateaudun, one of the men led me into his room without a word, went to an old wind-up phonograph and put on a Spanish record. He stood by the window and looked out. We didn't speak, but when it ended, we shook hands.

Besides raising morale our visits sometimes brought practical changes. I visited the Hospital at Cahors with Teresa Palacios in 1969 and we talked to Jose B. He longed to move out of this overcrowded and ancient place. Teresa was able to arrange for his transfer to Hyeres, which was very modern and well run, and the refugees there were allowed to come and go as they pleased. Later, Teresa wrote me that "Life has completely changed for him, and he can't find words to thank us for arranging the move. It was hard work but worth it to see him so happy."

At the Hospice of Chateaudun conditions were very poor. We complained to the authorities and Suzanne wrote me that now "the food is good, it no longer rains in the rooms, and they are allowed to cook in them, there is enough heat, they are free."

In 1963 Suzanne visited Agustin O., a fifty-six-year-old veteran of the Civil War, who had lost one leg fighting for the Republic and the other leg in France in 1957. He was living in a terrible asylum for mental patients in Chateauroux and she was so horrified by conditions (he had lost 26 pounds in 3 months and was in despair) that she moved him into a hotel room immediately. In Paris she found a place where he could "live again in dignity. It will be expensive to move him, but when it is a question of saving a life, the money doesn't count. He is beginning to come out of the tunnel, as he calls it, and can see the sun." Later our Swedish friends were able to give him a motorized wheelchair and he was "crazy about his car (he called it 'my Rolls')."

In October 1967 Chloe Vulliamy visited the Domaine de Tribomont in Belgium where 21 Spanish refugees had been transferred from Morocco. When she visited there were 16 there and she wrote us that conditions were very bad. By May 1970 there were only 12 refugees left. Diego M. had just died after a long illness and Celerino Arroyo reported to us that "they only send us to the hospital when it's too late. Every day things get worse. Before, we had a radio and billiard table but they took them away. We don't even have a book to read. This center is set up so that the directors have all the comforts, in the name of political refugees. Soon nothing will be left of us but the documents which you preserve of our testimony of international injustice."

In June I visited Tribomont with my friend, Virginia Chamberlain, who was traveling with me. By then SRA had found "adopters" for all 11 of those who remained. Poor conditions still existed: not enough to eat, no hot water, spartan conditions in winter, and unpleasant atmosphere in a beautiful spot caused by an inhuman woman, who exploited these victims of the Spanish Civil War. Lilacs were in bloom and when a number of the refugees took us to the station to catch our train back to Brussels, Sixto Fernandez disappeared for a few minutes and returned with a large bouquet of lilacs which he had swiped for us.

Thanks to letters of protest sent in all directions by Celerino, Suzanne, and SRA, by 1972 Tribomont was closed and the remaining 9 refugees had been moved to La Hulpe near Brussels.

Celerino wrote me: "We are all well for the present and all very happy, if only to have gotten away from that bunch of thieves—you know how it was. Here we each have our own room with a basin, very nice. The food is pretty much the same but cooked better, although there's very little at night. Between you and us, we were able to overthrow that nest of bandits, who stole so much from us and mistreated us."

I visited them that summer at La Hulpe and saw how they were well cared for in a pleasant place. When Virginia and I arrived, Sixto was standing in the rain outside the *Home des Refugies* waiting for us, and Celerino had gone to wait at the bus terminal. Celerino at seventy-five looked very frail but he was still full of fight and proud of his victory. He said it would be the last time he would see us and he died in August of 1973. Sixto remained in exile in Belgium. The rest died or returned to Spain.

SPECIAL HELP—MEETING THE NEED

When SRA began its work, the Spanish exiles had a great many special needs. During our first year, April 1953 —March 1954, we paid for 10 artificial limbs, 2 wheelchairs, 14 dentures, 75 CARE blankets and household linen packages, 2 hearing aids, and travel expenses to bring together a family separated for 7 years.

Over the 32 years we were able to supply:

artificial limbs, as well as an artificial eye[1];
many wheelchairs, even a Lambretta;
an accordion with Braille music lessons for a blind veteran;
a mandolin, 2 trumpets, and a piano for other musicians;
typewriters for journalists, paint for artists;
work tools and sewing machines to artisans;
for households: beds, mattresses, stoves, and washing machines;
in clothing: everything, from a wig to a cassock;
for entertainment: radios, phonographs, TVs, tape recorders, cameras and books;

We paid travel expenses, as for a trip to the frontier "to see my dear mother, whom I have not seen for 21 years," or to help arrange the meeting of Juan and his two daughters in Andorra, who had been separated for 27 years. We paid for legal fees, debts, key money for apartments, house repairs, and even a telephone for eighty-nine-year-old Francisca C., who was almost blind and on crutches—thus enabling her to live at home for another 5 years.

During 25 years, we distributed roughly 102 tons of clothing. Some were bought, like 130 sets of winter underwear in 1955, 76 dozen sheets in 1968, and $2,000 worth of clothes for our office in Toulouse in 1974. Most of the clothing was donated—a ton of clothing and 370 lbs. of soap from Germany in 1957, clothing from England, Germany, Japan, New Zealand, and Switzerland in 1958 and 1959, and $1,000 for sweaters from England in 1964. We were able to buy 250 sheets with trading stamps donated to SRA by contributors in the seventies. Spanish Refugee Aid also bought and distributed food. The first large donation came from CARE which gave us 720 15-pound Christmas packages in November 1954. Later we bought food at wholesale prices for the Foyer in Montauban and for winter distributions in Toulouse.

On my second trip to Europe for SRA in the summer of 1954, I took with me on the boat two secondhand typewriters, one ultraviolet lamp, and two hearing aids, of which one went to Admiral Valentin Fuentes, one of the few high-ranking naval officers who had sided with the Republic. He came to my Left Bank hotel room in Paris to pick it up. I will never forget his face as he turned on the hearing aid and said to me, "Say something" and the big smile that followed when I spoke a few words in French.

Antonio Gomez Baños:
"One day I had the good luck to find a hovel."

The ultraviolet machine went to Antonio Gomez Baños, an aviator for the Republic who had lost his legs during the Civil War. His story (taped in 1967) follows. I found him in 1954 living in a damp cellar room when I brought him the lamp, which Suzanne thought might lessen the pains in the stumps of his legs. When I interviewed Antonio in 1967, he was living more comfortably on the outskirts of the city.

Antonio is a vigorous and attractive man with broad shoulders, strong muscular arms and chest. His hair is curly and graying and he has laughing, mocking eyes. He wears a bracelet he made of twined copper wire which he claims keeps away rheumatism. He lives with Mireille, an attractive young French woman, her son, Patrice, and a large dog, in a one-story adobe house with trellised grapevine over the door and a view of vineyards and cypress trees. The house belongs to his brother, José, who works in a doll factory and often comes for meals. There is a small swimming pool in which Antonio exercises. Next to the

22. *Antonio Gomez Baños, an aviator for the Republic.*

house is the workshop, with its earthen floor, where Antonio makes, out of cattle bones from the local abbatoir, beautiful architectural scale models, accurate in every detail. His model of Notre Dame de Paris is massive and contains 900 statuettes, gargoyles, and chimeras as well as 140 windows which can be lighted up at night. José has fixed up trucks to carry this work (along with two others, Notre Dame de Lourdes and the Arc de Triomphe). In summertime Antonio makes trips around France to exhibit his models and to sell postcards describing them to supplement his tiny French Government pension.

Antonio's "chariot" is an old 4 CV Citroen which José fixed up so it can be driven manually. Antonio can hoist himself from his hand-propelled wheelchair into the driver's seat. When he picked me up at my hotel the first time, he was accompanied by two adoring small boys who ran errands for him. We drove out of the city and then off into the fields, through vineyards, to his home. In the distance are the Pyrenees, and beyond is Spain.

23. *Model of Notre Dame de Paris made by Antonio Gomez Baños.*

I interviewed Antonio in his shop. In his wheelchair, his "knees" covered with a blanket, he spoke rapidly, without hesitation, in good French. He laughed a lot and spoke with irony in a gravelly voice about his situation, without self-pity. I asked him why he didn't get artificial legs. He said he had had them during World War II but that it wasn't possible at that time to get them properly fitted and they were painful to wear. Also, the amputation was too high. Now he's used to being without them and gets on well as he is. Antonio says he's not ambitious. Unlike most of the refugees, he dislikes politics. His dream would be to sell his constructions and retire to a desert island where he would find peace.

When the Spanish Civil War started, Gomez was a member of the very small and poorly armed air force, most of which sided with the Republic. That is why a private English plane, piloted by an English mercenery, had to fly Franco from the Canaries to Morocco when the war started; at the air bases of Tetuan and Melilla the aviators resisted the rebels and many were shot, the rest imprisoned. The following is Antonio's account of what the Air Force was like then and what his life was like after the war was over.

Gomez: "I am Antonio Gomez Baños, a former aviator of the Spanish Republic. War came, and although I had no political background, I was on the side of the Republic and continued to fight, until I had the bad luck to fall in a naval air battle. One day at about 6 p.m. I sighted a boat at Palamos, bombarding the Catalan coast 30 or 40 miles from the French border, and I was shot at and fell near Arenys de Mar. There were three of us in the plane. The tail gunner was killed. I lost my legs, had a fractured arm and several head wounds, and the machine gunner, who was in the back of the plane, was hardly hurt at all. When we fell in the water, it was he who saved me, who held me in his arms, until a hydroplane flown by Manuel Martinez Padilla came to pick us up and took us to Barcelona. I spent almost a year in the hospital, until the end of the war.

"I was born on June 16, 1914, in a little Mediterranean village

called Mazarron, near Murcia and Cartagena. It's mining country and my father worked in the tin mines.

"My father had no politics. He worked for his children and that
was all.[2] He was a pacifist. He didn't like to get mixed up in
politics, rampant in the working class districts of Spain and specially in Badalona. There were many Anarchists. One had to be
either an Anarchist or else get into a fight. As he brought me up,
naturally I was never involved in politics either. My father established himself in Badalona, an industrial outskirt of Barcelona, where he found work in the chemical industry. It was from
there that I left at the age of fifteen.

"A friend told me that he was going to study to be an aviator.
And I said: 'Me too.' And I made an application to a school of
naval aviation in Barcelona. There were 50 places, and 3,000
young people applied. They found 50 with the physique and the
possibility of becoming aviators, and among the 50, happily or
unhappily, I was chosen. It was there that I studied for 3 years.
After that I became a spotter in naval aviation and then I asked
to become a pilot and I took courses at Alcala-de-Henares for
planes with wheels. Subsequently I took courses for hydroplanes at the naval air base in Barcelona. I finished my studies in
1935 and received my license as an international war pilot. From
there I went to join the squadron at St. Javier near La Union. We
were there during 1935 and 1936.

"I was in the Government Naval Air Force. And there the war
caught us by surprise and no one knew where to turn. In 1934
there had been a revolution by the parties of the Left, against the
government of the Right which was in power. At that time, we
military men obeyed the legally constituted government. We had
taken an oath to defend the Government of the Republic. It was
a right-wing government and we defended it against the Left revolution. Two years later, elections were held and the people voted
for a left wing government. Then as military men we had to obey
the will of the people. We were with the Left because the people
wanted it. And so war came.

"We were isolated in the base for some days and Cartagena
was waiting for our decision, because at that time we had the

fabulous number of 60 planes. Today this would be ridiculous. Then it was strength. We were for the Republic, not for the Left or the Right. This was one reason why the war was able to last 3 years, because 60 planes on one side or the other counted. Later it wouldn't matter when intervention came from abroad. Then Cartagena, which was 18 miles from St. Javier, decided for the Republic, and then Malaga, Valencia, Alicante, Barcelona, also took account of our decision.

"I don't know exactly how many planes the Republic had but I know that it had a lot more than Franco's side. At that time all the civilian planes were requisitioned, but at the decisive moment, we had the most. All our aviation was organized to cooperate with the army and navy. And, surprisingly, our side also had most of the Spanish fleet and their side had practically nothing. But with the cooperation of the German and Italian boats they managed to annihilate all the boats of the Republic.

"Aviators were needed on all the fronts. I, as a naval pilot, went to the Madrid front as soon as the war started and later to Granada, Almeria, and Cordoba, and always with land planes. It was only much later in the war that I went to the Balearic Islands with two hydroplanes. Mallorca was in the hands of Franco but our base was in Mahon, Menorca. We stayed there for some time to watch over the island. But our strength was insignificant next to theirs. Franco made an agreement with Mussolini and the Italians were in command in Mallorca. They had fantastic little pursuit planes, Fiats. We had only three hydroplanes and practically no defense. We stayed in Menorca for several months but then were recalled to Barcelona, when it was clear that the island couldn't hold out, although it was well fortified. When we were in Barcelona, I was in charge of the convoys and the protection of all the boats coming from abroad.

"They came from Marseille, they came from Russia, and from everywhere. But the point of entry was always the French coast. There were a few brave ones which crossed the Mediterranean in a straight line, in the spots we weren't watching, but they arrived safely. But there were many, many boats that were sunk through stupidity. Because if the Navy and Air Force had cooperated, many boats could have been convoyed as they were in the war of 1939–1945. But we were disorganized. An airplane would be protecting one or two boats, but when boats under Franco's command arrived, protected by the German and Italian Navy, our Navy, for lack of decision, didn't come out, and that is why so many boats were on the bottom.

"We were being watched by the foreigners to such a degree that one fine day I discovered the Hindenburg, the zeppelin which with the Graf Zeppelin were the two collosi of Germany. This zeppelin came in past Rosas above Spanish territory. I was in Barcelona when the Ministry of War and the Ministry of Foreign Affairs were notified. I was told: 'Go out, go out, and chase it away, make it go, but *in no case* shoot.' So I left Barcelona and found this mastodon over the coast. There were women seated in the cabin, as if on a pleasure trip, looking around. I saw no one armed. Then I passed by two or three times the full length of the airship and made signs to them that they should leave. But they didn't make a move. Then I said to my two observers, one in front and one in back: 'Bring out the machine guns and I will pass very close. Don't shoot, simply show that we are armed.' Then I passed very close, made signals for them to leave, and then the zeppelin, very slowly, mounted the Pyrenees like a horse and departed towards the West, towards France. When I saw it go, I made a half turn and left for Barcelona. Then a few days later, this zeppelin, arriving in New York, caught on fire as it was landing[3]. I remember it was in the beginning of 1937.

"When the war started there were 101 pupils in my group, and we had just begun to go out with the squadrons. We were young, active, courageous, and everything was rosy. We had no fear and so they made use of us right at the beginning. Our first sorties were on the Andalusian front. You will be amused when I tell you that we went out in Vickers without machine guns, without even a revolver, *nothing, nothing*.

"We went to drop bombs. On the Cordoba front, there was a General, not well known at that time but *very well* known later, General Miaja[4], with his General Staff. He used to telephone: 'Eh there, go out and bomb such-and-such, please.' Then we would go out and drop bombs and made reconnaissance flights to see if there were convoys on the route from Cordoba to Seville. And we went out without a stone to defend us.

"One day I went out with a pursuit plane to protect me, to bomb the route. I was in a Vickers, slow-speed, but it could carry almost a ton of bombs. The pursuit plane was disabled, but didn't notify me, because we didn't have a radio. All these things are modern. When I had gone a long way, I discovered that I wasn't protected and an enemy plane had appeared. It approached, and seeing that I wasn't armed, signaled that he wanted to stop me and to make a half turn. I said to myself, *No*. I made the half turn, deciding I would return home. Then he attacked me three or four times and I swerved as I could and forced him to use all his ammunition and we were hit. But neither I nor my pal were hurt and the plane was still flying. He made a half turn and left, and we went back to Andujar, a small town about 15 miles from Cordoba. As we landed, our left wheel broke and I made two turns but I and my pal were OK. There was another plane there which was supposed to go out immediately. But the pilot was sick. So 15 minutes later, after our little accident, I went out again with another plane and again without ammunition. The sick pilot had to leave the base and I kept his plane.

"One day we were informed from Madrid that two large civilian planes were bringing us printed material to drop over Seville. I was to go and protect them. I took a pursuit plane and started off towards Seville. But before arriving, I asked myself, does the machine gun work? I tried it and nothing happened. I recharged it, and again, nothing. I wondered what was going on. Then the planes were ready to leave, since there was someone protecting them! But I had nothing to shoot with. When we arrived I passed close to them and said: 'Quick, quick, finish fast and let's get back.' Luckily they worked quickly and they threw out the propaganda papers over Seville.

"Then, as they were making their half turn, a Nieport of Franco's appeared and attacked them. I intervened and the civilian planes left. I found myself with him shooting and I couldn't shoot. But instead of running, I went towards him, since if he had gotten behind me, he would have shot and killed me. He feinted to one side and I to the other and we played cat and mouse. I was sweating blood, but at last he left and I did too. I arrived at the base and said to the ammunition men: 'There, that doesn't work.' They tried it and *brr, brr*—it shot. And why? Another day I went out and climbed 2 miles and tried the machine gun and—nothing. Finally, after much study, we found out that the grease on the machine guns was of poor quality and at 2 miles it froze and the gun jammed.

"It was summertime, but if you go up 2 miles you can't imagine how cold it is. Nowadays the airliners are heated and pressurized. But in a plane then, it was completely open and when you went up you froze at 2 miles in August and down below one was perspiring. That is why we were dressed so warmly. Sometimes I am asked if I was an aviator and I say, 'Yes, I was the pilot of ox carts.'

"Now when you see planes arriving on an airstrip at night, there are flares. They land as if it were daytime. But at Andujar there were no lights. When I arrived at night they put out four piles of burning straw and it was a miracle that I landed. But I said to myself: this won't do. So I arranged to have a line of three electric lights attached to poles at a height of about 5 yards. When I came in at night, they lit a pile of straw. I would go towards it and when I saw the three lights at a distance, I knew that I was near and I fumbled and fumbled and slowly, slowly, I came in.

"Once I talked with an aviator who flies a Caravelle and told him about it. And he said: 'My God, you had to have the touch. Now one doesn't have to be an aviator. You must study a lot but the planes fly by themselves. They have an automatic pilot, as you know.' Often we didn't have a compass or altimeter. It was war. That is why among the one hundred and one students that were at the aeronautical school, many disappeared and the ones who are still alive are total wrecks. There is one at Narbonne who has a fractured spine.

"If we, young aviators, had had good planes at the beginning of the war, the results would have been different. I would have liked to have fought with the enemy planes when I had an equally good one. You know, to explain our war, it's not the same as to have seen it. Our camp was a football field which had been lengthened a little. When the first plane arrived in Andujar, the people came rushing out crying 'Long live the Republic.' All the representatives of the political parties came to see us. But we had to sleep under the wings of the planes; we had to fuel them, and put in the bombs which were brought to us in trucks. In other words, we had to do everything. We would get up at 3 in the morning to go out on duty. For 15 or 20 days we had nothing hot to eat. They gave us a bottle of wine, a piece of cheese, some bread, and a box of sardines. Everyone was sick, but I had a strong constitution. So I had to replace first one and then another. (I am explaining this to you so that you will see what a state we were in.) We had no clothes, or pocket money, because when the war started, we didn't wait for anything, for pay or clothes or anything. It was thought that it would only be for 8 days but after months and months we had only one pair of shoes and these were worn out. We went almost barefoot. And another thing: we were used to a military life but at the camp we were at the orders of a civilian committee. We had to agree with them and say UHP.

"'UHP—Proletarian Brothers Unite [Unios Hermanos Proletarios].' It was a revolutionary slogan [used by the Asturian miners during the 1934 revolution and later by the Popular Front]. I myself didn't know what it meant but I saw that everybody said it and I said it too. Then we would arrive somewhere and knock on a door and ask for food. 'Oh, but we are finished. Go and eat like everyone else.' Yes, but where? The bombs and drums of fuel arrived and we had to pump the fuel and place the bombs and even sew up the plane, because the rear ends of them were made of heavy cloth which looked like aluminum. One of my friends had the tail of his plane broken by gunfire. We had to borrow a needle from a woman in a house nearby, and sew it up lying under the wings of the plane.

"It was like being in the middle of Africa. The people had never seen a plane near at hand. Everybody loved to touch them and go in—it was a people's plane. We couldn't say anything.

Everybody was armed except us! Later there were sentinels to guard the planes and a depot of arms and everything. But when I arrived there was nothing. As I said, it was a football field and the gateways had been taken down and it was lengthened and that is where we came down.

And the amputation, how did that happen?

Gomez: "When our plane fell, the boat we had been attacking left, but came back at night. [This was on June 7, 1937, while he was attacking an armored cruiser which was bombarding the Catalan coast.]'' An alarm was sounded in Barcelona and all the lights were shut off. The hospitals had no electricity. At that time I woke up and found myself in an operating room (I didn't know it was one) and I saw four candles [whispers]. Naturally I knew that when there is a corpse there are four candles put by it to illuminate it [laughs]. I opened my eyes and saw these things and said to myself: 'But I'm not dead yet, what are these candles doing?' And they said: 'Keep quiet, keep quiet.' Then I felt as if someone was sawing wood, and it was my legs they were sawing. I didn't know because I had been given a spinal anesthetic. They put me in a room, my legs felt badly, but I didn't know they had been amputated. A little nurse talked to me through the night since I couldn't sleep. I was still drugged and I felt pain in my legs but nothing like the pain I was to feel later.

"When I was awakened by the pain, it was a disaster. I didn't have the luck to fall into good hands. When someone called from the base asking about the condition of the aviator, the doctor replied: 'He's dead.' So at the base they ordered a coffin and sent it to the hospital morgue. Two or three days later they asked in the morgue, 'Antonio Gomez, when are you sending him down here?' The answer was: 'He's not dead yet.' They replied, 'Well, what should we do? Return that thing, the coffin, or what?' [laughs]. They said, 'No, no, don't return it, since he's going to die sooner or later.' Since they thought that, they amputated like a butcher cutting up meat in a butcher shop. The way they cut the hoof of a lamb. Like that! [demonstrates]

"At the time they were amputating (I learned this later), a doctor named Harcourt, who seems to have been at Oxford University, passed by. This man touched my legs and asked, 'Who amputated these legs?' 'That doctor there.' 'But that's madness. You didn't have to do something like that!' The doctor touched my leg to see if it was gangrenous. When I had the accident they had made a ligature and the blood had stopped circulating and the lower part of my leg turned blue. And the so-called doctor said that he confused it with gangrene. *I* could be confused, I'm not a doctor. But a doctor? In any case, this Dr. Harcourt, when he knew this, called together all the surgeons and gave a lecture on amputations of arms and legs, based on those two legs of mine."

Did they think the doctor was a Fascist?

Gomez: "It seems there were many fifth columnists as they were called [The term originated during the Spanish Civil War. The Spanish Fascist General Emilio Mola said he had four columns attacking Madrid and a fifth inside the city.]. I consider this a base thing. Because if one makes war, one makes war. But to settle with a man who is in an operating room, that's not fair. I don't want to say to you, yes it's true. But it's something to think about. Anyway, someone confided in me and said, 'My poor friend, you have been the victim of this injustice.' But there was a doctor who was nice, Dr. Olivares, an honest man, a man who didn't amputate a leg until he saw it dropping off. And the other doctors in the hospital treated him as if he were crazy, until in the end he was locked up like a madman. These others amputated arms and legs and everything—it was a way of fighting as if they were in the trenches. It is a little questionable, a little hard to say something like that but unhappily it was true."

Was your wife with you when you first left Spain?

Gomez: "Yes, my wife and daughter were with me [The Gomez family came to France in February 1939.]. (Margarita's little one is called José Antonio—Antonio for me and José for the father of her husband; he comes to see me.) We stayed together until the war broke out in France. I was included among the old people and the women and children. We left for the Hautes Pyrénées and we found refuge in a small village, St. Savin. There were about twelve of us, my wife, my sister-in-law, my daughter and I, the brother of the poet, Antonio Machado[5], his wife, a friend of theirs and the wives of two aviators. We stayed there until the rout of the French army. Then we were sent to a French concentration camp.

"The floods of 1940 caught us in the camp of Argeles and there we saw everything [Antonio told me that it was in the concentration camp that he realized how inhuman people can be. He remembered only two individuals who helped him. One, who had caught and killed six rats, gave him one. Another gave him some bread.]. My wife said: 'I'll go to Spain and see if I can arrange for you to come back.' She left with the little one and when she got there, she asked what my penalty would be. They told her I wouldn't be condemned to death but that I would have 30 years in prison. I told her: 'Listen, for 30 years, let's wait till the end of the war.' When the war ended she tried to arrange to come to France to be with me but the frontier was closed. She tried everything but then she fell ill and died. I was in the concentration camps until the arrival of the Germans. Then I was able to escape and went to stay with a sister in Port Vendres, on the Mediterranean.

"When the Allies started to land, the Germans fortified all the coast and came to Port Vendres. At that point I was in despair and didn't know where to go. I didn't want to return to the interior and I said to myself that no matter what happened I would go to Spain. So I wrote to the Consul and asked to be admitted but was refused. The French authorities would have to take care of me and send me somewhere. With all the uncertainy, I decided to go to the hospital and have my left leg reamputated; that is to say, they fixed up the stump. I didn't really need it but we were to be evacuated and I needed more time to make a decision. I said 'My leg is hurting me.' So I entered the Hospital of St. John in Perpignan and they reamputated my left leg. In Spain they had amputated roughly but I could have borne this all my

life. But I needed time, because the Spaniards (all of us) thought
that once the war ended in France, our problem would be settled.

"I spent 4 months there because the reamputation didn't go
well. In those 4 months I made friends. When they realized my
situation, that I had nobody and nothing, they didn't want to send
me away, and they kept me at the hospital until the Liberation.
And when the Liberation came, despite the amputation of my two
legs, I wanted to pull myself up in some way. I couldn't think
about aviation. I didn't consider working in an office since I
didn't know the language perfectly. But I had to do something.
There was a wartime lack of everything and I noticed an advertisement in a paper for women's shoes. [laughs] I realized there
were none in France. So I took a shoe, put it in the wash basin,
took it apart and said to myself: 'It's not hard to make shoes.'
That is how I made a little money making shoes.

"After 2 years in the hospital I couldn't stand it any longer and
I came out. At that time the Quakers [American Friends Service
Committee] were helping us a little, but I couldn't make a go of
it and soon went back. That time I had myself operated on for
appendicitis. [laughs] It was nothing. You know, each time I saw
something going badly, I had an operation. I knew the people in
surgery and I preferred to be there than in the medical section
where there were contagious diseases. This went on for 8 years—
8 years!

"There was one thing I really needed, to find a place where I
could live. I knew I had to find something to do to pull myself
up. My morale had been very good, because even without both
legs one sees such miseries in the hospital that two amputated
legs was nothing. If I had looked ahead I would have been un-
happy because I would have seen people who were living the
good life. But always looking back, I kept seeing people who
were worse off than I was. And that gave me the courage to be
able to struggle.

"So I searched, and one day I had the good luck to find a
house, a hovel, a kind of cellar in the rue Pierre Troué. And it
was there I found out what I could do to pull myself up. I had

seen a boy who had made a little model of Notre Dame de Lourdes out of wood and that made me think, because in the concentration camps we had amused ourselves by making things out of bones. Although bone was an attractive material to work with, it was not possible to make massive things with it. But with small pieces one could make a construction.

"As a pilot I had to know mechanics (the radio, and how to fly a plane). If I had had my legs and had not been able to fly, I could have been a mechanic, worked on radios, or been an electrician. If I had had my legs I could have been a civil pilot in France because after the war there was a need for pilots. But all these things were no longer possible.

"So I began by picking up bits of wood thrown away by cabinetmakers. But that didn't work. I bought the motor of a sewing machine and a saw and I found bones at the slaughterhouse and the tripe shops. I cut the bones into tiny pieces and started to make constructions. First I made Notre Dame de Lourdes. I had some success with it, but in my state I couldn't tour France. So I gave it to someone to take around for me but he played me a bad turn and I had to take it back.

"By then I had already started Notre Dame de Paris [Antonio spent 6 years making it. At one point the municipality of Paris considered buying it, but that did not eventuate.]. I started it without knowing that soon there would be an 800th anniversary. When I learned that this would be in 1953, I said to myself that I would have success. I worked with a great deal of faith, thinking I would arrive in Paris magically. Unfortunately when I did arrive in Paris with my truck I was not allowed to show it. I had to exhibit it in the suburbs and try to find a buyer, but I never found one. I went from town to town and in the end I was discouraged because in my state it was very painful, going around like that. I had to go to a town, get permission to show Notre Dame, show it there, stay all day waiting for people to come and give me their good intentions. Many people had good intentions but no money, and others had money but no intentions. [laughs] It was the time to show it, put it in the summer centers, in the festivals, in the store, but they didn't allow it. They gave permission only if you knew the ropes.

"Already I have made the basilica of Lourdes and Notre Dame and when I have finished the Arc de Triomphe of the Etoile, there will be three magnificent works. I will try to show them at a great fair, the fair of Paris. At this fair there are many people who come representing other fairs from other regions of France and even foreign ones. And I will try to find four or five fairs where they can be shown. And I will earn enough money to allow me to live, if not in opulence, at least peacefully."

How did you get your car?

Gomez: "My youngest brother, José, is a mechanic, and when I had been here for some time, he said he wanted to come to France. We were lucky enough to find a place next to mine and he moved in there. And he bought this car; it's not a Cadillac [laughs], but he had the idea of making all the controls hand-operated. It's very convenient, this car. It's good to be in one where you are a person like others, while in an invalid's car you are always an invalid and it's sad to say that people regard you like that very often. Understand? Consideration—respect—and all that—is a result very often of the way in which you present yourself. But with an invalid's car there is already discredit.

"I noticed this because I lived in a hospital and I saw Spaniards who couldn't even read, while I, more or less, finished my studies and had an important enough job in Spain. Anyway, these people, who couldn't even read or write, who morally had little value, in seeing themselves physically superior to me would always slap my back and say: 'How is Antonio? How is it going? Poor Antonio!' It didn't make me angry—it made me laugh. I looked at them and would say: 'OK, OK.' But deep down I said to myself: in life there are men who are poor and men who live poorly. These people were mostly men who lived poorly, while I am a man who is poor but I don't believe I can say that I am a poor man."

NOTES

1. "Please accept my sincerest thanks for the artificial eye. Thanks to you, I have been able to dissimulate a physical defect, not because of vanity or a justified embarrassment, or to avoid that feigned compassion which we Spaniards call a 'rabbit's smile'. But only so that I would be treated like a normal person and considered as such at work."
2. Antonio was one of 6 children. He and José are in France and another brother is in Morocco. He has three sisters (two in Badalona and one in France). His eldest sister and her husband brought up Antonio's daughter, Margarita Gomez Carbajal, born January 4, 1938. They are like her parents, since her mother died when she was five. She is married and has two children.
3. The Hindenburg was destroyed while landing at Lakehurst, New Jersey in May 1937.
4. General José Miaja was Military Commander of Madrid when the Civil War broke out. He refused arms to the workers but later was famed as the defender of Madrid. Before the war he had secretly belonged to the right-wing military organization the *Union Militar Espanola*.
5. Antonio Machado, one of Spain's greatest poets, died in exile early in 1939 and is buried in Collioure, P.O., France. His family refused to permit his body to be returned to Spain while Franco lived.

PART III

11

The People We Helped

PRISONERS OF FRANCO

At the beginning of the Spanish Civil War, on 30 July 1936, Franco stated: "I will kill half of Spain if necessary." Executions began at once. In Seville alone, it has been estimated that 6,000 were killed by the end of 1936. Franco's specific enemies were officers of the Republican Army (if captured, they were always shot), members of the Popular Front, Free Masons, CNT and UGT officials and members of the Casas del Pueblo. But there were also mass court martials and large scale executions such as the frightful one in the bull ring at Badajos in August 1936. It has been estimated that 200,000 Republicans were executed during the Civil War and another 200,000 from 1939—1950.

It is believed that 2 million people passed through the prisons and concentration camps of Nationalist Spain by 1942 and that there were 3 million Spaniards living in conditional liberty in September 1951. This "liberty" was granted when prison terms were finished or after three-quarters of the term had been served. Remissions of sentences were granted to some after 6 months in prison: for 2 days' work, one day of remission was given, but it was denied to those who had tried to escape or were guilty of persistent misconduct. Provisional liberty was abolished in 1968.

How many amnesties were proclaimed in Spain is uncertain: those noted are of September 1945, July 1947, September 1949, May 1952, October 1961, November 1966, March 1969, and October 1971. Since the death of Franco on November 20, 1975 there have been others, the latest on March 11, 1977. The amnesties were farces; each applied only to specific cases. For instance, the amnesty of 1961, to celebrate Franco's 25th year in power, applied only to those who had been in prison for at least 20 years. The general pardon of October 1, 1971 didn't apply to prisoners convicted for acts committed prior to July 1965. Fernando Carballo Blanco, for example, who had been in prison off and on for 22 years, was released on January 13, 1977. He had been in prison this time since 1964, having been sentenced to 30 years, and had not been released until 1977 despite the intervening amnesties.

In February 1977, torture was still being used during police station interrogations. The prisoners were beaten everywhere, including the testicles; there was a water torture, running the gauntlet, hanging from hot water pipes. Some died or committed suicide under torture. There were no limits to the inhuman treatment of both men and women. At the end of the Spanish Civil War there were at least 300,000 people in Franco's prisons. Nine months later on January 1, 1940, there were still 270,710. Fifty-eight members of the Republican Cortes had been shot.

During the SRA's active years, the question of Franco's political prisoners was raised a number of times. Could we help them? How? In 1956, our first attempt to get information about Spanish prisoners in the USSR met with complete frustration. We wrote to some two dozen individuals and organizations and learned nothing. In January 1961 I had a note from one of our sponsors, Prof. Robert Alexander of Rutgers. He had been appointed an adviser to Kennedy on Latin American affairs and he asked if SRA could do something about the families of political prisoners. He had been in Spain during the summer and said that their situation was terrible and he felt that SRA was the outfit to do the job.

Morally, it seemed to me imperative for us to act and realistically it seemed to be the right time. I raised the question at our next Board meeting in May. Carmen Aldecoa offered to organize an evening of entertainment and dancing to raise money for the families of political prisoners in Spain, the proceeds to be sent to the Alianza Sindical Espanola. On June 9, $1,000 was raised, sent, and eventually acknowledged. But we never received a report on how the money was disbursed; and SRA's Board decided not to do anything further at that time.

Again the question of prisoners in Spain was raised in February 1967, when I called a special meeting at the home of Hannah Arendt to discuss the question of forming a separate committee to disseminate information with these purposes.

1. Americans could be better informed
2. To give the opposition in Spain the realization that the Communist Party was not their only ally
3. To show the opposition that we did not think that the Communist Party versus Franco was the only solution

The United Automobile Workers (UAW) was interested, and I met with their representative, Louis Carliner, several times. At a meeting called by Norman Thomas, Allard Lowenstein spoke about prisoners in Spain and played the taped stories of several, but such meetings produced no practical response. However, the UAW did contribute to SRA from time to time and they also directly helped the Socialists in Spain.

In March 1972 we thought of making the project to be called *Spanish Prisoner Aid (SPA)*, part of SRA's corporation. To do this we had to change our by-laws, with the consent of all our corporation members. The only dissenter, Jeanne Hall, offered to resign if this was needed. During the summer I talked to a number of people in Europe about SPA, including Jordi Arquer, Dan Gallin, Hans Matthoffer, Alicia Mur, Carlos Pardo, and Jordi Vilanova.

I returned home with the conclusion that there were only a very few prisoners to help, and that it would be hard to assure that money got into the right hands. Matthoffer cautioned me that if too much money were sent to one prisoner, it could fall into the hands of the Communists, who controlled prisoners' funds. In addition, we found an impediment in the U.S. Our incorporation papers, needed to make this change, could not be located. (They turned up when our first lawyer, Ernest Fleischman, who had retired to California, sent us our full file.)

But SRA helped many refugees who had been in prison in Spain. In 1977, 68, or 4 percent, of our Spaniards had been in Franco's prisons. One woman, Libertad, spent 5 years there; her husband was shot; she was beaten so badly that she was left totally disabled. Joaquin, a writer, was in prison for 7 years, and was brutally tortured. In France he was in and out of psychiatric hospitals. While Carmen was in one of Franco's prisons, her children died. Manuel C. was in prison because he was the secretary of a trade union. Ramon A. was in the prison of San Juan in Pamplona for 20 months where "there were 25,000 prisoners and they shot 15,000." Manuel M. fled to France on one leg, a crutch, and the clothes on his back, after years in Franco's jails. "I decided to quit the Francoist hell and reach freedom."

The stories of Faustina Garcia de Castro and Primitivo Sion Velasco give a picture of what prison life was in Fascist Spain.

They both spoke in Spanish. Chloe Vulliamy translated the tapes into English for me.

Faustina Garcia de Castro: Women in Franco's Prisons

Faustina Garcia de Castro lives in Montauban with her husband, Juan. She is a pretty woman, with soft, deepset, kind eyes and a generous mouth and jaw. Her white and wavy hair is short. She stands with her head forward and her shoulders bowed, but she moves about quietly and efficiently and is never too busy to help with anything.

She is very proud of her two boys. Luis, the elder, born in 1954, is married, has a baby girl, and works as a designer. He is a direct sort of person, affectionate and practical. Juanito, born in 1956, is more complex and brilliant. He is working in Venezuela as an engineer.

24.   Faustina Garcia de Castro was in Franco's prisons for over 12 years; Juan lost his right arm in the battle of the Ebro. Luis and Juanito are men now.

Their father, Juan Castro, is short and stocky. He was a farm worker in Spain and energetically continued to work on the land in France despite the loss of his right arm on the Ebro front in September 1938. He speaks an incomprehensible mixture of French and Spanish. For a while he cultivated his own piece of land with his sons, as well as working on the land of another farmer. He walks with a swagger, jerkily, sure of himself, but not boastfully so. He laughs a good deal, and he, too, is proud of his two big boys, now men.

Faustina worked part-time at the Foyer Pablo Casals as assistant to Teresa Palacios, helping keep the foyer in order, making up packages of food for the 300 refugees once on its rolls, mending and making clothes, and tending the garden. At home, she cooked for years for her family of four men, including Juan's brother, who helped pay the rent. They had two bedrooms, a kitchen, dining room, and bath. At one time the boys and their uncle slept in one small room and Faustina and Juan in the other. In her spare moments she used to make clothes for the family, including pants for the men. She embroidered exquisite linen gifts for special friends and their babies. When my grandson, Zachary, was born in 1969, she sent him two beautifully embroidered sheets for his crib. She wrote me: "I hold a needle in my hand with much greater ease than a pen." She had 12 years and 4 months of prison in which to perfect her skill.

She recounted her experiences to me in 1967.

Faustina Garcia de Castro: "My name is Faustina Garcia. I was born on July 29, 1915 in Alcocer in the province of Guadalajara. My parents were country people, small landowners who worked hard for a living, always just a little better off than the farm workers, who have always been poorly paid in Spain.

"I married Juan Castro on January 15, 1937. My husband was born on June 24, 1913, also in Alcocer. When the Civil War broke out, my husband and a brother of mine went off to the front. My poor brother died in the first battle, shattered by a cannon blast. My husband was wounded first at Brunete, [the battle of Brunete took place from July 6–28, 1937] shot in the kidneys. Once he had recovered, he continued to fight. Then in the battle of the Ebro [July 25, 1938–November 15, 1938.], where they died by the thousands, he was critically wounded on September 27, 1938, and they had to amputate his right arm.

"I could not even go to see him, because the Fascists had already encircled and cut off communications with Barcelona. He was in the hospital when the war was beginning to be lost, and finally he had to be evacuated to France. He came on foot with many other wounded from the hospital. They had to leave in spite of their injuries.

"When he arrived in France, he entered a hospital to recuperate. Then he was put in a refugee camp for the wounded in Caussade. In this camp they let him go out to work, and he went to pick strawberries on a farm. He was working there when they came to get him and put him in the concentration camp at Septfonds. But after being there for about 2 weeks, his boss arranged his papers and came to get him, so that he could continue to work on his farm. He worked there for 23 years without interruption.

"On March 28, 1939, the war was lost. I was with my mother in my village, Alcocer. I had gone to take care of her because she had broken her leg. At that time I was working as a servant. The people I worked for were from my town. My employer was executed in the Republican Zone. Once Franco won the war, this man's wife denounced me, saying that I must have known that her husband would be arrested and that I should have warned him, that she knew very well that I could have prevented his death. She accused me of being a spy in her house. She based this opinion on the fact that my husband's eldest brother was a political leader in the town. The poor man had died fighting at the front. Before the Civil War the Rightists had made him suffer in every possible way. He was always persecuted and refused work, and when by chance he happened to come home, the Guardia Civil was waiting to question him.

"My accuser couldn't take revenge on my husband's brother because he had died in battle. So she said that I was a spy in her house, and it was as such a spy that I was judged. This was the denunciation that she made against me. But she denounced so many people that one day the judge, tired out, asked her if all these people had been involved in the death of her husband.

"On May 3, 1939, I was called for questioning and on the 5th they came to arrest me, taking me to the emergency prison at Alcocer. This wasn't a prison, it was a stockyard. They put the men in the stables and the barn and the women in a room. Twelve women were detained there, sleeping on the floor and eating what our families brought us.

"From there they took me to the prison at Sacedon, which was the capital of the province. We were there only a few days when we were transferred to the men's prison at Guadalajara. A few of the women were in cells, and others were in a room that opened into a courtyard. But many of us had to spend the night outside because of the lack of space in the heat, rain, or snow. There was only one toilet for 600 women. We slept on the ground and drank a ladle-full of water, which had the good fortune to contain a little potato. We suffered a great deal in this jail, because, beside all these calamaties, we suffered hearing the screams of those being tortured to make them confess.

"In the month of August, at its hottest, we passed 5 days without water. Among us there were six mothers. One had two baby girls and the poor children begged for water all day long, crying like thirsty little birds. But no one took pity on the big or the little ones. After 5 days when we were all half dead, they brought us water from the river in a water tank. But this tank had been used before for gasoline. And when they gave a dipperful to each one of us, we drank it with anxiety because of the bad smell of the gasoline. We all fell ill with a terrible diarrhea. It was horrible.

"They transferred us from this prison to a nuns' convent, which was also being used as a women's prison in Guadalajara. The nuns were our guards. We were full of bedbugs, lice, and fleas in the heat—a horrible misery.

In September 1939, they started to judge and condemn to death most of the men. The men that were condemned were lined up in our corridor, and they spoke to us and left us, to die. They killed two men from my village, whom I had known from childhood. At that time they were executing a great many every day, stopping only on Sundays.

"Up to that time we were at least lucky enough to be treated as political prisoners, but from that time on we were thrown in with criminals, thieves, and prostitutes.

"I was in the prison at Guadalajara, when I went before the War Council on January 26, 1940. I was sentenced to 12 years in prison.

"But when the judge called me to confirm the sentence 9 months later, they took me in with those 10 who were being sentenced to death. Seeing my frightened face, the judge told me not to be afraid, that I would only be sentenced to 30 years. I couldn't believe it, and thought that there must have been a mistake, because there was another prisoner named Faustina, who was being sentenced to death and was executed. It couldn't be true that it was 30 and not 12 years. I thought that it must be a mistake, because in spite of all the trouble my denouncer went to, I couldn't believe that there could be such great evil or injustice in Spain. They didn't kill me, because in those months many inquiries had been made about me in the village and all reports were favorable. I had never been involved in political or trade union activities. For this reason I was saved. Otherwise I would have been shot as so many innocents were.

"They accused me of everything, including not being married, of being the mistress of a Communist agitator, because we had been married only in a civil ceremony, not a religious one. He was my husband. We were married for 2 years after a 5-year courtship.

"The official in charge of sentencing who took charge of the reduction of sentences and who had an office in the prison, was there when I went before the judge. He was very surprised to see that I had been sentenced to 30 years, when his file only showed 12 years. It was impossible to reduce the sentence through work of someone with a 30-year sentence, and the nuns were admonished for having put me to work in the kitchen. Then the nuns went to the office to see why this sentence had been imposed on me. They were informed that I had been given the death penalty, that it was only 9 months before that it had been commuted. It was fortunate that I didn't know, because I would have died of fright.

"While I was in this prison they killed five women. Among them were a mother and her two daughters. First they killed the mother. The day they executed her, we were all made to go down to the courtyard. As her daughters didn't come down, they were forced to. We all gathered together and the Mother Superior told us indignantly about the bad way the woman had died, because she had refused confession. The poor children had to listen while their mother, who was not even buried, was reviled. A few months later, they were both executed, at the ages of thirty and twenty-four. The oldest left an orphaned child. In that family five people were killed. They had only 30-year sentences and had never even been condemned to death; but they were killed.

"After my sentence was fixed at 30 years, I was moved to Saragossa with about 60 women. We were in Saragossa about 2 weeks and from there they took us to Barcelona, where we stayed only a few days before going to the prison at Gerona.

"I was at Gerona a year. From there we were taken to Santander, because the prison at Gerona was abandoned. They took us to an Oblate convent, which had been set up as a prison. Those nuns gave us a terrible reception. They received us as if we were wild animals, telling us that the Mother Superior wouldn't receive us until we had cleaned ourselves. Imagine what we looked like after a 3-day trip during which we were hauled in trains in which we slept and ate the little given to us. Our clothes were shipped ahead by rail, because our hands were bound as we were being taken through the streets and so we couldn't carry any packages. They walked us from the station to the jail, one woman bound to another and each guarded by two men.

"Later they closed that prison and transfered us to Saturraran, which had been a seminary at one time. There were 2,000 women imprisoned there, among them mothers of small children, whom they had the right to keep up to the age of four. Then if there were no relatives willing to take care of the children, they were taken to an orphanage.

"In this jail there were three pavilions of healthy women, but with that kind of life no one could really be healthy. I had a friend who was vomiting blood. We all slept close together, because the space they gave us was only enough for each body. We were piled one on top of another, and when she had to vomit, she did it on me. There was an infirmary, but when they took someone there, no one was cured. Most died of tuberculosis, as a result of the bad food. Malnutrition was rampant because of the poor quality and the small quantity of the food. We all looked like skeletons. We didn't die, because our families sent us food packages at great sacrifice to themselves.

"We ate in a huge dining room, and when we left we were hungrier than when we went in. We were hungrier in this prison than in any other, because we were close to the sea. When the nuns saw that one was thinner than the others, they put her to work in the prison store and kept her there for 2 months until her hunger was lessened. There they were given double rations. After the store, they put me to work in the kitchen, so that I would get better. But then I saw the filth that we had to put in the cauldrons; for 500 women, two ladles of oil and lentils full of vermin. One day they gave us two jars of preserved beans full of insects, but we had to put them in the pots anyway, or there would have been only water to eat. Seeing these things filled me with such disgust that, instead of gaining weight, I got thinner.

"The nuns, seeing the awful food they had to give us and the great numbers dying of hunger, decided to go out themselves and beg the neighbors to give vegetables as charity. They were given leeks, cabbages, whatever they could get. When they got potatoes occasionally and ordered the women to peel them, two nuns stood guard so that the women wouldn't eat them raw. If someone lifted a morsel to her lips, she was punished by being deprived of her meal and going without a piece of bread for the day. That day she only had the right to sing *El Cara al Sol,* the Fascist hymn, which we had to sing before each meal.

"From that prison I was taken to the prison of *Ventas*[1] in Madrid. There I started to work, because there was a factory in operation. In that factory we made blue work clothes, linen goods, and embroidery. We were paid 1.35 pesetas a day, money which we spent at the store in order to relieve some of our hunger. In this way they gave us money with one hand and took it away with the other—selling us food that was necessary for survival.

"One day, in despair at such an unjust life, two fellow prisoners bitterly protested the bad food. So the administrator decided to lock them up in solitary confinement to punish them. When the other prisoners found out, we declared a hunger strike as our only means of defense. The hunger strike lasted 4 days. We didn't eat; we only drank water. After spending 4 days like that, the administration insisted that we eat, because this was a discredit to it. But the prisoners wouldn't eat without establish-

ing certain conditions. We asked for the release of the two prisoners, that there be no reprisals against anyone, and that the food
be improved. The director agreed to all these conditions and we
started to eat again. After that, whenever there was burned food
or an unusually bad meal, the administration came to make apol-
ogies.

"As a result of this strike we were transferred to Segovia where
there was an infirmary for tubercular prisoners. They put us there
without disinfecting anything and scarcely cleaning it. They
moved 500 women from the prison of Ventas to Segovia and they
took us in handcuffs. It as very humiliating for me, being dragged
along through the streets like a thief or criminal.

"In the prison of Segovia we were worse off than at Ventas in
Madrid. The food, as in all the other jails, was inedible, scanty,
and bad, but in this place we faced something worse, the cold,
because we were in the middle of the mountains. The water froze
in our cells. However, none of this was so bad; another problem
appeared and we suffered a real calvary.

"One day, a young woman of Chilean nationality, a lawyer,
arrived, accompanied by a delegate of the Ministry of Justice,
Maria Topeta, who was the director of the prison of the *Madres
Lactantes of St. Isidro* in Madrid. According to the prisoners
there, she was terrible to them and knew no pity. Other representative of the Ministry came, along with the director and other
officials of the prison.

"This Chilean woman went around asking the prisoners about
conditions in the prison, and she addressed herself specially to a
very young inmate, asking her where she was from. The political
prisoner replied that she was from Madrid. The woman told her
that she had just come from the capital and found it marvelous.

"Then the prisoner asked for permission from the Director to
reply. The Director agreed. The girl told her that it was surpris-
ing that she had found so much beauty in Madrid, but was certain that she had not visited the *La Elipa* slum and others like it,
where people lived in hovels and slept in the crypts of an abandoned cemetery.

"The Chilean woman asked how someone so young could be

there, and why. The girl answered that she was a political prisoner, like all the others present. The lawyer insisted again that she didn't understand how it was that in Spain, which was so prosperous in comparison with other countries—even the prisons were the best—there were so many women in prison. Why did she in particular, who was so young, fight against the regime? The girl replied that it was not the first time that she had been judged and imprisoned, it was the second. And she would return as many times as she had to, as long as the regime didn't leave her any alternative. The attitude of that Chilean woman was a provocation to all the prisoners and only a provocateur could speak this way to so many women living in such awful conditions. She could see very well that we didn't even have a miserable bed to sleep on, that we slept on the floor.

"She continued asking about the treatment the prisoners received from the administration. The prisoner answered that we couldn't complain about the administration, because we had a warder, who was present, from whom we received bad treatment and worse words. And, she asked, the medical care? The prisoner answered that when we went to see the prison doctor, whatever the illness, he gave us sulfa drugs. She didn't say that we had nicknamed the prison doctor 'Dr. Sulfa.'

"When this woman left, Maria Topeta, who was the head of the Madres Lactantes de St. Isidro, immediately reported to the Ministry of Justice in Madrid, omitting none of the answers the prisoner had given. She didn't even give the Director time to do it. The Director had already told some of the prisoners that he was afraid that those answers would cost them dearly.

"As the declarations of this prisoner reflected the same general feeling of all the political prisoners, when they came to lock her up in solitary confinement, the whole prison protested. Even some of the nonpolitical prisoners joined the protest. The shouting prisoners demanded that she be released from the cell, and all the women marched through the halls and asked for her release. Then the Director said that he couldn't do this, and that he would have us all locked up. But the prisoners didn't give up, because there had been a rumor that she was going to be shot.

"The Chief of the Military Police, from whom the Director had asked for help, refused to enter with his men to restrain the women, because his duty was to guard the entrance. In the face of this refusal, the Director brought in the guards from the men's prison. These were not guards, but cruel savages. They beat us without pity or shame, but the women resisted without submitting, because we knew that the life of a comrade was in the balance, and that she might be shot, as had been done under similar conditions.

"Finally they succeeded in putting us in our cells by sheer force. Then we realized that our only means of protest was not eating, and everyone without exception refused food. Immediately they took away our thin mattresses—from those who had them—our coarse dresses, our blankets, and all our things. They left us only a towel and soap to wash with. In this way we protested for 5 days without eating a morsel. When they came with the food, everyone refused to eat. The strike was complete, all for one. There was a prisoner who had only been there a few months and was pregnant. She didn't want to be different and also joined the strike. We opposed the old prisoners taking part in the hunger strike. There were some over seventy years old and they were so weak already that all of them would have died.

"This hunger strike took place on January 18, 1947. It was terribly cold. Some died of hunger and cold and others couldn't hold out any longer. So we decided to eat, once they had already promised that the prisoner, who had spoken out, was not in danger.

"When we ate, they returned our clothes. But it didn't end like that. Afterwards we had to spend 3 months without exercising in the courtyard. We were held incommunicado, receiving no letters or packages from our families. The punishment was lifted on the Day of our Lady of Mercy:[2] in other words, from January 18 to September 24, 9 months went by without any correspondence or packages.

"I was in this prison at Segovia nearly 2 years, leaving once again for the prison at Ventas in Madrid. The transfer was arranged by my family through the Ministry, so that I could be closer to them and in better conditions, because, however bad, there we had beds to sleep on and weren't crowded.

"In that prison we had some very bad times, because those who had been recently arrested came there. Having been arrested, they were sent to the Home Office and to the General Security Office, where they were horribly tortured to make them talk and denounce their comrades. I saw a young woman of thirty-four with both lungs crushed by a beating. Fortunately there was a good doctor at Ventas and it had a special infirmary for tuberculars where he took care of her. She was cured after 2 years, but the poor thing always remained delicate. Five of us in our cell decided to live together as a family, and she was one of them. We divided and shared everything that we got from our families.

"Among these five was a prisoner who had had her toenails pulled out. Carlitos and Mario, two of the nine policemen who tortured her, were famous for their cruelty. These nine men beat her without pity. In order to be able to hit her better, they stripped her so that her clothes couldn't protect her.

"I also saw a poor girl come from the General Security Office, who had received electric shocks through her breats. You could put a finger in the hollow of the scars. There was another girl, a pretty eighteen-year-old, who was brought in ruined, half dead from being repeatedly raped. The doctors were horrified when they saw her.

"In my cell there also were two sisters from Toledo. The husband of one of them had had his genitals cut off, and then he was nursed back to health. When he was better, they shot him. The husband of the other was also shot. I was also in prison with the wife of the Mayor of Valladolid. Her husband had been tormented like a bull and speared, before he was murdered in the same bull ring. His wife was imprisoned and sentenced to death, but later her sentence was commuted to 30 years.

"I was imprisoned with women who had been arrested for siding with the guerrillas from the region of Badajoz. They received letters from their husbands, which was permitted, telling of the horrible tortures inflicted on them to make them inform on the guerrillas and tell where they were. They castrated the husband of one of them, who was sixty years old, but this old man grieved more that they tortured and mutilated young men as well.

"If I kept on talking, I couldn't finish telling of the horrors that I saw or heard about after the war in Spain, which were as cruel as the tortures of the Gestapo, only they were not as publicized. They gouged people's eyes out; they fed castor oil to men—even more to women—so that they would die of diarrhea. It is almost impossible to believe that there were human beings capable of such evil, and the horrible details don't end without recounting the many kinds of humiliation to which we were subjected.

"They forced us to go to mass, to confess and receive communion whenever ordered. There was a prisoner, who was very much opposed to Catholicism. To humiliate her, she was assigned to the job of cleaning the sacristy. They couldn't keep her there alone because, when she was asked to clean a saint or the Virgin, she let it drop and broke it. When they saw that soon not a saint would be left, they took the job away from her.

"They couldn't handle that one. One day she was in solitary confinement and she started singing the *International*. Frightened, the chaplain asked her if she knew what she was singing. She answered: 'Yes, I'm singing the *International*. I have been condemned to prison and solitary confinement. What more can you do to me?'

"The Catholic religion has been very responsible for all that happened in Spain because everything has been done in the name of God. Even the tortures were performed to defend the Holy Faith. The Inquisition lived again in these years in Spain, with its same refined cruelty. They always killed with the crucifix in hand, and to the many who refused to kiss it, they forced it into their mouths, even injuring them with it. Before taking people to be killed, they took the men as well as the women and put all sorts of pressure on them to make them confess their sins. But the indignity made even those who had beliefs, refuse to receive any sacrament under such coercion.

"In spite of the horror and the surveillance that we lived under in prison, committees of all the political organizations functioned and held meetings. During the war between the Allies and Germany, we received daily news via Radio London. Talent was put to work in setting up communications between all the prisons, using all kinds of schemes. We read the news many nights by the light of a wick made with a cloth and lard. We had to read it the same night in order to pass it on to another part of the prison, so that all the prisoners would be informed. This did much to maintain morale.

"I finally ended this prison odyssey on September 29, 1951. I spent 12 years and 4 months in prison. When I got out, my health was almost ruined and I regained my strength only very slowly. I had a terrible infection in my mouth, but I was cured of everything. Then I went to work doing embroidery.

"I left the prison on parole and had to present myself to the police once a month. It was impossible to leave Madrid, because a police permit was needed to travel, so that they could know every moment where we were. Under these conditions, it was impossible for me to get a passport to join my husband.

"So, my husband in France looked for a guide to take me secretly across the border. The year that I left prison, I contacted this guide. I had come from Madrid to Barcelona without police permission, and again I was in danger of being arrested. I went through Barcelona on foot with this guide.

"The passage through the Pyrenees was the worst part, because, aside from the danger of being arrested, we had to fight against the cold. The first snows had already fallen as we were leaving Barcelona on October 25. We didn't arrive at Andorra La Vella until the first of November. We had to crawl through the mountains and I entered France with a serious injury, because of frostbite.

"Finally on November 1, I succeeded in joining my husband in Andorra La Vella, after a 15-year separation. My emotion was intense because it was the first time that I had seen him without his arm. This was very painful for me.

"Afterwards my husband worked in the country earning very little, and I as a helper, wherever I could. Later we had two sons, the oldest, Luis, born in 1954 and the second, Juan, in 1956.

"Now despite the sorrow which is part of living in exile, we are not badly off. We live as a family. We have all that we need. The boys are good students and now our only desire is to be able to give them as stable a situation as possible. That is, if humanity doesn't commit the folly of preparing another war that will create a life that can only resemble the martyrdom that their poor parents had to go through because of a civil war."

Primitivo Sion Velasco: A Man of Asturias

Primitivo Sion Velasco, whom I tape-recorded in his one-room apartment in Bordeaux in 1968, is a man of Asturias. It is the leit motif of his experiences. His story keeps harking back to himself as an Asturian, his meetings with other Asturians. He offered me cider from Asturia, gave me a can of typically Asturian beans to give to an Asturian friend of mine, and they had been given to him by a friend who visited him from Asturias.

Sion lives in a spotlessly clean, cheerful, sunny room, full of books and documents. "My favorite books are those which deal with freeing men from the tyranny which they have suffered throughout history: Bakunin, Proudhon, Tolstoy, some Marxism, Victor Hugo, Albert Camus, Dostoyevski, Gorki, Louise Michel, Blasco Ibanez and the Spanish classics." He was very hospitable, as are almost all the Spanish refugees, and insisted on my tasting a prune liqueur he had made, a mint drink, and candies.

Friends often come to stay with him, and they sleep on the floor on his mattress. He does his own sewing, and I noticed an elegant darn on his shirt. He has a soft, gentle way of speaking and is a sensitive and decent person. He told me that he gets on well with young people and mentioned a boy who told his father: "You slap me, but Sion explains and is loving." His room is full of artificial flowers because, as he said to me: "I am tired of looking at bolts and bars and I try to put flowers in every spot where my eyes come to rest." He signs his letters "your unconditional friend."

25. Primitivo Sion, a man of Asturias. "My favorite books are those which deal with freeing men from the tyranny which they have suffered throughout history."

Primitivo Sion Velasco: "I come from the Asturias, and was born on July 7, 1907, in the town of La Felguara. All my family lived there. They were, and are, all miners. My brother is a miner and my sisters married miners, too. I started work when I was eleven, with false papers, because no one under sixteen was allowed down the official mines. But I was working further away in a makeshift mine, and when I was fifteen I moved to one of the main pits, El Fondon. And so I began to get the hang of things and became a man. I started to play some football and take an interest in sports. When I was twenty I left the mines and went to work in the building trades.

"I never went to school. Once I went to see a teacher and my mother asked him to take me as a pupil. I went to the school but my hands were dirty and the teacher told me to hold them out and hit my fingers with a ruler. So I ran out of the school and because we were very rebellious in those days, I threw stones at the door and everywhere, and I never went back. Later on I learned to read in various prisons and hospitals. That was where I got an education.

"Asturias is an industrial area, where strikes occurred often. In spite of my interest in football, I leaned toward collectivist, libertarian ideas, somewhat Quixotic, but easy to realize if only men were not so egoistic. Then in 1934 there was an uprising against the repressive forces of reaction, headed by the President of the CEDA [Jose Maria Gil Robles]. Asturias was the only region where the struggle went on for 15 days against the army of Moroccans and the forces of General Lopez Ochoa.

"I had joined the militia, and after a strong resistance, we were obliged to flee to the mountains. After spending 2 months there and in neighboring towns, I went to Madrid. From there I went to Valencia and then back to Madrid. We were being persecuted and had to use false documents, so I was not working; in any case, work was scarce at that time. But when I got back to Madrid I met a friend who had worked with me in the building trade during my last years in Asturias, and he arranged for me to be taken on by his firm.

"On June 1, 1936, a building workers' strike began in Madrid. It was a mass strike because it was backed by both unions, the CNT and the UGT. It continued for some time and I went to Asturias, getting back to Madrid in the last train at the outbreak of the revolution, or rather, the military uprising. Already the loudspeakers were calling the people to join their unions or their political parties. I presented myself at the offices of the CNT, which I belonged to then as I do now. We organized ourselves into groups for defense, and went off to the various fronts. I was wounded at Guadalajara and was sent first to a hospital in Siguenza, then to one in Guadalajara and finally to Madrid, where I was treated for very serious wounds. I was not expected to live. I also had a mental breakdown lasting 3 weeks. The psychiatrists who treated me sent me to a clinic for rest and nourishment. They wouldn't let me read the war news in the papers for fear I should become more disturbed. Later I went back to the front and was wounded again, this time in Madrid in the Casa de Campo [an area of the city]. Soon after this I was sent to Valencia where I spent the rest of the war.

"I was still sick, or rather suffering from my wounds, when Franco took Madrid [March 28, 1939]. But being in Valencia I tried, like all the others, to get to the port of Alicante in the hope of boarding a boat. But instead we were surrounded. The troops of the Italian General Littorio pounced on us and took us to the beach at Alicante. A loudspeaker announced 'Those whose hands are not stained with blood have nothing to fear.'

"That very night we escaped before they had put up barbed wire barricades. There were many who fled; some were killed, but I was lucky enough to get away into the orange orchards with another Asturian and from there we reached Valencia. In Valencia we found they were giving everyone a safe-conduct pass to his place of origin, because that was where he would be tried. I opted for Madrid instead of Asturias, because I had fought there during the war and because I thought I had no enemies there who would denounce me.

"So we went back to Madrid and that was where we were charged. There was a group of wounded Asturians in the same freight car with me. Two were intimate friends and with one of them I am still in close touch. As I thought of the house where I had lived for 3 years as my own, I said, 'You must come home with me.' It was 8 or 10 days since Franco's entry. All this time we hadn't been able to shave and had had very little to eat or drink.

"I was surprised to see that the house was occupied by a couple, as well as by the man whom the owner had taken in during the siege of Madrid. I felt there was something odd, but I didn't pay much attention. So the comrades shaved and had tea and then I took them to the North station where they could get a direct train to Asturias. When I got back I found three uniformed police and two plainclothesmen in the house. They arrested me, very correctly, searched the packages I was carrying, and took me to the police station.

"The reason for my arrest was a denunciation by the man who had been taken in by the landlady. He not only denounced me but also my landlady and her husband, a man incapable of offending anyone. In the police station there were so many people that we could scarcely move, and were immobilized like living statues. There I found a watchmaker who had been involved in the uprising against the monarchy in Jaca in 1930 (the captains of the garrison, Galan and Garcia Hernandez[3] had been shot in consequence.

"I also met there a captain of the Assault Guards from Jaca. I had no sympathy for the crimes he had committed in his short history as a mercenary, but he had defended the Republic with great daring. He called himself 'The celebrated captain of the Assault Guards.' Because I was an Asturian and we have the reputation of being different from other people (I don't know whether we are supposed to be more foolish or braver), the captain said to me: 'Come and join us; we know what's in store for us.' We spent 3 days there. During that time I didn't see any ill-treatment.

"Then I was moved to the station of the Castellana and I saw the most horrifying crimes. In the short time I spent there, I saw men coming away after being questioned, pulverized. In one case I had to let the poor fellow have my blanket because he was in such a bad way. Still they didn't touch me. There were two magistrates; one asked my name, and I gave it. He knew my family because of our playing football. He told me I was accused of entering a house that didn't belong to me. I said I hadn't done this, and explained that I had come from Asturias and joined the confederated groups in order to fight the enemy wherever he was to be found. But he said, 'No, I mean now, when you all arrived from Valencia.' Then I understood that we had been denounced by that man. I said the house wasn't mine but belonged to my landlady and that I had been living there for 3 years. I gave them the rent receipts I had kept and went out. They behaved very well and didn't touch me.

"But soon afterwards another young man who had been with the magistrates came back to the prisoners' room, and they had assaulted him. He must have been charged with something serious because he was terribly battered—his nose was bleeding, and he was terrified. He asked me if I was the one who had been before the other interrogator and when I said, 'Yes,' he said, 'You will be freed'; because the military judge said that the one who should be imprisoned was the denouncer.' They took us to the prison that night. People were frightened, thinking they would take advantage of the darkness to shoot us. This was common practice, but there were women and children with us, which gave us hope.

"I was brought to the Torrijos prison in Madrid at midnight; it's called after the street it's on. It's a former convent which was taken over during the war and used for transient troops. Afterwards, the Nationalists turned it into a jail. It was in a shocking state, without water, or beds, or anything. We had to sleep on the tiled floor. Later they began to fix it up, but there were no kitchens and the meals came when they came. We were very hungry. I was in a bad way: I had two suppurating wounds, one in the collarbone and one in my thigh bone. There was no infirmary and I had neither bandages nor cotton. I had to tear my underwear into strips and wash them in a flask of water so that I could use them to bind up my wounds.

"The man who betrayed us was naturally afraid that I might be released, and denounced us again. This was a serious accusation of having come from Asturias with a group of dynamiters to attack the Montaña barracks [a center of the Nationalist uprising in Madrid at the beginning of the war], of having shot people in the streets and seized their property. So they came to the jail to get me to sign the accusation, but I refused.

"On October 4, 1939, they moved me to the Salesas in Madrid, a prison notorious for the crimes committed there. There I found myself in a room with some Falangist youths. It was the fashion for boys to join the Falange, I hardly know why. Anyway, they began insulting me, perhaps because I was an Asturian and so believed to be rather special. They called me *chulo* or *ponce* [pimp], a most disgusting name for any decent person. I answered back that they were the only *ponces* there. They began to attack me, and I took the typewriter that was on the table and threw it at one of them. In the morning I was lying in a pool of blood, a complete wreck.

"The next night they strung me up and did such horrible things that I was in despair, feeling I couldn't stand any more blows. In the end I pulled the metal tip off one of my shoelaces and tried to cut one of my veins, hoping to die. Early next morning they came to wake me because the lieutenant who had brought me was going to take me elsewhere, or so I heard. When he came in I seemed to hear a vague sound a long way off. He gave me a kick and then shone his torch on me and saw the blood on the floor and that I was helpless.

"He began to shout that he had brought in a man and now there was nothing but a carcass and that it was disgraceful. I was taken back to the hospital at Torrijos and nursed there. My comrades in Madrid were very good to me. When a kitchen had been equipped, seeing the condition I was in and being fond of me, they saw that I had an adequate diet, though food was scarce. They also got permission from the officer in charge for me to sit in the patio outside the kitchen and sunbathe, which was very good for my wounds.

"I was in that prison from 25 April, 1939, until early in 1941. I was condemned to death on December 25, 1939. I want to stress the intervention of a lawyer, Sr. José Serrano Batanero, who was a prisoner himself. I first knew him in the Torrijos prison. He was not very communicative. As time went by we got to know each other, until I believe I was one of his closest friends in prison. He was a man who hated the dictatorship for the crimes committed in its name and who chose honest men as his friends regardless of their ideologies.

"He belonged to Izquierda Republicana and was among the chief defenders of the men who were fighting for the freedom of their towns and villages. He bore his imprisonment with stoicism, although he suffered many privations. I believe I owe him my life, as I will explain. They took me from prison to the court, but he had advised me that as there were three of us, only two should go each time we were summoned, so as to prolong the trial and avoid being shot. Because others accused of the same thing were being shot at dawn each day in the Montaña barracks; we used to hear the firing in the suburbs.

"We were able to refuse to appear on account of the woman, who was the landlady of the house where I used to live. She had a brother in Franco's army. He was a Falangist. This young man tried to get his brother-in-law out of prison, but it was impossible. However, they did free his sister (conditional liberty), and it was she who washed her husband's clothes and mine, and visited us. He and I were in different prisons. So I told her on the first summons, it was Gerardo, her husband, who shouldn't appear; then it was her turn, and then mine. And the fourth time, they sent me away, because I was feverish from an abcess that had formed in my leg wound.

"In spite of our delaying the proceedings for 2 months, the prosecutor asked for a death sentence. The woman was acquitted, but her husband and I were condemned to death, as well as 15 others among the 32 who were in the hall on trial. This was on December 25, when Jesus Christ was born from heaven. I know that when they had all 32 of us in court at the same time, the only defense brought by our lawyer was, that it was the anniversary of the birth of Jesus the Redeemer, and that therefore the 17 who were condemned to death should have their sentence commuted. Actually, the sentences were upheld and I was under the death penalty for 11 months.

"After we were sentenced, I was back in the hospital, and this was when Don José Serrano Batanero suggested my appealing in writing against the judgment. He composed an appeal addressed to Franco. But when he read it to me, I found it said, "May God preserve you, for the good of religion and your country.' So I naturally refused to sign it. He said that it was only a formality and of no importance, but I insisted that I would not sign. It was then that he put his hand on my shoulder and said, 'With men like you, we would not have lost the war.'

"From that time on we became great friends. As I didn't

smoke, I used to give him my ration of tobacco when we got some. I knew that he had two daughters. The eldest, who had been his secretary, had been arrested, and the youngest, who was working, used to come and see him once or twice a week, after work. Once he told me that certain neighbors had offered to help his daughter, but she had refused because she knew they offered in order to enjoy her submission. A month after my trial, he was tried too, and 2 months later he was shot. When they came to shoot him, fearing a scandal, they called him out for an interview. The Civil Guards were waiting to take him with some other comrades to the wall of the cemetery. He was a man we loved, superior, but friendly too, and of international renown. To my mind he was quite outstanding, a real man, what we call a *macho.*' When they shot him, I felt as if it had been a member of my family.

"Although I was in the prison hospital and not in the room with the condemned men, I saw them taken out to be shot. It was tragic; there were many shootings nearly every night. I told the chief warden of the hospital that I had been sentenced to 12 years and a day; I didn't say I was condemned to death, so that they wouldn't take me out of the hospital. This was a trick agreed on by a group of my friends.

"On November 25 they called me out about 9 o'clock at night. This wasn't the time that prisoners were usually taken to be shot or to have their sentences commuted. I had some packages of tobacco in my knapsack which I was keeping so that my comrades could dedicate a cigarette to me the day I was shot.

"I had many friends by this time and they all gathered round thinking it was the end. Of course, they said just the opposite, that my sentence was going to be commuted, but all the same— Anyway, I took out the tobacco and divided it among them, saying: 'If they shoot me, smoke a cigarette for me, and know that I am well aware of what I have done. I have only defended freedom and for freedom I am going to die.' Comrades came from other rooms as well, because it was suppertime and they were allowed outside. There was a great crowd, above all of Asturians, who always seem more like members of the family. Some I had known since the revolution of 1934. They all followed me with their eyes, because they couldn't go with me.

"When I entered the room, I was surprised to find myself alone with the chief officer of the Guards. He gave me the feeling that they didn't mean to shoot me after all. He said: 'What would you think if Franco commuted your sentence?.' I answered that the sentence should never have been passed, and that no one deserved to be shot for what I had done. After a lot of talk, he told me that my sentence had been commuted to 30 years. When I got back, the room was full of prisoners who were waiting for me, which I will remember forever.

"On January 1, 1941, a large number of prisoners from all the Madrid jails were moved to the Dueso in Santander, a prison for 3,000 men between the ages of eighteen and seventy. The transfer was worse than if we had been animals, and the vigilance as excessive, as if we were gold ingots. To transport a thousand or more prisoners, there were at least as many mercenaries armed to the teeth. It took a trifling 6 days to get there! hungry, thirsty, and in rags. The building, large and seigneurial, is several miles from the nearest station and surrounded by the sea. It has an aspect appropriate to crime and the desolation in which we were to live.

"Our first trial was being held incommunicado for a month in what they called the 'period' room, isolated from the rest of the penal colony. We were in a cell meant for one and I had eight companions. Afterwards we were put in wooden barracks. At the beginning of February 1941 there was a violent storm in Santander which tore off roofs and laid waste to the city. We were terribly hungry in the Dueso; men were actually dying of hunger.

"The authorities made a regular habit of exchanging prisoners, moving southerners to the north and vice versa. Those from the south, from Andalusia and Estremadura, who were used to a warm climate, found themselves in a place where they were cold from 6 or 7 p.m. onwards. There were strong winds, because the jail was on a sort of island, separated by a little swamp, and there was only one bridge. In the mornings it is sheltered and sunny and very pretty, with a large outside enclosure. But we were starved there, so much so that as a road divided it from the cemetery they arranged to make a door in the prison wall so that the dead, who numbered up to 14 a day, could be taken across without the townspeople being aware of it.

"As to the men who died of hunger, it wasn't possible to know the exact number, but there must have been a great many. The doctors diagnosed starvation as the cause. We were kept in groups in large rooms. There were small cells too, and at one time we were at least eight and up to twelve in each. When I was there, from 1941 to 1944, food was scarce. We had mostly cabbage soup with a few beans they had scavenged from the pig bins. There was no oil. I had a discussion about the food with the judge at my last trial, and he wouldn't believe what I told him about conditions at the Dueso.

"I was released on parole on September 24, 1944. I was the only political prisoner freed that day. It was the day of the Feast of the Virgin, who is the prisoners' patron saint. Weak from malnutrition, I was able to reach La Felguera which I had left 9 years before. My family welcomed me with the greatest affection, but where were my friends? Very few remained. Because of economic difficulties I started working. Two friends who were bakers gave me my ration of bread—they had even sent me things in prison from time to time.

"I wasn't free long. I was rearrested on January 14, 1945, for clandestine activities, which I don't deny. I told the police who arrested me that if I had had a pistol in my pocket, I should have gambled my life with it. They asked me why and I explained that I dreaded the hunger more than the captivity, because I had suffered so much of it.

"They took me to Oviedo. The police commissioner appeared to be the same type as the one in Madrid 6 years ago. His agents used the same means of 'persuasion' when our depositions weren't those that they wanted. They were not able to 'persuade' us, thanks to a play on words between the comrade who was with me and I. I had been accused of sending propaganda into the prisons to encourage the comrades and raise their morale, and I was also accused of setting up organizations of the CNT.

"What interested us was to be sent to prison where they couldn't beat us. When they moved us to the prison, we changed our statements. It was a serious accusation, so the judge kept us more than 4 months in solitary. As I had once been condemned to death, they said that this time I would have to complete my previous life sentence.

"When a death sentence is commuted, one is given a life sentence; but because the trials had been rushed through, they found later that my 'crime' should only have carried a penalty of 12 years and a day. And there is a law that prisoners can gain remission by working. I couldn't work because of my wounds but they allowed the remission, one day in three, so that by serving 5 years they reckoned that I would have completed the revised sentence of 12 years and a day. In this respect I have no quarrel with their findings in Oviedo. They didn't mistreat me and once we were with the other prisoners the food was good. I could tell some stories about the place, but I think I had better not because they involve people who are still in the country.

"My wounds were very troublesome and I tried to get into the hospital and have an operation, the main idea being to escape. They did operate, and did it very well. All the doctors and nursing staff were good to me and looked after me properly, particularly the surgeon. I was in contact with the Resistance movement, and when I realized there was a chance of getting to France, I escaped from the hospital.

"It was easy. We had a couple of guards, but when the doctors came to make their rounds, the guards had to wait at the door. I took advantage of this moment to go to the toilet just inside the door, where I knew there were piles of dirty linen. I fastened three sheets together and tied one end to the radiator and dropped from the window. I did this in 1946, on June 24, the popular Feast Day of St. John, which we celebrate in Asturias too. Everything had been arranged. Our plan was to seize a small private plane belonging to an engineer, who amused himself by making trips through Asturias with it. But because of the holiday he hadn't come that day. So we had to leave and go to the mountains."

How did you live in the mountains?

Sion: "After the defeat of the Republican army, this making for the mountains was in desperation, a forlorn hope. It was the only place for a last stand and for several years they were full of fighters. Naturally, whether the comrades were in prison or outside, we had hopes of a liberation. But we had no help at all from the French or anyone else. Such hopes were illusory but they die hard. In those days the men in the mountains had to risk their lives to get food. They operated in small groups of six or eight, or three or four, and they organized holdups wherever they went because of the necessity of buying themselves something to eat. They couldn't force the peasants to feed them. A peasant is like a dog, friendly if you give him bread but if you steal from him he becomes your enemy. In fact there were comrades who sometimes helped the peasants with their jobs in the fields when it was necessary.

"It was only the first three or four years that our comrades were concentrated in the hills. The Guardia Civil and the Army in their efforts to wipe out the guerrilla fighters in the mountains claimed many, many victims in Asturias. From about 1946 the numbers fell quickly and the men began to go down to the cities. It was easier to work there. This is why I have more comrades now in Madrid and Barcelona than anywhere else.

"On my arrival in the mountains, I had a bad spell with an abcess in my leg, and I was taken to a house near Aviles where the people were absolutely reliable and very good to me. The night after I left this house, at daybreak, it was entirely surrounded by Civil Guards and uniformed police and they had even set up mortars to blow it up, if there was any resistance. They had been denounced and accused of very grave crimes. It was said that they had had a lot of people there preparing false documents and counterfeit money for the men who had left by boat from the nearby port of Aviles. None of this was true, but they had certainly sheltered a good many refugees. I wish I could give the name of the family. I'm deeply grateful to them. It was very risky for them to have us there.

"From there I went to another house and was visited by a comrade from France, who came over from Gijon. He had a friend on the committee in Madrid and brought me false papers to enable me to travel. A contact from the Gijon resistance came over to tell me when we were to set out, and we left as arranged. I went with him to Madrid, from there to Bilbao and San Sebastian, and finally to Behobia, a place I was often to revisit. I went to Madrid first because the headquarters of the organization were there and it was for them to decide whether a man should go or stay. If they needed him, they kept him, but as I was wounded and no great shakes, as you might say, as a propagandist, it was best for me to leave. When I was in San Sebastian, our comrades in France sent money to pay my passage on a boat, but several boats had been stopped about that time for carrying contraband, and the crews were afraid to take me, so we went overland instead to Behobia.

"On crossing into France on November 1, 1946, we encountered the obvious difficulties. We forded the Bidasoa river near Hendaye, where it's easy to get over. A contact acted as guide and we managed all right, but we were stopped by the French police, who asked for our papers. I and the comrade who had come to meet me, were the only ones without documents. They locked us up for the night but the next day they sent us to Toulouse via Hendaye and Bayonne, where we met some good friends. In Toulouse it was painful to me to see how needy our comrades were. As I say, I belonged to the CNT, and the principal leaders were sleeping on mattresses on the floor. They had only one sheet and were short of everything; it was pitiful. They all ate together with the money that was earned by the group. I had been given a good suit in the house where I stayed, but it was a summer one, and I was cold. There was no chance of a warm coat, and having nothing else in view, I got myself admitted to the hospital, Hotel Dieu, where I spent more than 4 months.

"I had four operations, three of them bad. It was the iliac bone which had been broken as well as the femur. The collarbone wound which had suppurated for 3 years was cured while I was in prison. Some friends from Bordeaux came to see me and invited me to stay with them here while I convalesced, so I came early in April of 1947 and I've been here ever since. At first I was concerned about finding work, but when I had a job and found that I could do it, that problem was solved. And now I have a pension; it's a mere pittance, but given my situation and that of so many others, I have no right to complain. I've been lucky, very lucky."

REFUGEES TO AND FROM THE USSR

It is estimated that from 5,000 to 15,000 Spaniards went, or were sent, to the U.S.S.R. during and after the Spanish Civil War. The main categories of those who went comprised:

1. 1,700 children taken during the war to protect them from bombings, and as refugees afterwards. (Elsewhere it is said that there were 5,000, and that 2,000 died).
2. 102 adults accompanything the children.
3. 52 seamen of the *Cabo St. Agustin* and *Sebastian Elcano,* boats interned by Russia during the Civil War.
4. 60 aviators sent in 1938 to be trained in Russia.
5. 3,961 refugees after the war.
6. 400 men of the Blue Legion, captured while fighting for the Nazis on the Eastern front.
7. a few Spaniards taken to Germany from France by the Nazis and then taken from Germany to Russia at the end of World War II.

The pilots and seamen and a few civilians (a total of about 110) were sent to the concentration camp at Karaganda between 1941 and 1942. By 1948 only 59 had survived the climate and forced labor. By 1956 the 35 who remained were transferred to a camp in Odessa. Eighteen, who agreed to sign a paper saying they wished to work as free workers in Russia, were released. The three, who were considered heads of the opposition, vanished. The other 14 were sent to a concentration camp of German prisoners of war near Leningrad where there were also 400 members of the Blue Legion.

In his book, *La Grande Trahison,* Jesus Hernandez (1953) writes: "It would take a Dostoyevski to describe the infinite sufferings of my unfortunate compatriots lost in the four corners of vast Russia." (p. 215) In speaking of the 5,000 children sent to Russia, he says that they were well treated until the end of the Civil War, but after that they were put to work in the woods and fields and that by 1941 50 percent had tuberculosis.

In 1950, 2,500 Spaniards went back to Spain, helped by the International Red Cross. In 1954, 286 men of the Blue Legion returned on the steamer *Semiramis.* At least 1,407 were repatriated during September–December 1956 on the *Crimea,* the *Krim,* and another ship. Included in the figures were Russian wives, and children born in the U.S.S.R. By February 1967 there were said to be only 4,000 Spanish exiles still living in Russia and of these 1,000 had been born there.

Recently I was told by two Socialist deputies of the Spanish Cortes that there is a Casa de Expaña in Moscow, and that there are 1,500 Spaniards who want to return to Spain. But they must wait until they receive their Russian retirement pensions. Like all other Spanish exiles, they will have housing and medical cost needs if, and when, they do return.

Agustin and Felisa Trueba Calvo

The Truebas gave me their account speaking in French, of how they lived in the USSR as exiles and how they left for Spain and became exiles again. Agustin Trueba Calvo was born in Santander in 1923 and his wife Felisa was born in Spain in 1929. They had two children, Dolores (Lolita), born November 28, 1955, in Russia, and Agustin, Jr., born in Madrid on September 1, 1959. Trueba's brother was shot by the Spanish Fascists and his mother spent 13 years in Franco's prisons. Exiled in Russia, Trueba worked as a metalurgical rectifier and later as a lawyer. Felisa was also a lawyer.

After returning to Spain in 1956, they became exiles again in

France in 1960. When I first met them in 1962, these four were living in a tiny hotel room in Paris, all sleeping in one bed, the father out of work and Lolita tubercular. SRA bought beds for the children, provided clothing, found them an apartment, and arranged to send Lolita to a sanatorium. Trueba had a heart operation in 1962 and died in the early 1970s. Dolores recovered from tuberculosis and is married. The boy worked when he could and Felisa worked in a factory for many years to keep the family going.

Agustin Trueba Calvo: "The first time I left Spain I was thirteen. I came here to France with my four brothers. I left them here in Paris. They were to be taken by French families and adopted. I went back to Spain. After that I was in the army, in the 15th International Brigade. It was called the Mackenzie Papineau Batallion. It was mostly Canadians and infantry from North America. We were on the Ebro front and from there we retreated right up to the French frontier at Port Bou. That's where I entered for the second time. At first they were going to put me in a concentration camp, Argeles-sur-Mer. But as I wasn't yet fifteen—"

How many years did you fight?

Trueba: "Four or 5 or 6 months. There were students on all the fronts. And when I passed through Gerona on my way to the frontier, I found a cousin of mine, who got me a passport to enter France and then to leave for Mexico. But once I arrived at the frontier they didn't ask for papers. Everyone went together: 'Go along, move,' like that. Afterwards I showed my papers and they took me out of the concentration camp because I was a minor and they sent me to a little village in the Lot and Garonne, called Casteljaloux. And from there I left for Russia. I was claimed in Paris by a special committee for the Spanish Republicans."

And how many children left with you?

Trueba: "There were only three Spaniards. One was very well known in Spain during the Civil War, he was a division commander, Barrios. He belonged to the PSU and was secretary general of the UGT of Barcelona. He was an important military man."

Felisa Trueba: He is in Paris now. He was not a Communist but he was close."

Trueba: "Yes. After him there was another Catalan. He was an important leader of the PSU, that is to say, the Unified Socialist Party. And me. And there were about 40 people, all from the International Brigades. They were French, Germans, Italians, Poles, everything, from all countries. Most of them were wounded. But there were only three Spaniards. We left on a boat called *Cooperative,* which was later sunk by the Germans. That is how I arrived in St. Petersburg-Leningrad, via the Baltic, the Channel, Calais, the Atlantic, all that. From there we went to Moscow.

"What did they do with me? That's a long story. Because when I left I had a big illusion. I really thought that I was going to fall in an earthly paradise. But when I arrived, everything collapsed immediately. I only had to look at the port."

Felisa Trueba: "It was of wood."

Trueba: "Because I was born in Santander, a clean and big port. And when I arrived in Leningrad, I saw the tiny port, and the men all old. It made such an impression that I was disillusioned. But next to me there was a Yugoslav, who had been the head of the International Brigade of Yugoslavs in Spain. This was his second time there and he spoke perfect Russian. He understood from my face that something had happened inside me.

"And he started to explain: 'No, it's not like that, you haven't understood. It's because Russia is too old a country and in 21 years they were unable to remake things there.' He explained everything, but he couldn't raise my low morale. And in that moment I understood. I am going to try and keep my mouth shut, and wait for the day when I can leave. Despite that, they were very nice to us. But I looked around and thought a bit.''

Were you put in school immediately?

Trueba: "No, no. I was put in a rest home. They say it was formerly the home of a great Russian singer, Chaliapin. It was a city mansion and it was given over, half for Spaniards and half for the International Brigade. It wasn't far from Moscow. There were about 25 or 30 people there, half Spaniards. But all of them were special men, chosen to be sent to military school, the Frunze Academy, and political schools. The nephews of Dolores Ibarruri[4] were there.

"Then they started to send us, one to the military school, another to the political school. But I had an uncle there, Escobio. He was, at that time, a member of the Central Committee of the Communist Party of Spain; he was a founder of the party. He was a very cultivated man: a medical doctor, engineer, captain in the marine, and also a lawyer. He had studied in France and Germany and Spain. Good, as they had made him Medical Director of the International Brigade, they sent me with him and I stayed there a month.

"But they didn't want me there and I was sent to the automobile factory at Stalino. It was the largest automobile factory in Moscow. I had to learn the trade of adjuster. Good, this continued until the World War started. Then I left for the army. The war in Russia started 22 June 1941. I was in a special camp for commandos, which had missions as partisans. Also, we defended Moscow when the Germans arrived. In 1942 and 1943 we were defending the Caucasus and we made the tour of central Asia to avoid Stalingrad. We got as far as Baku.''

Were you with Spaniards?

Trueba: "Yes, yes, and with Russians too. But there was a small independent Spanish group. At that time there were 124 of us, because there were Spaniards in the other army in the Crimea. But we weren't actually in the army, we were in a special state security force. They told you: 'Good, you must defend this, and if you escape, you are finished.' We were obliged to fight to the death. They put great trust in us and that is why we were entrusted with defending the Kremlin."

Felisa Trueba: "And Stalin."

Trueba: "There were a little more than 6,000 of us and we were in the Red Square. I remember very well. It was 16 October 1941. They say that Stalin didn't know where the front was. He lost his head. Nobody knew where the front was at that time. They didn't know where the Germans were."

Felisa Trueba: "There was a panic in Moscow."

Trueba: "It reminded me of Barcelona, when everybody was burning papers and documents. They were afraid that the Germans would arrive, and papers were flying everywhere. In Barcelona we left at the last moment and the Francoists were entering, if I remember on 25 January. They came from the north on the Diagonale and we left from the other end. It reminded me of all that. And afterwards for a month, we patrolled Moscow every day and every night. There was great confusion."

When did you leave Russia, and why?

Trueba: "It was my wish for 18 years."

Felisa Trueba: "For me it was different, all went well."

Trueba: "For us, it was our salvation when the war started, luck."

Felisa Trueba: "Because all the Spaniards of his age and older understood that this wasn't the life they were longing for, and that the Spaniards had fought a war for nothing. There were some Spaniards who said, 'Good, as for me I prefer to live in Spain. We lived better in Spain before the war than here. Why did we fight the war?'

Trueba: "Everyone was saying that."

Felisa Trueba: "But then the war started and we were lucky."

Trueba: "Otherwise we would have landed in Siberia. Because they started to plant spies everywhere."

Felisa Trueba: "Among the aviators who came to Russia to become pilots."

They were in Karaganda?

Trueba: "Yes, in Karaganda."

And they all died there?

Trueba: "No, no, there are a few who are still alive. After the war, I read in a paper in Paris that there had been a big campaign in Mexico and France in favor of the pilots who had been sent there."

And your family in Spain, were they political people?

Trueba: "In general, no. The monarchy fell in 1931, the Republic came, then the Revolution of 1934 in the Asturias. That's when the Moors and the Legionnaires came, to destroy the Revolution. After that there were great repressions against the workers. And the rich, if you wish, the capitalists, sabotaged the Republic. They closed the factories and left everyone without work, nothing to do. It was normal that we should be disillusioned. I remember, it was February of 1936 and my family, like all the workers, they voted for the Popular Front."

What was your father?

Trueba: "My father was a sailor and my mother was a wholesale fish dealer in the market. She sold all the fish that was brought in, in certain boats. She would call out the prices. And then there was my brother, who was twenty at that time. He was in metallurgy. He was shot during the war, 1937. He was in my batallion on the Burgos front. He was taken prisoner and killed. But no one can tell me what they did to him, they don't dare until Franco has gone. And my mother was in prison 13 or 14 years."

Felisa Trueba: "Yes, and his sister too."

Trueba: "My father, that's another story. He was in the army too but he had time enough to catch a boat and get out of Asturias. He came to France via Santander and Bilbao. He got to La Rochelle. He remained as a guard for the boats until the end of the Spanish Civil War. Then he was sent to a concentration camp near Perpignan, St. Cyprien. And something else happened. I was in Bordeaux, 90 kilometers away and he was with other Spaniards, guarded by the police in a house. The French comrades, who lived near me, had taken me to see my father. But when we got there, he had left 12 hours earlier."

He had left for Spain?

Trueba: "No, no, no, no, for the concentration camp at St. Cyprien. From there they had sent him to make fortifications against the Italians. It was there that my father became a prisoner of the Italians and they sent him back to Franco. He died 3 years later in Spain, of tuberculosis. Yes, dead. They didn't shoot him. At that time my mother was in prison. I had a little brother, who was taken in a charity school. My grandmother was very old, ninety. My father was all alone, sick and had nothing, without work. That is the way they liquidated people. It's the easiest. Because at that time they couldn't shoot people as they did before. My little brother is twenty now, completely illiterate, strong enough for the life of a dockworker, that's all, he's a dockworker."

Is he still in Santander?

Trueba: "Yes. My mother is still alive, but just barely, and her sister, they put out her eye with a gun and broke all her ribs."

When did you leave Russia?

Trueba: "In 1956. And in those 10 years after the end of the war, I did everything. I did 2 years of technical work in textiles in order to go to the University. I went to the Law Institute and so did she. We met, yes, in the Institute in Moscow. When we finished, we both went to Siberia, in Magadan, across from Alaska. We had become naturalized Russians there because otherwise it was impossible to live. Every 3 months you had to go to the police, 100 kilometers away. And if you wanted to go farther than 100 kilometers, you had to get authorization of the police. So we were obliged to become naturalized. When all that was settled, they wanted to send us to Ivanov, a big city of about three or four hundred thousand inhabitants, as an investigation judge for criminal trials. But as they didn't pay much there, I said no. I had learned from some comrades that there were places in Siberia. It was better there because after 5 years you earned four times more than in Moscow and there were greater possibilities for advancement. The climate is bad, but if one eats well and is well clothed, it's better than if one stayed in Moscow or Ivanov."

How many years were you there?

Trueba: "Twelve and a half years, until Spain. They offered her a job in Moscow, as lawyer, but not good conditions. That's why we left. Russian friends wrote us that there were people starting to leave for Spain. Authorization had been given and the first boat had left, and a second boat. We wrote to the Red Cross and they sent us papers to fill out."

But why did they let you leave then?

Trueba: "It's all a mystery, because before we left, the prisoners of the Blue Division went in 1954. And afterwards we went, after the death of Stalin, when Khrushchev was in power. We don't know at all if they made a treaty or contract with the Spanish Government."

Felisa Trueba: "They sent us off with a tiny amount of money, $75 for him, $35 for me, and $35 for Lolita."

Trueba: "We had a lot of money that we had earned, because we had worked a lot—almost 2 million French francs."

Felisa Trueba: "We spent it in one month in Moscow. We bought things like good cameras, Leicas, which we sold in Spain. And we bought prismatics and tape recorders. We were given special permission to take out 600 rubles because we had worked at the North Pole. So we were able to take a little more than the others."

And where did you arrive—in Santander?

Trueba: "No, no, after leaving, everything was done in complete secret at night, in a special train from Moscow to the Black Sea, Odessa."

Felisa Trueba: "The secret police was everywhere. When our train arrived in a big city of the Soviet Union, all the stations were empty, there was not a person. We embarked on the boats and stayed in the Black Sea for a night before passing through the Bosphorus. Only a few hours before we reached Spain, we knew the port where we would arrive. It wasn't even Valencia but Castellon de la Plana. All the port was full of Spanish flags. They took us to a big Spanish castle.''

Trueba: "Near Teruel. We were there 3 days.''

Felisa Trueba: "They put a big number on us here'' [points to her chest].

Trueba: "They questioned us.''

Felisa Trueba: "They photographed us.''

Trueba: "The first files were made on the boat. I remember 12 people got on the boat at the Turkish port of Istanbul and that's where they started our biographies and all that.''

How many Spaniards were there on the boat?

Trueba: "Not more than 400. Everything was free. I don't know who paid for it, the Red Cross?''

How many days were you with the Spaniards who were questioning you?

Trueba: "Three days. They asked for basic statistics, birth, profession, when did you go there. Then they sent us off in buses, some to Bilbao, others to Santander, Asturias, Barcelona.''

Felisa Trueba: "We went to Bilbao because my parents were there.''

Trueba: "When we reached Bilbao, the police began to question us about what we knew about Russia, what we knew about the aviation and military matters. They explained that these questions were being asked from Madrid. When we got to Madrid, they continued; it was worse."

Felisa Trueba: "In Madrid there was a special office organized for the repatriates from Russia. They called us in every month for a questioning."

Trueba: "There it was very different, the office was called 'The fight against unemployment.' But it was in the offices of the Francoist trade unions. It was headed by Lt. Colonel Vallin who after the war had been ejected from Mexico as a Fascist press correspondent. There were three offices and one was headed by a General of the Spanish Army, who had been a prisoner in Russia. He had been in the Blue Division. He wrote a book on Russia called *Ambassadors in Hell.* A film was made of it. They worked together with an American information office. We were called in three or four times a month by the Spanish police. After that it wasn't Spaniards, it was Americans."

Felisa Trueba: "Once there was an American of Russian origin, who spoke with us in Russian. But he was American."

They were probably from the C.I.A.?

Trueba: "Yes, yes, yes, from the Base at Torrejon. We were questioned by one and then another. The Russians weren't Russians. They were from Riga. They spoke Russian well. And after all this, I said to the Spanish General Palacios, that I didn't want to be questioned any more. And it finished badly. Because since we didn't want to be questioned by the police, we didn't have the right to work, or get a home."

Felisa Trueba: "In the end we refused to be questioned because they would call us in one or two days and they would pay you a little for those days and then it was finished. They promised us work, but in 6 years we had no work."

Trueba: "Oh, no. I taught some little courses in Russian at local unions. And then I wrote a few things about law for magazines."

And you were able to cross the frontier easily?

Felisa Trueba: "He got a passport as soon as we came to Spain. We got as far as the frontier, Irun, showing our identity cards. He presented the passport only at the frontier. Because if you show your passport 3 or 4 hours before arriving at the frontier, they have time to telephone and go get the black dossier. One person did that and they were finished."

SPANISH EXILES IN THE FRENCH RESISTANCE

For every five Maquis, three were Spanish Republicans.
—Anthony Eden addressing the House of Commons.

The Nazis in France had been unsuccessful in getting volunteers to work for them on the Atlantic Wall. On February 16, 1942, a law was passed called the *Service de Travaille Obligatoire,* which permitted them to seize from 15 to 25,000 Spanish exiles alone as forced laborers for their Todt organization. Some of the first groups of maquisards were formed by the men escaping from this slavery. Others joined them from the woods and mines, where they had been doing forced labor for the French.

At first the Spaniards had their own organization called the *Guerrilleros,* which entered the F.F.I. (*Forces Francaises de l'Interieur*) en bloc when it was formed. In Spain, during the Civil War, there had been a XIV Corps of the Republican Army, a special battalion of 500 *guerrilleros* designed to infiltrate enemy territory. So the Spanish exiles in France were already prepared for this kind of fighting. They were also knowledgeable about making weapons and from the beginning they took part in sabotaging railroad tracks, bridges, transformers, and attacking German patrols and factories. They were everywhere—in the Haute

Savoie and Haute Loire, Lot et Garonne, and Paris, but they were specially active in the South of France, in the Hautes Pyrenees, Ariege, and Gers.

One of the most active Resistance groups was the Reseau Pat O'Leary. The Spanish Grupo Ponzan (seven men headed by Francisco Ponzan Vidal) formed part of it. Ponzan could have gone to America, but he felt it his duty to stay near Spain. He actually returned once to his country briefly, and fought there as a *guerrillero* but was forced to flee in 1940. Then from Toulouse he organized a group of guides to take people across the Pyrenees. His group took 1,500 resistants and escapees over the mountains and often had to carry women and children and even old and sick men on their shoulders. Ponzan was eventually caught and killed by the Nazis just before the Liberation.

26. *Monument in Annecy, France, to the Spanish Resistance fighters.*

During the Liberation the Spanish resistants helped free cities such as Toulouse, Clermont-Ferrand, La Rochelle, Vichy, Paris, and many more. At this time there were six Spanish divisions with over 10,000 armed members. During the war they had destroyed 80 locomotives and 150 railroad bridges, cut 600 electric lines, took part in 51 attacks against the enemy, seized 9,800 prisoners, and killed 3,000 Nazis. They also worked in underground organizations, centers for liaison, food, information, propaganda and recruiting. About 3,000 Spanish resistance fighters were arrested by Vichy or the Gestapo and deported to Germany. After World War II was over, a number of the Spanish Maquis went back to Spain to fight against Franco and many of them were caught and shot.

On June 6, 1944, when the Allies landed in France, there were about 800 Spanish *guerrilleros* in the department of Gers and the most important group was active in a forest in the district of Vic Fezensac. They were in contact with the P.C. of the Commander in Chief of the Resistance, the English Colonel "Hilaire." This was the group that José Luis Mata Lobo fought with and he told me in some detail about his life in the Resistance. Unlike Mata Lobo, Francisco Pinos and Manuel Palacios worked with groups who were involved with liaison, propaganda, etc. And Juan Parra resisted on his own, wherever he found an opportunity to make trouble.

Jose Luis Mata Lobo:
"We saw a way to defend an ideal."

José Luis Mata Lobo, a gaunt, sick-looking man unable to work because of all his disabilities (including pulmonary sclerosis, lumbar and intercostal neuralgia, and stomach trouble. His pretty wife, Isabel, born in 1934 in Ronda, went out to do housework while he minded the three lively daughters, Elizabeth, Sylvia, and Ida. They lived in Bordeaux, all five sleeping in one airless inside room off a small kitchen. He spoke in very strongly accented French (as though it were Spanish), quite slowly and with some hesitations, but fluently.

27. *José Luis Mata Lobo and his family are happy to be back in Ronda, even though it is hard to find any work.*

Mata was born on October 19, 1917, in Seville. His father was a sailor, who disappeared at sea. His mother had to go out to work as a cook in a bourgeois home to support her son and two daughters, who were still very young. José went to school until the age of twelve, when he started to work. He became a member of the Libertarian Youth, because most of the farmers in the region were libertarian syndicalists and were starving. He was nineteen and living in Ronda when the Spanish Civil war broke out and he volunteered for the militia.

José Luis Mata Lobo: "I was in a battalion consisting mostly of peasants, whose commander was an Anarchist, Pedro Lopez. He had a brother, who was a lieutenant in the Guardia Civil. Perhaps out of respect for his brother, he went over to the Republican side with a number of the Guardia. He behaved very well, because, you know, the Guardia Civil was usually for Franco. Lopez was Mayor of a village, Montejaque, near Ronda. He was in a very good position there. He made pork sausages and he didn't need to take the stand he took. But he did it because he was an idealist. I had a great admiration for that man, who abandoned everything. I saw him later in France where he was in misery like all of us. He was nostalgic for his family, most of them having stayed in Spain, and he hadn't any news. He wanted to leave for Casablanca. I don't know if he was taken, I had no news of him. His brother, the lieutenant in the Guardia Civil, joined the Spanish Maquis and was shot.

[Mata, when being evacuated from Malaga, was wounded in the leg and was hospitalized for some time in Valencia, Benicarlo, and Cambrils. From Barcelona he left for the front and was in the battle of the Ebro.] "I was with Lister [Enrique Lister Forjan, Commander of the Vth division who after the death of Franco, became head of one of the Communist Parties of Spain]. He was the commander of the 5th Army and before that he had commanded a division. I was in the 11th division which was commanded by Rodriguez. I became a lieutenant, although not really named as such, but to fill the place of one who had fallen. I wasn't too eager to be in that division as it already had a certain reputation and I wasn't a Communist. Most of the soldiers in that division were Communists, a good number of them. I didn't feel at ease in this kind of formation. I wasn't even an Anarchist. But I was a man, who wanted to think for himself, without having to follow a doctrine. I felt that I was a democrat but in my own way. I didn't like dictatorship. I wanted to be free without being called a Communist or an Anarchist. It's as if you had to be called a Christian to be good. I think it's one's conscience which defines one's thoughts. I wasn't very happy there, but there was a certain camaraderie and a solidarity in the face of danger. Later I got used to it, I had to. I missed my pals and all those who disappeared every day.

"Then I was put in a special battalion which had to cross that famous river, the Ebro [The Battle of the Ebro lasted from July

25 to November 15, 1938.], to get information and to see if the Nationalists were waiting for us, and if they knew about the offensive that the Republicans were preparing. I went across a number of times in rowboats before the great offensive. When all was ready, we crossed. Many were drowned in the crossing because the boats had been standing in the sun and were unseaworthy. We crossed at Miravet, where there was a castle we were to take. From there we went to Pinolls and then to Mont Pandols. It was there that I was wounded in the arm and I was ferried back across the Ebro. I ended up in the hospital at Cambrils and was sent to the Military Hospital in Barcelona. I left there 2 days before it fell [on January 26, 1939].

[Mata crossed the border into France on February 6, 1939. He was sent to recuperate from his wounds at Lamalou-les-Bains near Montpellier and later was sent to the French concentration camps at Agde and St. Cyprien, from there he joined company number 190 of the *prestataires* [which, unlike the work companies, were militarized]. He had to sign up for the duration of the war. He dug trenches, helped to build factories, and took care of cavalry horses. After the German Armistice his group started retreating to the south.] "Our dream was to get to Bordeaux and to leave in a boat, because we were going towards the Pyrenees and we were always afraid of being taken by the Germans or being handed over to the Francoists. One fine day, in February 1941, in the Haute Loire at Maserat, a so-called control commission of Germans came, and with the French command they chose the workers that they needed and we were ordered to leave with them. It was my first contact with the Germans. We were taken to the station, closed up in cattle cars, and sent to Rouen, where there were a number of companies, and later sent to Brest to the submarine base."

When you went to Brest, had the Germans taken all of France?

Mata: "No, not completely. The demarcation line was at Montpan in the Dordogne. From there we were taken directly to the concentration camps at Brest. We were considered prisoners, and were not free to go out. We were lined up for work, taken to the submarine base, guarded by Germans with submachine guns and returned 12 hours later. We ate at the shipyards. Work went on 24 hours a day. There were about 3,000 men in each group constructing the submarine base.

"We were always thinking about escaping, it was our idée fixe. There were some Jews at the base and they were treated worse than we were. But of course we were threatened with death if there were escapes. Then one day I began to notice that a number of young men were starting to disappear, and I began to think seriously of escaping too. I was in the camp called Saint Pierre Quibignan, which was an old fortress in Brest. I was able to escape from there at night."

Wasn't it well guarded by the Germans?

Mata: "Yes, but the English, the Tommies, came to bombard the submarine base almost every evening. [During the Occupation, Brest was bombarded 165 times by the British and American Air Forces. Their objectives were the submarine base and the three enemy cruisers in the port.] There was a certain amount of disorder because the Germans would leave when the planes came, for they too clung to life. So it was quite easy to escape. There were women, Bretons, who came to work there in small trucks. Already there were quite a number of French who were thinking of resistance, and these women were in touch with the Resistance. They came to the camp to prepare the food and they took the laundry away to be washed. And I and two Spanish brothers, Daniel and Joseph Nieto, were able to leave the camp in a truck covered with laundry. We left quite easily at nightfall. We went to a restaurant in town where the escapees used to go.

"When we were in the restaurant, a German policeman came with an interpreter, who had been in the International Brigades in Spain. I don't know if he was playing a double game, but in any case, we were afraid. But they left and he said nothing although he knew us all. Later we heard that he had been shot. I don't know if it is true or not. But in any case he behaved well toward us.

"One day we were in a cafe and there were a lot of German sailors there. They thought we were Francoists and said: 'Spaniards, have a drink?' But we didn't want to get drunk, as we knew the camp police could come in and they would know we were 'Reds' and not free Spaniards. While we were talking, we saw the German police and we wanted to escape at once but we got to the door too late. We were seized and they asked us how we escaped. We pretended to be naive and said that we had just walked out the gate and came into town to buy some underclothes. It was more dangerous to say that we had escaped. One of the policemen had been in Argentina and spoke Spanish well. I don't know if he took pity on us or what. But he appeared to believe us.

"But we still wanted to get out of Brest. At that time the Germans were preparing to evacuate some wounded and useless people to Toulouse. They were unable to work and would be sent off to Germany and death, or back to camps like St. Cyprien or Argeles. These were no longer reception centers but disciplinary camps, where they let people die. There was nothing to eat. We managed to get into a box car of the train. We didn't know if it was going to the South of France or to Germany. It took 6 days to go to Argeles-sur-Mer and we remained several days in that camp. Then there was a flood in the river and they needed men. I was lucky enough to know an old Spanish officer, who headed a work company and who came to the camp to ask for men. He asked where I came from in Spain and it turned out that he came from Seville. Thanks to him I was saved.

"We were taken again, and we had no papers. We said we had been working in the timber yards and the woods and had wanted to go to Toulouse. They really didn't know who we were, so they put us in a camp called La Poudrerie, in Toulouse. I made my last escape from there with a woman I knew at the time, who helped me. I went to the village of Eauze in the Department of Gers, where my mother and sister were. There was a distillery where they made liqueurs like Armagnac. D'Artagnan and the Three Musketeers came from that region.

"It was there that I started working in the underground. There were people organizing the Maquis, specially the Gaullist Secret Army. I worked for a producer, René Fouillouse, who distilled Armagnac, and there were Alsatians, Spaniards, and Poles too. There were almost 150 workers and my boss had gotten them from the work companies which were controlled by the Minister of the Interior. One day we really made contact with the Resistance and the French were very glad to see the Spaniards. We had a certain popularity, having already fought in the war before.

"Our boss, of course, traded with the Germans, but he knew that all his workers were with the Resistance, and he was too. One day we received orders from a Colonel Parisot and we left for the woods. We started to be in contact with agents who came by parachute from London. As soon as there were enough arms to create a small formation, we were ordered to join the Maquis. We had grenades, machine guns, and submachine guns, and we started to patrol a large sector.

"We were in the area between Toulouse and Bordeaux and there were two or three hundred of us at the beginning. In the end there were about 3,000. This was called the Battalion of Armagnac (which became the 158th Infantry Regiment), and there were about 700 Spaniards in it. I was there for 7 months. Usually we were on the road, but we went on missions to destroy bridges and telephone lines. We had to harass the Germans as much as possible and to get nearer and nearer to them. We had several engagements at Aix-sur-Adour and Estang, and a very big one at Castelnau. At that time we had with us a British agent named Hilaire. I don't know if that was his real name. He was sent as liaison to ask for arms and to plan.

"I was in the Secret Army [De Gaulle's group] and there were 300 Spaniards. We were commanded by the French. Nearby there was a typically Spanish battalion commanded by Spaniards and they were called Franc Tireurs. They leaned towards the Communists. We gave them arms but they were on their own. We could have joined with them but we didn't want to, as we didn't think the way they did. I was with my brother-in-law, Luis de la Rosa, at that time, and he came from the Socialists and Republicans and he didn't want to be with them. We were better off as far as food was concerned, because our people were of the region. But when there was a special thrust to be accomplished, they were always in the vanguard and they behaved admirably."

How did you live at night?

Mata: "We moved around a lot, but we stayed near a house in the country. At night, while some slept, others stood guard on the roads or made roadblocks. We knew that when anyone arrived, it was either the Germans or the Resistance. No civilians circulated at this time. There were no cars except perhaps for a doctor, and we knew more or less about them, and would let them through. But except for them, it was either friends or enemies.

"I remember one time at a crossroad, there were two of us guarding the road at night, and I had a submachine gun. When one knew that a convoy of Germans was coming, one either had to wait for them in ambush, or if they were more numerous than us, not attempt a confrontation. Because there was no talk, if they took you, you were shot. Or they tied you across of the front of their trucks so that they could circulate freely, because they knew that our pals would have to pay if they were attacked. So we were guarding the road that night, and four trucks came along, full of people, and they were maquisards. But they forgot to give the password, which was 'Nothing new, always the same.' And we thought it was the Germans and we shot at them. A number of them were wounded, people of the Maquis. That was bad. Later we controlled perhaps 50 kilometers. That was quite a lot because the Germans were not far away. Their headquarters were at Auch. And having seized several maquisards, they knew our positions and were preparing a big offensive against the maquis of the region.

"That was when the battle of Castelnau took place. There was a Spanish battalion with us, led by the famous Camilo. He had only one leg, but he managed to find himself in the middle of the conflict. Have you never heard of him? He was a Communist. And we were surrounded and had to get out. Our company was commanded by a Dr. Vincent. He is still alive at Eauze. Our headquarters were in the center for protection and it was we who took the blows. It was hard, very hard, because they had planes and we had only arms. But at least it was easier for us to run! And we managed to escape and reach a large forest which was near Panjas [There is a monument there to the 158th resistance group in which Mata served]. The commander of this village was Abbe Tales. He was a wonderful man, who had been deported to Germany and escaped and had taken command in the Maquis. The big bourgeoisie in that region, who were believers, well, they were part of the Resistance, passively without wishing it, since the Germans were forcing them to give chickens and eggs and food to feed them.

"So the Germans had to break out. Then they threw down leaflets from planes, saying that all those who wanted to return home would not be harmed if they turned in their arms. It was demoralizing, because there were men with families who imagined themselves already taken and shot. But you know, we were there because, dead or alive, we had to stay. We were not going to give up.

"And I tell you, not because I am one, but I think the Spaniards were a source of great morale to the French Resistance. They were cheered, feeling that these people had already experienced guerrilla warfare and things like that. Perhaps this is an impression but I was very satisfied with the French comrades where I was. We got along very well with them and there was no question of nationality. There were no Spaniards, no French, there was only the Resistance, we spoke only of that. We slept together, we suffered together, we fought together, and sometimes we were shot together. I don't know of any group of Maquis where there were no Spaniards. They were everywhere. Because by instinct they were obliged to join. We saw a way to defend an ideal, to defend ourselves."

It was a little like the continuation of your war?

Mata: "Yes, it was the continuation. The first time I had a machine gun with me I felt free. Before they were hunting men everywhere. Now it was equal to equal, because we had the means of defending ourselves.

"Then one day they came to attack us in the woods. Quite a few had left us after the German planes had thrown down their propaganda. There were people whom I had thought would stay to the end, but no. Our French commander said to them: 'If you want to go, you had better go now, rather than be bad soldiers.' Then one morning we were attacked in the woods, first the planes, then Germans on motorcycles, and after that they came in tanks and trucks. They surrounded the woods and beat the woods for us. We were able to escape. There were many deaths and also among the Germans, yes, many, many dead. Because we wouldn't let ourselves be taken like that. It was a question of life or death. We knew what was waiting for us. Our group was able to break away and retake the sector of road where we had been before. Our specialty was the destruction of bridges and lines of communication.

"Then one day we heard echoes of the landing. Then the Germans started to evacuate and we left some roads open because it was better that way. But little by little the patrols met the Resistance. The Germans were demoralized and we made quite a lot of prisoners. Then we received orders to come to the Poche de Royan, it is near the Pointe de la Grave. There was a big concentration of Germans there. The Americans had been ordered to bomb Royan and it had been completely destroyed. It is a big city by the sea. We were sent there because the Germans were beginning to surrender. There were some big battles there and I was lucky enough to come out alive. I don't know, but I did what I could. I had a citation [the Medal of Free France, awarded for taking part in the Liberation]. But out of modesty, if you like, I can't tell you the details of what I did myself. I speak of the whole.

"It was in 1945 that we felt that at last we were going to be free. Because until then we had always been controlled on one side or the other, except for the time in the Resistance. It was really there that we felt free. We had the impression that we could defend ourselves, that we were fighting for something, for the continuation of a democracy which we had seen completely threatened with slavery. Once the debarkation took place, since we were not professional military men, we wanted to return home. But those who were too young, went on. They left for Indochina. Unfortunately I had some pals who never returned. You know, for them, war had become a habit. Elsewhere there was no stability. For them, life was war. But I understand it. They were not educated when they were young, they saw nothing but war. So they wanted to continue the war, and they went here, there, anywhere, as mercenaries.''

I wanted to ask you, why you don't go back to Spain?

Mata: ''I could go back to Spain. I left when I was very young. As far as responsibility, I consider that I have none. Besides, I felt that I was a Republican, a democrat. There was a Republican Government and then one day the military overthrew it. That was what the people with big interests wanted. Yes, really, sometimes I have wanted to go, but after all, I didn't like the mentality of the Spaniards who are there. And I couldn't be in Spain as a favor and be told, you can come back, you have nothing to fear. I feel well here. If some day I have the possibility of returning with a really democratic government, then we could talk, then we could discuss, then we could say many things that it is impossible to say now. Frankly, I don't go because I don't want to, as long as the present regime is there.''

Mata and his family returned to Spain on July 10, 1983. They settled, where they had their origins, in Ronda. He wrote me: ''We had to start again from zero.'' They were lodged for a while by family but otherwise ''received no help from our compatriots.'' Work has been a problem. His wife, Isabel, who is fifty-one, can find none. Sylvia would have liked to continue her studies at a university, but there is none in Ronda and they can't afford to send her elsewhere. She teaches English in the Ronda Cultural Center. Elizabeth gives French and English lessons at home, Ida is out of work. But the city is beautiful and the climate good and they are happy to be back.

Juan Parra Gonzalez:
  "Every day I threw a handful of sand into the
  motor."

Juan Parra Gonzalez lived with his family in Septfonds, Tarn et Garonne, the site of forced labor camp 21 bis. I met and taped him in 1968. He spoke in Spanish and Teresa Palacios transcribed his tape for me, retaining the Andalusian phrases. Chloe Vulliamy translated it into English.

At that time, Parra and 35 other Spanish refugees in Septfonds were planning to fix up the cemetery of the camp, giving up their Sundays to work on the project. Eighty-one men are buried there, Spanish refugees and Jews of the International Brigades. Out on a country road, in a field, when I saw it in September 1968, it was completely overgrown and covered with weeds. It was hard to

28. *Juan Parra with his little friends, the canaries. ". . . spoke with assurance, especially when talking about injustice."*

see the crosses and small memorial pillars. Today the cemetery has been transformed. On September 26, 1976, 500 people came to see the first stone of a monument to the Spanish Guerilleros placed and a moving speech made by the representative of the National Federation of Deportees, Internees, and Resistant fighters, M. Désirat. The monument was designed by Angel Hernandez, a Spaniard who had been deported to Mauthausen. Twenty thousand Spaniards had passed through forced labor camp 21 bis.

Juan Parra was a tiny, lean, gray-haired man, soft-spoken and gentle. He has a lopsided-looking face, as though it had been made for two people. He spoke at the beginning of the tape in a monotonous and melancholy way, rather tremulously. But as he went on, he became excited and spoke with assurance, especially when talking about injustice.

Parra: "I was born in Almuñecar, province of Granada, on October 9, 1903. My father made espadrilles, but he died when I was eight, and at sixteen I went to work in a sugar factory with an uncle and aunt. Later I joined the Navy where I did a bit of studying, because I could hardly even write. We had no father and my mother had to work, and though I went to school as a child they taught us nothing. The only thing we learnt there was how to say our prayers. In the Navy I learned some mechanics and I went to work as a second engineer on the fishing boats that went on 15-day trips from Malaga to Gibraltar, Ceuta, Tetuan, and Casablanca, and all around there.

"I got married when I was twenty-six, and went back to the factory as a mechanic, but a monh later we moved to Oran and spent a year there. Afterwards I worked on the fishing boats again."

Where were you before the war started in Spain?

Parra: "I was in Oran and when I got back to Spain I went to my village of Almuñecar. I belonged to the UGT, and to the Committee for the Defense of the Republic. When the rising began I was a delegate and my wife represented the Socialist Party. When Franco declared war we were both in the Town Hall. At first there was a phone call from the town council in Granada: 'Nothing is happening, everything is quiet.' But at 3 in the morning they rang again and this time it was: 'Comrades, we call on everyone to support the social revolution and the general strike. *To the streets!* The army has risen against the Republic.' And immediately we all rushed out into the streets.

"When Malaga was burning, the Committee for the Defense of the Republic went to join the struggle, because the Fascists were there already and controlled part of the town as well as other places. Salobrena, Motril, and Nerja were partly in their hands and we went to all those places. The people fought back and managed to save some of the towns, but Motril and Salobreña had already fallen to Franco and the Fascists.

"Then with the help of Don Nicolas Chave, the head postmaster, and the teacher, Don Francisco Moreno, we of the Committee got hold of a small gunboat, the *Pelayo*, and another called the *Arcila*, which had a 7½ bore gun and went up the coast from Malaga to Motril firing shots in support of the people. I went along as second engineer, because we didn't have anybody to depend on but ourselves. Don Nicolas Chave organized it because he had been working in the Navy like me[5]. So we managed to reach Motril at 9 in the morning and there the resistance was terrific. The Republicans had set fire to the house of the Acostas (she was a marquise) and to lots of others, and we managed to regain possession of Motril.

"We tried to get up to Granada but we had to stop at the tunnel of Izo because the truck wouldn't go any farther. For a year we were holding out and fighting on the Andalusian fronts. We made two counterattacks to win back Orjiva and Lanjaron and all that countryside, but we couldn't do it. We failed because there were so many traitors. When we were planning a counterattack, these creatures went to our enemies and said 'They are going to attack!' And that was how our Civil War started.

"Then came the fall of Malaga [February 8, 1937] and it was terrible, it was really terrible. I can tell you that I walked 80 kilometers with my brother-in-law, who died here in France. I walked from my village of Almuñecar, where I had gone back to my family after leaving the front, to Almeria—on foot the whole way. On the road to Almeria I saw women and little children throw themselves down in the ditch in each other's arms; I saw three sisters holding each other and falling to their deaths. It was dreadful when a plane came—mule carts, women and children all destroyed and massacred. They had no pity, and then they can talk about God! Such people can't be forgiven, they can't be forgiven.

"They destroyed our Republic. Why? What harm had the Republic done to those people? Why? It was because we wanted liberty and they wanted oppression; they didn't want the people to be free. This is not right, and there is much that needs to be said about it in Spain. There were massacres in my village. In my village *we* only killed the real Fascists, the cruel enemies of the people, not all the thousands who were shot by the other side. I know, because people from my village came and told me, that the President of the Socialist Youth, a brilliant and wonderful girl of eighteen, was seized and taken to the slaughterhouse where the animals are killed, and there all those scoundrels raped and then shot her.

"This isn't just. These things should be written in books and recorded in the history of the Spanish revolution, because they were crimes and there were many of them. And when I remember these things I think chiefly of my own experiences, and of how they crushed us because we wanted freedom. I want freedom for all the world, for the common people, freedom for each one to think as he likes and to go his own way. A lot of Spanish Republicans wanted just this. We wanted no truck with criminals or evildoers or anything like that, just freedom for the Spanish people. This is what we fought for, but it's the other side that has been in power all these years."

What did you do when you left Malaga?

Parra: "When I left Almuñecar for Almeria, my wife, my mother, and the whole family were taken to Borjas Blancas in

Catalonia and they stayed there while I went on living in Andalusia after the retreat from Malaga. Later, as my group hadn't been called up, I asked Captain Benavente whether I might go and look for my family, as I didn't know where they were. I left Almeria and went to Alcantarilla and there I met one of my uncles. So I stayed there 2 days and we wired and telephoned all over the place to try and find them. At last we heard they were in Catalonia. So I went to Catalonia and called on my comrades there, and they said, 'Stay here in Barcelona and we'll see later.'

"I stayed there and they sent me to work soldering 'Laffite' bombs in a town named Sitges, where they had set up a bomb factory. But soon afterwards there was general mobilization. The International Brigades left and everyone was called up. My friends said I could ask for a job with the police, so I applied and was taken on as security guard in Catalonia. Later I was moved to Granollers where I left the police force. Then we went from Barcelona to Gerona and from there they sent us to the front. But it was already broken when we got there. So we took six Guardias and a Sergeant named Pastor and crossed the mountains. The Fascists were there already and civilian refugees were on the road. We crossed the frontier at Bourg Madame and came to France. They kept us there for 3 weeks in a meadow and then took us to the camp at Vernet."

Were there many Spaniards with you?

Parra: "There were about 17,000 Spaniards at Vernet, mostly from the Army, and for the 17,000 we had four old huts that had been used for German prisoners (in the war of 1914–1918), and the police of the Garde Mobile told us, 'Plenty of Germans died here.' Some of us slept in the huts and some in rough shelters, and we each managed as best we could until the camp was organized. For food, all we had was a little boiled rice and a small ration of bread. A lot of food parcels came from Paris for us, but they didn't give them out, because they said we had all we needed. This was the French Government! At Vernet there were various kinds of refugees, including political prisoners. Many, many Spaniards died while they were interned there. When I left the camp after 9 months, I had to spend 4 months in the hospital.

"Later they sent us to another camp at Espagots to work in the fields, in the Work Companies. I don't remember the number of my company, because I was only there a short time, not more than a month. As a mechanic I made pipes, and then a call came for a mechanic and an electrician and two of us were sent to the Camp at Caylus with an interpreter. I was working there for a year. They only gave us our food—no clothes, nothing at all, not even 5 cents.

"After 5 months I asked the Commandant, a Frenchman named Berlosan, whether I could send for my family and whether he would give me a certificate to say that I belonged to the Engineers. It was the Engineers who were responsible for the water supply. He said I could ask the captain of the Engineers for permission to claim my family."

Where were they?

Parra: "They were in Belle Isle, which was occupied by the Germans, but they let my wife come to Caylus. I wasn't earning anything, so she went to work in a café where they paid her 30 francs a month, which covered the rent of the house they found for us. It was lucky they fed us well at the camp and gave us tobacco. The Commandant said they would provide her with food too, and we were there until the Germans left.

"Before that happened, I was repairing a car for one of the French Police at the time when the Germans were rounding up all the Spanish Republican refugees to send them to work in Germany. Because I had fixed his car, the policeman said: 'Look here, what you should do is find work on the land,' because the Germans didn't deport agricultural workers. I said, 'I can't do that kind of work, I don't know how.' But he said 'I'll find you a good employer who will teach you.' He found me a job, and I went to Lacapelle de Livron and they gave me two oxen and sent me out to plough. I didn't know the first thing about it, but I set to work to cultivate the land. Then came an order from the Germans to round up all the Spaniards.

"They set me to work on a concrete mixer and every day I threw a handful of sand into the motor, just a bit of sand every day, and like that we broke 12 mixers. I carried out all the sabotage I could. One day a German from the Gestapo called Frick came up and said 'You're a Communist,' but I said 'No, Franco, Franco.' I had a fake letter from Franco and I said 'Franco, Franco.'" I said to myself, 'I'll soon deal with you,' and one night we caught him with a noose of steel wire and left him dangling. There was an Asturian mechanic who was employed in pulling out tree stumps with a tractor. Do you know what he did? When he pulled one out he would arrange for the chain to break so that he couldn't do any more work. And the Germans kept calling him a Communist. In Bordeaux you could get letters from Franco, letters from the Spanish Consul and passports to travel all over France, all made by the Resistance.

"The Germans thought more of us than of anyone. A Frenchman said to the Germans 'Why not round up all the Spaniards and put them in a concentration camp?' But one of the Germans had fought in the Spanish Civil War, and he said, 'You don't know the Spaniards. They're not just bad. If we interned all the Spaniards, within 2 days they'd have machine guns and trucks and planes as well. Better leave *them* alone.'

"This is what we did in the Resistance. All of us Spaniards fought with all our might to defend the Spanish and French Republics. All the world should know it."

When Juan Parra had finished, he said: "I want to show you something." He led me upstairs and on the top floor of his house, opened a door. Inside were hundreds of canaries in all sorts of elaborate cages which he had made for them. Made of wood, they were all different sizes—hotels, houses and rooms for these little friends. He spends all his spare time with them, and I went off with one, "a good singer" in a painted cage, a gift for the Foyer Pablo Casals in Montauban and for all the old Spanish refugees who went there.

Francisco Pinos Vidal: 36 Wounds

Francisco Pinos Vidal was born in 1896 in Tortosa, Spain. There were 24 children in his family and five died for lack of proper food and medical care. When I first met and taped Pinos, he was living in a sort of closet in the walls of a quai on the River Garonne in Toulouse. He sat in his wheelchair in the doorway (there were no windows) and inside were his mattress, stove, old clothes, and mementos stuffed into suitcases. He wore a big ancient beret, faded old trousers and shirt, and canvas shoes. It was hard for him to speak and he looked very ill.

He was taken to the Hospital of La Grave in Toulouse, after trying to commit suicide by slashing his wrists. He was found unconscious on the street with festering wounds in his legs (eventually both his legs were amputated). Pinos missed his closet, and the Garonne where he used to fish, and the passersby with whom he used to gossip—and his freedom.

Speaking to me in Spanish, he told me as much of his story as he was able.

"I am Francisco Pinos Vidal, of Tortosa, province of Tarragona. I was a sailor in the Merchant Marine, the big boats, a worker like the others. During the Civil War I was mobilized by the Republic. As I had done my military service, I was a sergeant and I reached the rank of captain, not for excellence at school but for merit in the war. I was wounded 36 times. I will show you, all over my body. I had to go everywhere in Spain because I was in the 13th International Brigade, the 4th Battalion of Juan Marco. I was employed in communications, because in Spain at that time we didn't have what we have now, radios. Franco had them, as a Fascist he had everything. But we only had telephones with ground wires and telegraphs. I knew a little about them because when I started in the Merchant Marine, I used to spend my time with the telegraph operators on the boats, and so they put me in the Transmission Section.

"Don't speak to me about fronts. I was all over Andalusia, Madrid, Brunete, Loma Gorda, Sierra Gorda, Teruel, Granada, Malaga, and always with the same Brigade until we crossed into

29. *Francisco Pinos Vidal in his room, a closet on the Quai of Toulouse.*

France in 1939. The volunteers withdrew in 1938 before the last offensive. But I was Spanish. They wanted me to leave too, but I said 'no.' I stayed in Spain. It was not my duty to go to France, only to remain at my post like a good Republican. Well, like all those who were good, because there were many, many.

"I crossed the frontier on 10 February 1939 at Port Bou and Cerbere. I was among the last to leave. And even if I was wounded and very sick, I still had the courage to let my comrades pass quietly. From there they took us to St. Cyprien. I had a high fever and couldn't eat. Then we were taken to Barcares where there were barracks, but we had to sleep on the sand, full of lice, full of misery, the water bad. But still I was sheltered a little. We were very badly treated by the Senegalese and the French Moroccans who were guarding us. They didn't flinch from cutting off a head. They cut off heads for the gold teeth. This happened, I saw it. It didn't happen to me because I didn't have gold teeth. But I saw it. I buried the bodies in the sand. It was worse than in the German concentration camps, those times. I suffered a lot.

"After that they made us go into Spanish Work Companies. I was in the 115th Company and because I didn't want to go, they called us terrorists—Republicans! The Fascists were good people! Well, many went back to Spain. I don't know why they crossed the frontier, to return later. I didn't want to go. They took me in a train to Argeles, in a horse car, me and many, many, who didn't want to go into those forced labor companies. From there once again, they took us to Barcares. And there we had to give in. We couldn't go on because they beat us, and didn't feed us, and we were forced to go into those Companies. They took us in wagons meant for eight horses, 40 and 50 men, like ants in there, without food. They took us to the Department of the Ain near Bourg-en-Bresse. At about 40 kilometers there was a big administrative center and we were taken there to work. It wasn't bad. The work was obligatory and we did everything, worked as masons, carpenters, farm workers, making barracks, washing dishes—anything they wanted us to do. But there we didn't lack food. That was a good time before the war.

"When the war was lost in France, during the retreat, I was wounded in the foot and lost a toe in the bombardment of the aviation field at Amberieu. They machine gunned the fields but we were forced to work there, and he who was hit, was hit, that's normal. When the retreat started, I was taken from there to the hospital of Meximieux and then to Lyon, where they took care of me. As I was in civilian clothes, the Germans and nobody bothered me. On the contrary, they took me in an ambulance. And there were tanks and men and women going along the roads, just as it happened to us in Spain.

"Then when I was a little better, I went to the Company I belonged to, the 150th (first it was the 115th made up of Spaniards—the 150th was foreigners). The head of the work company

was a French captain who was very nice. He was a Republican
and didn't like the Germans at all. They had to substitute another in his place. But at that time the Company broke up and
everyone went where they could, do you understand? I left to
earn my bread, camouflaged. By chance I had this foto. It was
small and I had it enlarged. I made them to give away. I was an
officer, but you don't see the braid, but you can see that it's
clipped. I made it this way so that they couldn't see that I was
an officer, because they would have shot me at once. And thus
I survived the whole occupation. (I could talk for 20 days.) I have
been everywhere, camouflaged by good Frenchmen, because
there were good ones, above all in Savoie, because they didn't
like the Italians. They prefered to feed us rather than the Italians. In the Ain too they were quite nice.''

Were you with a group of the maquis?

Pinos: "No, not at that time. It was later that I made contact
with the comrades, when I was sure they were Maquisards:
French, Spanish, they were every nationality. They said, 'You
can't be with the Maquis because you are wounded and can't
move easily. But manage as you can and tell us what you find.'
Actually, I was a *chivato* (informer), as they call it. It was then
that I started to be pursued and unhappily it was a Spaniard who
denounced me. I was picked up at the Fabes Bridge, which
everyone knows about. It is a few miles from Lyon in the direction of Clermont-Ferrand and the French and Spanish Maquis
were there together. But each group had its own job. This is when
the militia picked me up at Vic-le-Compte and took me to Clermont-Ferrand. They came at 5 in the morning and picked me up
at 6. I had gone to the stables to feed the horses and to hide. When
I came out, the whole town had been taken, and they took me
too and many Frenchmen. They put us in a truck and they went
through all the little towns picking up the people who were most
suspect.

"They took me to Clermont-Ferrand and I suffered from my
foot and the missing toe, which hadn't healed well. Nevertheless
they took me to number 92, the place where the Gestapo tor-

tured everybody and which is universally known. All the suspects among the Resistance fighters and members of the Maquis were tortured there, unimaginable tortures. To make me talk, they put me in a big high chair made of wood, with my arms and legs bound so that I couldn't move. There was a big stove with a pot of boiling water, and there was another pot full of ice. Then they put my foot into the boiling water and afterwards into the icy one. At first, I tell you, I wanted to cry, I couldn't bear it any more, I couldn't, I couldn't.

"But after a while, by dint of being there 2 hours, and 2 hours, and 24 hours, they gave me shots to keep me going, so that I would talk. 'Where were you? Who was the leader of this one?—the leader of that one?' and so on. I understand French, I don't speak it well, but I speak it. But I pretended that I didn't understand anything. Naturally interpreters came, interpreters by day, interpreters by night, and they talked to me in Spanish and I told the French that I knew nothing, that I was obliged to work and that I worked, that I hadn't done anything, that I knew nothing, patati, patata. . . . And finally after so much torture they took my foot and I said to them, 'No, don't bother, I'll do it myself,' and I put it in and took it out and put it in and took it out. And the one who was torturing me said, 'There's nothing to be done with this one, this scum.' I understood and said to myself, now they'll give me a little peace. But peace until death!

"In those days I was strong. Now I'm not worth anything. Then I always had courage. It was then they took me to Lyon. Here are the attestations if you want to see them. I got them when the comrades of the Resistance freed me. I remember, it was 5 in the morning when usually they came to the prison to take away 15 or 20, 4 or 5, to shoot them or take them to the occupied zone. I was lucky enough to escape that, because the Maquis freed me together with 150 politicals. I was freed because they attacked the jail. And the Civil Guards, who were guarding the jail, were Republicans on our side, in the Resistance. They didn't do anything, they said nothing, they opened the door. The head of the Department of the Masif Centrale was there, called Blenoit. I don't know his real name. I was called The Moor. Each one had an assumed name, you understand. I was called The Moor, another was called Paper, another Carton, another Black Beetle. It didn't matter what. That was so that our name wouldn't cause us trouble, so if they picked you up with some papers in one's pocket, one's real name didn't exist. It was a means of camouflage. They called me The Moor, because I've always been a little black from the sun, like most of the Spaniards. So then the Maquis called me The Moor, because there were always those who could hear and were spies and denounced us. They could dig into the files of the Work Companies where we had been when we came to France and then they knew you well and you couldn't escape.

"I can't speak any more, I'm tired. I beg your pardon but I'm tired. Please excuse me."

NOTES

1. For a more recent description of this prison, see the Duchess of Medina Sidonia's book, *My Prison,* Harper & Row, 1978. Ventas was closed in 1969.
2. The Order of our Lady of Mercy was founded in order to ransom captives in the thirteenth century and later did missionary work in prisons. The prisoners' saint's day is the most important fiesta in Spanish prisons. See the Duchess of Medina Sidonias's book, *My Prison,* p. 145.
3. A military uprising occurred in Jaca in December 1930 against the monarchy and in favor of the Republic. It was headed by Captains Fermin Galan Rodriguez and Angel Garcia Hernandez. They were tried and executed on December 14, 1930.
4. La Pasionaria, President of the Communist Party of Spain (Santiago Carrillo fraction) (in her eighties) lived in Moscow after the Civil War until she returned to Spain after Franco's death.
5. Before hostilities started there had been committees of Socialists and Anarchists, consisting of sailors and under-officers on almost every boat of the Spanish Navy, with a central committee on the cruiser *Libertad.* The sailors' committees were loyal to the Republic and they were ready for the rebels when the war began. Most of the officers had been for the rebellion and 70 percent of them were killed by their men at the beginning of the Civil War.

12

Deported to
Nazi Germany—
and Liberated

*I*t is not generally known that a great many Spaniards were prisoners of the Nazis during World War II. Twelve thousand (some say 30,000) Spanish Republicans, who were doing forced labor for the French, were taken prisoner on the Maginot line as the Germans entered France. The Vichy Government refused to recognize them as prisoners of war. Forty-eight thousand in all were brought to Germany, to the Stalags, the concentration camps (KZ's) and to work in industry and on the farms. Among them, one to three thousand had been in the French Resistance. A total of 16,000 died. In France, fifteen to twenty-five thousand did forced labor for the Todt Organization[1], which was in charge of constructing the Atlantic wall.

The most prominent Spanish captive of the Nazis was Francisco Largo Caballero, Prime Minister of Spain from September 4, 1936 to May 15, 1937. He was in the KZ of Oranienburg and died soon after he was freed. Spanish Republicans were also in Gusen, Buchenwald, Bergen-Belsen, Dachau and Neuengamme. But the greatest number, 9,985, were in Mauthausen[2] and 70 percent of them died. Of those, 95 percent died in the first terrible years, 1940–1942. They were moved there from the Stalags

30.   *Hitler's concentration camp—Mauthausen.*

31 A.   *1940 Hendaya: Hitler-Franco . . .*

31 B.   *1959 Madrid: Eisenhower-Franco . . .*

as a result of the representation of the Minister of Foreign Affairs of Spain.

Although the Commander of the camp gave orders that the Spanish should be eliminated through hunger, cold, and forced labor, most of them were assassinated. This same commander, Ziereis, wanted to force the Spaniards to put on German uniforms and fight the Russians, like the Falangist Blue Division.[3] He insinnuated that this was their only chance to get out of the camp alive. The Spaniards refused and expected there would be reprisals but there were only menaces. Barrack #10 was exclusively Spanish and its inmates regularly put aside a cauldron of soup at great sacrifice to themselves, to give to those prisoners who didn't have enough to eat. It was said to be vital to have a Spanish friend in this camp. Mauthausen was liberated by the Americans on May 5, 1945.

Juan de Diego:
   "If one blames others, it will never end."

There were only 2,398 Spanish survivors. One of these was Juan de Diego Herranz. At the suggestion of José Ester, I went to interview de Diego one evening in a small Right Bank Paris hotel in the Pigalle area. He was working as a concierge, and there were frequent interruptions of the taping, as the hotel clients came and went. Halfway through, de Diego stopped for some supper of sausages and mashed potatoes which he shared with me; and I had to leave very abruptly when I realized that I might miss the last Metro back to my hotel on the other side of the Seine. Several years later I interviewed de Diego again. In the meantime he had received indemnification[4] from the West German Government and he insisted that I come to see him in his new apartment near the Parc des Buttes Chaumont. He was very proud of the elevator, bathroom, the bright airy outlook, and as we sipped sherry he told me about his origins and childhood.

"I am just a common citizen, born on May 18, 1915, in Barcelona, the son of a railroad worker and a housewife. My father came from the province of Segovia and my mother was from a very typical small village in the province of Avila, Nava de l'Asunción. Segovia is the very heart of Spain both in spirit and language. If you like, it is still the Spain of chivalry.

"My father had three brothers and they all went into the army because there wasn't enough to eat. This was a common solution. My mother worked as a servant. I am very proud of my modest origins. My father, who was in the army reserves, went to Madrid to join up at the time of the big troubles with Francisco Ferrer, in 1909, the celebrated tragic week.[5] After that, my father took part in the war in Morocco and the Rif and afterwards became a railroad worker and met my mother. I was born in Barcelona but conceived in Madrid. I am happy to know this; my mother told me. My father was a cultivated and intelligent man and very kind. In our family he was my mother, and my mother was my father!"

What do you mean by that?

de Diego: "He was a good and moderate man, while my mother was courageous and capable of fighting. When the revolutionary strike took place in 1917 and 6,000 railroad workers were laid off, my mother went out to oppose the Guardia Civil and she threw herself in front of their horses. She was a member of a group headed by an extraordinary woman called Sra. Antonina. This woman weighed 264 pounds, but despite her weight was light on her feet. She and my mother were pals and they went out together to fight the scabs (in Spain they are called *los amarillos*). Surprisingly, this Antonina was the widow of a Colonel. And when she stood in the middle of the street, the strikebreakers were afraid of her. This was a woman's strike and the Spanish women at that time were very courageous, there was no one like them. Do you know what they did? They suckled their babies while demonstrating. It was a maternal gesture, not an erotic one. It was beautiful. My mother told me that. At the time she was breast-feeding my brother."

How old is she now?

de Diego: "She lives in Barcelona, is almost ninety, and has a very good memory. She was a woman who liked to fight, even in this last war. When my brothers said to my mother 'we are leaving,' she said, 'You are accepting your responsibilities. Do as you wish.' She never cried. And without much education, she still had a great feeling for liberty. During the Franco years, the police came to ask for her children. Do you know what she did? She hit the policemen. She had the courage to do it. Fortunately, they were not bad, and only said, 'Because you are an old woman, we respect you.' And during the elections she went directly to the election bureau to show her opposition and to vote *No* (although voting yes or no was all the same). But she wanted to declare 'I am against you.' My sister, who was very worried, said, 'You are compromising me.' But my mother answered: 'I am compromising nobody. I am profitting by the liberty given me to say what I think'."

How many years did you go to school?

de Diego: "I was privileged because I went to school, and this was rare in 1922 in Catalonia. Some Catalan intellectuals had founded four or five schools and I went to one called the Guinardo School. It was very, very good as it followed the Montessori method for the youngest children and the Pestalozzi methods later on. When the weather was fine, our work was done outside under the chestnut trees. For that era, the spirit of the school was very progressive, even more so than education in France today. The children of the big shots in the mayor's office and in the Administration went to these schools. But there were also places for the children of the poor and I was one of them. I was the only one among my brothers and sisters who was able to go to this school. I now realized how much I got out of it. It gave me a taste for good things, literature, music, and other fields."

How long did you stay there?

de Diego: "Until I was fourteen, when I went to work as an apprentice in a pharmacy. And my first days there were comical. Like all children, I loved sweets. And I took some santonine lozenges and poisoned myself! But it wasn't serious. I had another misadventure when I smelt the contents of a large bottle and almost fainted from the fumes of ammonia. Well, I learned something, but I wasn't satisfied about being in a pharmacy. So I went to do the sweeping in the Koch Academy of Commerce. I was paid to sweep, dust, and run errands for the students. I followed the courses at the same time, so I learned what I know while working."

And you were there until when?

de Diego: "I stayed there until I was sixteen or seventeen and my real education began. I worked in a commercial enterprise in Barcelona and made contact with all sorts of rich people. Bourgeois contacts are not bad, because these people know how to live well and have good taste. And through them I learned to like good things. Then the war in Spain came."

Were you in a political party before this war?

de Diego: "I had belonged to a group called the Republican Left of Catalonia. But I was more interested in being in a workers' organization. So I joined the Socialist Union of Catalonia and during the war I was in the century called Rosa Luxemburg, which was part of the Thaelmann group.[6] That was the first international group that came to fight for Spain before the International Brigades were formed. It was by chance that I found myself in it. We fought at Tardiente on the Aragon front. There were a few Germans, Poles, and Bulgarians in the group. But I was there only by chance, not by choice. At Tardiente there was a terrific attack by the Moors. One the eve of the battle there was a big storm and I got very wet. I fell ill and had such a fever that I was delirious and wasn't even conscious of the bombardment. Most of the men in my century were either killed or taken prisoners. By chance my life was saved. It's odd, a storm saved my life.

"After Tardiente there was a Colonel named Don Joaquin Blanco Valdes and he called me in and asked if I could write. I told him I could use the typewriter, so the political commissar took me with him and later the Colonel used me too because there were very few people who were educated or who could write. I was in the country of the blind, as they say in France and Spain. I became the secretary of the Colonel and we were in Barbastro, then Barcelona, and finally on the Madrid front. He went to Madrid because the Colonel who was in command at University City and Moncloa had been wounded. And by chance, 2 hours before Durruti died,[7] I was with him. All this by chance. I was sent to take some documents for Durruti to see. He saw them and I returned to my Colonel. All this was chance, the hazards of war. It was by chance too that I landed in the *schreibesteube* at Mauthausen. Everything has been chance in my life but I have been lucky [This is what Juan de Diego told me about his early life and here is what happened to blue triangle (the insignia worn by the *Rotspanier* (Spanish Reds) in Mauthausen) prisoner #3156 during the '40s.].

"Mauthausen concentration camp in Austria opened in 1938. Himmler [the leader of the SS or Elite Guard] was the creator. The camp was for Germans and Austrians and for people in the occupied countries who didn't conform to the German regime. Himmler wanted to transfer all the population of Holland to Poland. But there was someone who took care of Himmler because he had stomach trouble, a nervous illness, I think, and this person persuaded him not to do it [probably Felix Kersten, a Finnish expert in nature cures, who had been taught by a Tibetan]. But a first contingent of Dutch Jews was sent there and arrived around June 1941."

How did you arrive there?

de Diego: "I came in 1940 and I saw only German prisoners, yes, a few Austrians, but most were criminals. I was taken as a prisoner of war with a group of 392 Spaniards. We were in a company called *prestataires*. You know that when we crossed the frontier, one had to become a *prestataire* to have the right of asylum in France. Afterwards we would have the right to become French nationals. Good. At that time it was a period of speculation. They speculated with foreigners and with the French and with everybody. There was a lack of authority and when the Germans raised their hands, everything collapsed like a pile of sugar. The French let the Nazis and the Fascists do everything they wanted to do. They became victims themselves, and the consequences were what we knew until 1945."

What company were you in?

de Diego: "I was in the 103rd company and we were at Cambray making fortifications near the prolongation of the Maginot line, which was called the Lightning Line. We were volunteers and wore the uniform of the French Army. But as we were attached to the engineer corps, we didn't have a battalion number. This put us in a very bad spot, because if the Germans caught us, since we didn't have a number, we were considered partisans. You know we were in illegal units. Yes, yes, that is the way it was. But actually we were military enlisted men."

Why did the French do this?

de Diego: "They were negligent. They should have given us a unit number so that if we were taken prisoner we would have been covered by the Geneva Convention. You know that it says that anyone who doesn't belong to a unit is considered a partisan. When I was taken prisoner, a German officer said to me: 'Sir, what unit do you belong to?' I said: 'I belong to the 103rd work company.' He said: 'You are in uniform. We cannot recognize you as soldiers.' He was right. They considered us civilians and partisans and under these conditions they took away our category of prisoner of war and we entered the concentration camps.''

Were many Spaniards caught in this way?

de Diego: ''At Mauthausen there were about 7,000 Spaniards [the official figure is 9,985] from 1940 to 1945 and about 80 percent were in this category. Most of the Spaniards were taken prisoner on the fronts from the Alps to the Atlantic. There were also quite a lot who were seized in the Legion and the Battalion de Marche. They were officially military and were really prisoners of war, as they were in the French Army and were part of combat units. But these soldiers were treated in the same way as the *prestataires,* against all international law. But later we knew that the Germans didn't respect international law. So they weren't going to respect this law for the Spaniards, since we had made war from 1936 to 1939 against the Nazi spirit, against the racist spirit, against all that spirit which Europe followed afterwards.

''I don't mean to say that we were glorious, but just the same, we were the first to fight for a cause, and Europe should have followed. We fought, perhaps not intelligently, but at least with heart, and that's already a lot. I think from that point of view we deserve to be considered. Now when one studies the problems of the war in Spain, one has to recognize that the greatest injustice that Europe did was to abandon Spain at that time. We are romantics, scattered in countries all over the world. But we are not so bad, we don't blame anyone for that. If one blames others, it will never end. I still hope for peace in the world.

''To get back to the camp at Mauthausen. The Spaniards, arriving on 6 August, 1940, were the first group coming from outside Germany. Those in the concentration camps at that time were Germans, mostly common criminals, but also the old German Trade Unionists and Communists, that is to say, the first fighters against National Socialism. Most of the latter were from Munich and Bavaria. I knew and was close to them and I have a very good memory of them, because they were brave people. A few of them have important jobs today in politics but on the other side of the Iron Curtain, as it's called. Despite one's political opinions, to be just, I knew them as honest men. Now political opinion doesn't consider them in the same light, but I consider them still as the people I knew. It's difficult for me to believe that men who suffered in the conditions in which they suffered, could change and be bad. I don't believe it. I believe that the evil comes from those who didn't live under those conditions.

"I knew Novotny[8], who is President of the Czech Republic, and at that time he was working as an individual in the camps; Cyrankiewicz[9], who is the head of the Polish Government, lived in the same conditions. Another was Franz Dahlem, who was Minister of Education in East Germany, and Rau, who is no longer alive, was Minister of Economy. I knew all these people and I tell you, at that time I considered them good fighters.

"Novotny had come from Czechoslovakia, Cyrankiewicz came from Auschwitz, Dahlem was a refugee in France because he was a German Communist deputee before the war and took part in the Spanish Civil War. He had a very important position and when he came to Mauthausen, naturally in principal, the Spaniards were in debt to all those who had fought at our side, whether they were Communists or Socialists, or no matter what they were. When we were able, it was our duty to save the lives of men like these. They came as volunteers to give their lives for us and we owed them this life. We had Hungarian friends and Poles, who were in the International Brigades, who had different ideologies. There were Socialists, Anarchists, free thinkers, and everything. Because in the International Brigades, it wasn't just Communists, there were men of all sorts. There were Jews too. For example we had a Jewish doctor, who wore the number 1 in Mauthausen. This poor man died on the barbed wire. He was a doctor in the International Brigades, a man who saw things clearly and who fought against Nazism. He came to fight in Spain to defend, if you like, the cause of the Jews in the Spanish war. The war in Spain was extraordinary.

"So we entered Mauthausen 6 August, 1940, 392 men, *prestataires*. Travelling conditions? The prisoners never travelled first class! You know that prisoners don't even have the status of animals. They are kicked and beaten, they are given nothing to eat, they have no importance. You know, I think that man is always very primitive when it's a matter of treating someone who is inferior. I don't think this was just a German characteristic. Perhaps you will be surprised when I tell you that I make no exception for anyone, specially when one speaks of prisoners.

"When we arrived in 1940 until the end of 1942, life in the camps was very, very difficult. When we entered we were put in quarantine. This was already a kind of apprenticeship. We slept in barracks made for say 100 people and there were 600 of us, like sardines in a box. Naturally the proximity in which we lived produced vermin and provoked bad feeling among people. It is very hard to describe the life.

"For 40 days we remained isolated from everybody, with minimum food rations and insufficient calories to maintain a normal life. From the month of August 1940 until the 3rd or 4th of March 1941 I was like everybody. I worked in the quarry. [The famous 186 steps to the quarry were constructed by the Spaniards in the winter of 1940–1941. Each step was said to have cost a life.]. I carried up stones on my shoulders. In this conditions I realized that if I wanted to leave the camp, I must make a special effort. I saw that the only thing to do was to learn German. Most of us were of humble origin. I was an office worker in Spain but I had studied some and had tried to educate myself for my own satisfaction. I knew that I couldn't carry stones, my physicial condition wouldn't permit it. You see, I am not a strong man. I said to myself, you must learn German. If you speak German, you will be able to defend yourself better."

How did you do this? How did you learn?

   de Diego: "I learned while carrying stones. At that time one went down to the quarry and one carried stones. One carried them up, one carried them down, one carried them up, one carried them down. Well, there was a German next to me and I asked him to tell me how to decline the verb *to have,* for example. He said to me: *'Ich habe, du hast, er hat.'* So I carried the stones and recited as if I were reciting a prayer. That is how I learned the essentials of the German language. Having learned the essentials, they allowed me to be an interpreter. In 6 months I learned to get along rather well.

"When you had finished the day, they gave you your piece of bread, your little piece of margarine and sausage, and weariness prevailed and men fell on their straw beds and slept. You were like a dead man, a man drugged by work. The nights were very short in the summer, very, very short, because the sun rises early and sets late. So we slept very little. Personally, my greatest suffering came from lack of sleep. That is terrible. While I worked in the office, I worked many hours. Because it was a factory and there were a lot of goods coming in—because men were treated like merchandise. They spoke of *'stuecke,'* that means pieces. There were so many pieces, you understand? And when people began to arrive, it was 24 and even 30 hours that were needed, until one dropped. We had to identify, give numbers, file the forms, make reports.

"So during the 6 months I was in the quarry, I had been in almost all the commandos of the camp, until I entered the office in 1941. There I made the dossiers for the Spaniards and corrected many of the names because the Germans wrote them incorrectly. And since I had learned a little German, they gave me the book of the new arrivals. It had 10,000 numbers but at that time they only used the numbers up to 3,000. For example, when someone died, they erased the name, which was written in pencil, and they used the numbers two, three, four times. The Germans thought of the administration in a special way. The camp had to have 3,000 numbers, thus it wasn't possible to say that 30,000 to 40,000 men had passed through it. There were only 3,000. I am speaking of the first period in the camp. It was a way of concealing from the German population the number of people in the concentration camp.

"Then, as a result of the war in Russia, they needed a lot of people in the German war factories because all their troops were concentrated on the Russian front and in the different countries which had been occupied. So naturally they needed workers for the I.G. Farben, the Hermann Goering Works, Krupp, and all those big German war industries. So they used the deportees as slaves, which was unjust. The capital they have today stems from the exploitation of all those people who had been deported from all over Europe. Naturally, speaking about this 20 years later will not be pleasant. It is an old story. But for us it will never be old. It was unjust and will remain so. Also, they didn't respect human beings.''

Where did the Spaniards work in Mauthausen?

de Diego: "They worked principally in the quarry but some were used in the Hermann Goering Works in Linz and made tanks. Goering was the big 'Manitou,' as one says, of German heavy industry. The SS benefited from all this big industry. In reality, deportation was the first attempt to make slaves. We know what the world would have been like if it had been under National Socialism. Some people say: 'Oh, the Germans, they organized very well, they had Social Security.' But for those whom they took to the concentration camps there was no Social Security. There was only the bludgeon. And the conditions of life were the most horrible. They reduced men to nothing. They didn't even make them do real work, but things to be forgotten. Although conditions were better later, they were still so inhuman that the men couldn't resist. The proof is that during 5 years there were 200,000 deaths in Mauthausen. And you know that with the Jews their policy was for complete extermination.''

Was it possible to save some Jews?

de Diego: "The deportees who were not Jews did a lot to save them. Some people came with false identities and we helped them disappear from the camp to the commandos, where they were less disturbed and no one bothered them. I think men are more courageous in difficult moments and more quick-witted.''

Were there people who were able to escape from Mauthausen?

de Diego: "We had a group of three Spaniards who escaped from a commando. It was very difficult from Mauthausen itself. The commandos were groups of say 200 men, who belonged to Mauthausen but who worked 100 kilometers, or 50, away from the barracks. They were guarded but they worked for a concern or for the SS. Well, there were three Spaniards who escaped. Recently we honored one of these comrades, the two others are dead. One died in terrible conditions not long ago. He was called Leonte, and this poor fellow escaped twice. The second time, the war had ended and he was wandering in the forests of Yugoslavia without knowing that the war was over. He was eating grass and roots like a primitive man. And this poor boy, it was the second time he had escaped and under no circumstances did he want to fall into the hands of the Germans. He died about 6 months ago, atrociously, from an illness contracted in the concentration camp. I think he lived for a month in the forests and he was like a savage when they found him. And we paid homage to the only one of the three who has survived. He is called Santos. General Riquelme decorated him with a medal of the deportation and in memory of the two others who died.

"After the first escape, the Germans sent Leonte and Santos to an Arab-Russian camp at least 625 miles away. After 6 months they were returned to Mauthausen. And the Commander said: 'Since you escaped from the camp and you went 625 miles, I will pardon you.' But they were beaten, and each week they received 100 blows on their backsides. They also passed 41 days in the black cell. It was a miracle they survived. Once Santos left the black cell, he received a great deal of help from his comrades—solidarity saved his life."

Was he at Mauthausen until the end?

de Diego: "Yes, he was in a commando and we helped him a lot. We Spaniards are accused of having an individualistic temperament by people who don't understand us. I think this is a sickness of humanity. But still I think that as far as solidarity is concerned, in difficult moments, I believe the Spanish were the most exemplary. Without boasting, I think there is a great virtue in our temperament. The Spaniards were more civilized and there was a certain Quixoticism. *Quijote* was written to illustrate the Spanish attitude, a sort of Spanish Bible.''

Were you in the office until the liberation?

de Diego: "Yes, until the end. I had a very important job. I had to keep the card index of the camp, the book of the new arrivals, and especially reports about everyone who died. And so naturally it permitted me to know the mysteries of the camp.''

Was it possible to write to people outside?

de Diego: "At a certain time, another Spaniard, named Climent, took steps to see if we could write letters [Late in 1942, after almost 3 years, the Spanish Republicans were allowed to write to their families in France and Spain]. And it was arranged officially. Secretly I managed to get in touch with my family through a young Spaniard, who was freed and went to see them in Spain. I believe the Spanish authorities intervened; he must have had military men in his family. His mother was a widow and I think she had been married to a colonel, someone of high rank, and so he was freed. I don't remember his name but he went to my home. And my family got news that way.

"But my mother, who was a woman of great courage, got a lot of people moving and received the first news that I was in Mauthausen in a letter from the Spanish Ambassador, on 14 April, 1941. That was very rare. One must admire mothers because they are capable of everything. I have the letter at home and it is dated 14 April, 1941. That was the date of the proclamation of the Spanish Republic in 1931. And 10 years later there was joy in my mother's home because there was news that her child, a Republican, was in the hands of the Germans.''

Tell me, were you in touch with Germans outside the camp?

de Diego: "No, as I was only outside the camp on three occasions. I went out when the Merk Commando was bombed. The SS was unable to put it in order. So they sent me because I had all the dossiers for inside and outside the camp, and I had to go. I considered it a duty to bring order because in doing so I would save the lives of many men. Because the SS when they made roll calls, martyred the men with blows. They always did it this way. I was a prisoner, and they were my fellow sufferers. So I used calmer methods and prolonged the roll call as long as possible so that they would have some rest. But with the SS it would have been bludgeons and 30 deaths. They didn't know who was there after the bombardment, nor their names. That is why many Jews, who were thought to be dead, were alive."

You mean to say that during bombardments you gave them different identities?

de Diego: "The report of deaths was falsified, and remained so until the end of the war. That is to say, those who were called Meyer, who were alive, they weren't mentioned, because naturally the SS never made a mistake. And if they had known that there were people who were alive, but dead, they would have killed them so that everything would be in order. Do you see? It happened once like that."

What were the two other occasions when you left Mauthausen?

de Diego: "I also went to Steier when it was bombed because there too it was necessary to put things in order. The third time I went to Gusen. It was what was called a deportation center. It was there that people died like flies from 1940 to 1942. I received a list of 448 Spaniards who died at Gusen under terrible conditions. The first mass deaths there were Spaniards. I think it was the first 'final solution.' They killed them with injections of benzine in the aorta. They killed them with cold showers of 15–16 degrees. They killed them with kicks, with bludgeons, and they killed them even by putting their boots between the neck and chest. They killed them with dogs. I think, as I said, that it was the 'final solution,' they started it there, it was studied there.

"And you know that one of those who was most responsible was Serrano Suner [Foreign Minister, member of the Falange, and theoretician in the early days of Franco's rule] the former Minister, brother-in-law of Franco. When he was in Germany, the Germans asked him: 'What should we do with the Spaniards?' And do you know the answer? He said: 'You have only to eliminate them, you will help us avoid having to eliminate them ourselves.' There are documents which will only be published after 50 years, which will verify the truth about this. These documents are at the International Red Cross. They won't give them out because it's a law; certain documents must remain in the archives for 50 years. And when 50 years have gone by, they will have had 50 years to deceive us. Is this just? or unjust? I don't know if this is for good or for bad."

ROBERT DUBOIS, MANUELA RIQUELME, ANNE MARIE BERTA

How were the Spanish deportees received in France from Germany at the end of World War II? Captain Robert Dubois and Mme. José Riquelme described the return to Paris. Anne Marie Berta gave me her impressions of the repatriation in Toulouse. They all spoke in French as I taped them.

Mme. Manuela Riquelme is very vivacious and outspoken and is sometimes referred to as Mme. La Generale. Her husband, General José Riquelme y Lopez-Bago was a very cultivated man, who is said to have preferred negotiating to fighting. During the Spanish Civil War, only 200 out of 15,000 officers sided with the Republic, and Riquelme was one of 13 generals who remained loyal.

The Riquelmes fled from Paris when the Nazis entered since he was on the list, presented by Franco's men to the Gestapo, of Spaniards to be arrested. Riquelme was active in the French Resistance in the South of France during World War II. He died in Paris in January 1972 at the age of ninety-one and is buried in the Pere Lachaise cemetery.

Captain Dubois, a French army officer who had been captured on the Maginot line, was in military internment camps in Germany during the war. He was chosen by the Seine Prefecture after the liberation to take care of the Spanish deportees repatriated to Paris.

Riquelme: "The Hotel Lutetia was the center for repatriation and classification of all the Spanish deportees returning to France.[10] I was given the direction of the two camps which were set up for them: the Centre Gallet, formerly a garage, at 165 rue de Vaugirard in Paris, and the Centre de Montrouge, on the outskirts. I had about 1,500 people to feed and house, and there were a lot of difficulties since there was a shortage of food in the capital. But we were helped by the Government and the Prefecture of the Seine, which provided us with what was needed to put these men back on their feet, as they were in absolutely deplorable condition. The French Government paid for everything: food, clothing, and lodging.

"There was a French decree which said that the deportees should return to their former homes. But, alas, they had no homes; they had come from work companies or French concentration camps. It was difficult to make the Government accept the idea that these Spaniards were brothers and that they should receive the same advantages, rights, and pensions as the French. There were many with lung and kidney trouble and intestinal dysentery. To show you the frightful privations they had endured, a man who had weighed 176 pounds had dropped to 77. Some recovered completely but there are many who are not even well today despite everything. Some had families here and some in Spain. At Montrouge we were able to reunite 6 families, that's all. Either their families couldn't leave Spain for political reasons or lacked the means.''

Mme. Riquelme [represented the Spanish Republican Red Cross and worked with Captain Dubois as a volunteer]: ''It was my job to do everything possible to comfort the deportees and raise their morale. The centers were open until 1948. And for 2 years Picasso paid for 12 women who did the work at the centers. He also gave a painting for the exhibition of Spanish painters at a Gallery at 12 rue de Seine and we collected money there for the medical center at 47 rue Monge, which Dubois had gotten permission to open. There had been a French one but there was a language problem. Many of the Spaniards had been taken to Germany in 1941. They spoke German but not French. This center still exists and is the clinic of the Spanish Republican Red Cross at 11 rue Gerbier. There was another one in Toulouse, whose President was Dr. Marti Feced[11] and he had delegated powers for a vice president in Paris.

''Two years ago, some of the survivors wanted someone to go with them to Mauthausen and they paid the expenses for my husband and me. There is a stairway to the quarry, the place where they took stones. One had to go up the stairs 40 times with a stone weighing a minimum of 55 pounds, to exhaust them, and there were 198 steps. You can't believe it if you haven't been there. It's horrible.''

Anne Marie Berta tells what happened in Toulouse after the liberation:
''I knew Dr. Marti Feced. He was the only person who had the right to recreate the Spanish Republican Red Cross. The French gave us a place in the rue Pargaminieres and paid the rent. Commissioner Bertaut, who had been a prominent Resistant, was named Prefect of Toulouse and he chose me as delegate of the Red Cross for the deportees who were coming from Germany. There was a woman from the CNT, one from the Communists, one from the Socialists. Each party had a delegate, but I was apolitical. We worked in the Victoria Hotel across from the sta-

tion. And a little further on were the Quakers [the American Friends Service Committee]. The French Red Cross helped us, and were magnificent.

"When the trains arrived in the station and masses of people came, parents and family, and the military band played the *Marseillaise* and the *Song of the Partisans,* and children came with bunches of flowers, it was terribly moving. Then one saw terrific scenes, parents with children hugging the deportees who arrived, some who had to be carried because they were nothing but skin and bones, and the ambulances with their stretchers to take others to the hospitals. A 'Don Quixote City' had been created for the deportees and their families at Recebedou at Portet sur Garonne. You could see the Republican flag flying from far off. And those who were in good health were taken there. Others, if they were considered very ill, were taken to the Hotel Dieu or the Purpan Hospital.

"And sometimes among the deportees, someone came from the Blue Division[12] and pretended to be a deportee. They were easily discovered; it was flagrant. You could see that they hadn't suffered, and they had no papers as deportees. The French police gave papers immediately to the deportees but when they were suspect, I took them up to the first floor and they weren't seen again. They were liquidated. When I asked the French police, who had all been in the Resistance, about them, they said, 'Don't bother about them, they will do nothing more.' I understood. Once I had seven at one time together. Also, when they saw the Spanish Republican flag one felt they were annoyed. They were traitors.

"As for the Spanish deportees, everything went well. The Quakers gave them packages and clothes. The French Red Cross gave furniture when they had it. At that time there were a lot of things. The French *Entr'aide,* whose director was a wonderful woman, gave a lot of food packages for the deportees. It lasted for 2 or 3 months. They came from the camps of Dachau and Mauthausen. And the women were all sick, with big pimples. They had been given injections to stop their menstruation, and they were suffering from vitamin deficiency. They were in a terrible state, some very fat, others very thin, but all with pimples. They had to be hospitalized immediately for treatment.''

NOTES

1. It was named after Dr. Fritz Todt (1891-1942), a military engineer, who designed the Autobahn and the Westwall.
2. Mauthausen was in Austria on the Danube, near Linz. It was opened in 1938, was an extermination camp, and was called *'Totenburg'*, or the "mountain of death."
3. It was formed in Spain in 1941 and sent off in July to fight in Germany with the Nazis on the Russian front. General Munoz Grande led the 15,000 man division. It "consisted of Falangists who had been mixed up in murders or malpractices of some kind, adventurers, or uprooted people, and above all Republicans menaced with death or reprisals against their families . . . Reinforcements came from the prisons of Spain!" Out of 27,000 men who went to Germany there were 9,000 who deserted and 11,000 casualties. In 1964 the Bonn Government granted pensions to the wounded veterans of the Blue Division who fought for Hitler, and to their widows, orphans and parents. (For quotes and statistics see André Prunier in *Temoins—Fidelité a L'Espagne,* Printemps—Été 1956).
4. The Bonn Government has given indemnification to over 3,000 families in Spain for men who died in KZs in Nazi Germany. Gradually, many exiles who suffered at the hands of the Nazis have been indemnified with a fixed sum in addition to a monthly pension.
5. In July 1909, reserves had been called up in Catalonia to replace a column of troops recently massacred in Morocco. The people of Barcelona rose in protest and there were 5 days of rioting. When it was over 75 workers had been shot in the streets and among those tried and executed was Francisco Ferrer, the founder of the libertarian and anticlerical school, the Escuela Moderna, and a theoretical anarchist. He had not been in Barcelona at the time and there was no evidence that he had been involved in the uprising.
6. A century consisted of 4 groups of 25 men in the Republican militia. Ernst Thaelmann was the leader of the German Communist party, who had been imprisoned and killed by the Nazis.
7. Buenaventura Durruti, militant of the CNT-FAI, who came from

the Aragon front with 3,500 of his men to defend Madrid and died there on November 20, 1936.

8. Antonin Novotny, Czech Dictator (1953-1968) and Communist Party leader. When the Communist Party was declared illegal in 1938 he worked in the underground and was arrested and deported by the Nazis in 1941. He died January 29, 1975; the *New York Times* obituary called him a "cold, humorless, and often ruthless man."

9. Josef Cyrankiewicz became president of the Council of Ministers in Poland. He was in the anti-Nazi resistance in Cracow and was arrested by the Gestapo in 1941 and then deported to Auschwitz and later Mauthausen.

10. General and Mme. Riquelme gave me, for SRA, the Republican flag which hung at the Hotel Lutetia when the Spanish deportees returned from Germany. It has been used in the U.S. several times to cover the coffins at funerals of Spanish Republicans who have died here.

11. Dr. Marti Feced was active in reconstituting the Spanish Republican Red Cross in Catalonia during the Civil War and again in Toulouse in 1945. He was a member of the Catalan Government after the May days, representing the Esquerra Republicana.

12. See footnote 3.

13

Libertarians—
Anarcho-Syndicalists

*I*n the introduction of this book I have written I have a personal bias and that my sympathies are with the Spanish Libertarian Anarcho-Syndicalists. The Colonie d'Aymar, founded by Anarcho-Syndicalists, has been described as a place where some of the "comrades could find health and tranquility in an ambiance of fraternal affection and solidarity''; Organizing the town of Puigcerda was in Mariano Puente's account "according to the libertarian principles of equality for everybody.''

Three more libertarians with remarkable stories to tell are Miguel Garcia Garcia, Diego Camacho, and Pedro Duran.

Miguel Garcia Garcia, a libertarian, was very active in the underground resistance in Spain and spent many years in and out of Franco's prisons. Diego Camacho, at fifteen, worked in an agricultural collective for a few months during the Civil War. Under the pseudonym Abel Paz, he wrote a book about the Spanish Anarchist, Buenaventura Durruti, which I translated in 1977. Pedro Duran, a close friend of Juan Andrade, exiled in France and a member of the POUM, helped found with his wife, Pepita, a successful mattress cooperative in Toulouse. The libertarian spirit pervaded their work and their lives.

MIGUEL GARCIA GARCIA:
"Every man was his own leader."

Miguel Garcia Garcia was born in Barcelona in 1908, the seventh of nine children. He was a newspaper boy at nine and an apprentice printer at twelve. He was an active member of the CNT all his life. After the Civil War he was in prison for almost 2 years. Picked up again in 1949 for his activities against the Franco regime, he was condemned to death, but was released from prison in 1969 after 20 years. All his attempts to escape had failed. As an exile in London he spent his time trying to help the comrades he left behind in Spain. He wrote a book called *Franco's Prisoner,* published in England in 1972 by Rupert Hart Davis.

I met Miguel a number of times when I was in London. He took me to see the Centro Iberico, where he was very active, and cooked me a delicious paella in his cellar home in Upper Tollington Park. He was a generous and warm-hearted man, whose response to difficult situations was always, "We must *do* something." His motto was *dar la vida por la vida* (one must give one's life for the sake of life). He returned to Spain in 1979 where he opened a café, La Fragua (the forge) in the Calle Cadena in Barcelona. It became a meeting place for anarchists from all over. It was with sadness that I learned of his death from TB in London in December 1981.

Interview with Miguel Garcia Garcia[*]

Where were you at the outbreak of the Civil War?

Miguel Garcia: "I was living in Barcelona, and at dawn of the 19th of July those of us who knew of the military uprising began to prepare. Since the government had been afraid to arm us, particularly the CNT (National Confederation of Workers—a syn-

---

[*]First published by Black Flag Press in London in English in their *Simian* series.

32. Miguel Garcia—in his beloved Barrio Gotico (Gothic Quarter)—at the Plaza San Felipe Neri, where many comrades were rounded up and shot in 1939, and where many were arrested in 1949. Barcelona 1979.

dicalist union) for fear that since it was opposed to all authority it would make use of the arms for starting the revolution. It was necessary to take the guns from wherever possible, in armories and barracks. Barricades were thrown up and armored cars improvised in the fight against the army. On the 21st the military uprising in Barcelona had been stamped out.

"News came that our comrades in Zaragoza had not been successful, and we immediately made plans to go and help them in the street fighting against the military. On the 22nd a column was due to leave with Durruti at its head, but on the 23rd since nothing had happened, the six of us who formed my group set off in a car. In Caspe we came up against resistance and after a sharp fight with the Guardia Civil found that we could not get through. We fell back to Lerida for reinforcements. The following day again we tried to take Caspe and this time met with very little resistance. We pressed on, but it was now too late for Zaragoza. Nobody had arrived soon enough, and the military, which were very strong there, had taken the town. A front line formed before Zaragoza and it lasted right up to the famous battle of the Ebro. From there I went to Madrid in November 1936 with a Catalan force that was to help in its defense against the tremendous pressure from the Fascist forces. I spent the rest of the war there."

What did you do at the end of the war?

Miguel Garcia: "I went back to Barcelona where on 9 May, 1939 I was arrested and put into a hemp warehouse which had been converted into a prison, since the *Prision Celular* was by now brim-full. After 22 months, in March 1941, I was cleared and released."

What was the atmosphere like when you came out?

Miguel Garcia: "The atmosphere was good, though perhaps a little too optimistic. Although the Germans had pushed back the Allies, people were so confident in ultimate victory that they did not attach much importance to this, and everyone was preparing for a possible comeback of the CNT. We certainly were active, but we also had to work cautiously since the firing squad was hard at work every day. Trials condemning 30 or 40 people to death were quite frequent. The *Prision Celular* built to take 1,100 men, was at bursting point with 14,000—14 in a cell! There was hardly room for them standing up and they slept in turns. Eighteen thousand men were shot, according to the record, and it was unwise to hope for a mere spell in prison—people were automatically locked up for nothing more than having a union card. They were terrible times, right up to the fall of Germany. Much has been said about the extermination camps of Germany, but the systematic slaughter of Spaniards, particularly those of the libertarian movement, at this time reached proportions that have never been guessed at."

What did you do at the end of the World War?

Miguel Garcia: "We were all certain that the Spanish exiles, with the help of the Allied Forces, would invade Spain to smash the last stronghold of Fascism in Europe. But no, as everyone knows, the interests of economic investment came first, and Franco went happily on with his reign of terror. Many people accepted that nothing could be done, but others did not and carried on fighting in secret resistance groups."

How did these groups develop?

Miguel Garcia: "Well, in fact, as far as the libertarian movement is concerned, undercover resistance has never died; but at the end of World War II it was reinforced by comrades who had been fighting on the side of the Allies and wanted to fight on in independent groups. They crossed the frontier and made contact with comrades in the interior, and wrought havoc for the regime by sabotaging electricity plants, industry, and the banking system, and at the same time crossing and recrossing into France and making complete fools of the frontier guards. Occasionally there were the inevitable skirmishes with the police and the Guardia Civil, by whom they came to be regarded with terror.''

Were there many men lost among the guerilleros?

Miguel Garcia: "Yes, many comrades left their blood on Catalan soil, but many, many of the servants of the regime also paid with their lives.''

Was there any guerrilla who stood out from the rest?

Miguel Garcia: "Somebody will always stand out from the rest more or less in any life situation. There were men in the movement who, whether by luck or ability became famous and very much feared by the enemies of freedom.''

Can you give me any names?

Miguel Garcia: "I am not keen on mentioning the names of men who distinguish themselves, since we are opposed to all idols, but to satisfy your curiosity I will tell you of two who were renowned for their quick reflexes, their courage, and for the havoc they caused for the regime. These were José Lluis Facerias and Francisco Sabater Llumpart. Sabater's elder brother was with me in that hemp warehouse I told you about when I explained how I was arrested at the end of the war; he died in a police ambush—but not without making sure he took with him a police inspector.''

Anyone else?

Miguel Garcia: "Many. In fact hundreds, but there was one group that stood out because of the affinity that existed amongst all its members. It was called Los Manos. They were comrades who had known each other a long time and had weathered good and bad together—plenty of the bad.''

Can you tell me about any particular thing they did?

Miguel Garcia: "Can I? I could make a 100,000 page book about it. But I'll tell you one about Sabater; it's a good one and will give you some idea of his fast reflexes. It was in Barcelona and Sabater was riding on the platform of a tram. He was dressed as a poultry farmer and hanging on his arm was an egg basket in which his submachine gun was hidden. He thought one of the other passengers looked like one of the secret police and he got off the tram to see if he would follow him. Well, the other fellow got off too and started to follow.

"After a short distance, Sabater, in one of those lightning reactions that only fast movers get, spun round like a cat, grabbed the chap by the lapels and said: 'Who are you? Let's have your papers, pronto!' He almost snatched the identity card out of his pocket and seeing that he was a detective, picked him up by his jacket collar. He spun him round and sent him flying with a very powerful boot, thundering after him in raucous Catalan: 'Get out of here and don't bother me again.' The fellow took off as if the devil was after him and never dared to look back once. When you think that it was just like doing it in the middle of Piccadilly you'll get some idea of the nerve this man must have had."

How many men to a group?

Miguel Garcia: "It varied. Usually about six and never more than twelve."

Where were they recruited?

Miguel Garcia: "I don't think recruit is the right word when there were always enough comrades keen enough to form a group. But since the strength of these groups lay in their solidarity and affinity, they never approached anyone unless through heavy losses."

Was Sabater as good a leader as he was a fast mover?

Miguel Garcia: "We have no leaders in our movement. Every man in a group was his own leader and nobody took decisions without everybody's agreement. If the need arises to represent somebody on their behalf, the man chosen is no more than a delegate and his only authority lies in carrying out decisions agreed upon by the group members."

But didn't this create endless discussion and delay important decisions?

Miguel Garcia: "Any action is thoroughly discussed before carrying it out, but in a way so that every man states his opinion and we come up with the most appropriate and sensible decision, as is logical. As far as delaying decision-making goes, in specific instances of unforeseen circumstances the individual acts on his own initiative at the time. It's not done any old how. Each group member knows what he has to do and when to do it. These are determined men, with lots of fighting experience. Each man uses his own particular knowledge for the benefit of the group without attaching any more importance to it than that. In our society most people expect anyone with special knowledge to exploit it for profit-making, and it is perhaps difficult for you to understand the spontaneity and freedom of spirit in libertarian dealings. We are all brethren of the same family and our fatherland is humanity itself."

What exactly is the libertarian movement?

Miguel Garcia: "The word liberty has been bandied about quite a lot, and to say that a libertarian is a lover of liberty can be rather vague, but in fact it could be said to suffice. However, to avoid confusion it is best to say that the libertarian movement includes all those who reject imposed authority. Any individual who has sufficient insight to understand that his own rights end only where those of his neighbors' begin, who does not want to treat people any different from the way he would wish them to treat him, is capable of living without guards and policemen to impose rules on him concerning what he may or may not do.''

Yes, that's fine, but I meant the Spanish libertarian movement in particular.

  Miguel Garcia: "Well, it is composed of the Libertarian Youth (JJLL), the syndicalists (CNT), and the pure anarchists (FAI). The youth movement consists of just the young libertarians. The syndicalists are the workers and their unions in their various trades; the pure anarchists are the ideologists of the libertarian ideal.''

Are these three movements independent from each other?

  Miguel Garcia: "Completely—otherwise they would no longer be libertarian.''

And did they attempt to establish collectives during the Civil War?

  Miguel Garcia: "Yes, and it worked too, in spite of opposition from other ideological elements. It showed clearly that the idea of all living and working together as one family is perfectly feasible.''

Can you tell me about any specific case?

  Miguel Garcia: "Yes, certainly. In Lerida, for example: I spent 2 days there on leave from the Aragon front, on one of the farming collectives. The whole thing was running in harmony and perfect order; everybody looked happy in a way that I had never seen before among country folk. They now had no more problems, financial or otherwise.

"The same thing happened in industry. Factories and workshops were collectivised, and when the original owners moved back in at the end of the war they found them in better running order than when they had left them. Everybody knows how a collective gets under way so I won't bother to go into it again."

Perhaps, but I myself don't know much about it. For example, how did you organize the administration in a factory?

Miguel Garcia: "Just the way way it is organized now, except that positions in administration do not exist within a hierarchy which demands respect of inferiors. All we have to do is to get rid of a few prejudices and realize that it is no more difficult to work at a desk than on the production line."

But then won't everybody opt for the production line rather than the desk, since the money is the same?

Miguel Garcia: "Yes, perhaps an actor, seeing that he is not going to earn any more than an usher, would rather be an usher. And this is exactly what did happen in Barcelona in the case of a well-known actor, Enrique Borras, who tried to change places with an usher for a few days to see what would happen. He made his point, since as you can see it is not easy for an usher to do the job of a first-rate actor, and Borras would only have been cheapening his vocation. Every individual is born for a certain function in society in accordance with his aptitudes, and the idea of valuing one's function in hard cash is only a creation of our modern society. In real life we each of us follow, if we can, our impulses, and these are derived from what our organisms require. It is just as absurd to suggest that a man gifted in the arts should win glory as a dustman as it is to force a left-handed person into doing things with his right hand. You can be sure that in a free society production would become balanced to suit people's aptitudes.''

I would like to believe what you are saying, but it would seem to me to be very difficult to put into practice.

Miguel Garcia: "It's all a problem of education, and whether we want to live in shacks or palaces—that is, putting progress and civilization within reach of everybody. The solution to your doubts lies in the verse of an English poet:

> Labour is the one thing man has had too much of.
> Let's abolish labour, let's have done with labouring!
> Work can be fun, and men can enjoy it; then it's not labour.
> Let's have it so! Let's make a revolution for fun!''

Very original. But, tell me, how are you going to set about replacing the present structures with the new?

Miguel Garcia: "Whatever is not covered by the regulations is solved by logic, and the present laws are only the consequences of antisocial customs. You can be sure that mankind's ingenuity will not disappear just because of social change. Let the bird alone and he will find the best place for a nest.''

There is something that I have always wondered about. How did the libertarians take the militarization of their forces during the Civil War?

Miguel Garcia: "Very badly. Since we were opposed to war, we were opposed to all specialist organization for making it, but here is where that logic comes in. We found ourselves in a situation where the alternatives were war or revolution, but if we wanted to have a revolution we had first to win the war. There is no doubt that war is a subject for the specialists; a profession with its own necessary techniques that cannot be improvised.

Had we all been libertarians the process would have been unnecessary, but Spain has always been a country with a high illiteracy rate, more so in the ideological and political aspect. State power like church power was based on the ignorance of the people; there were people everywhere who knew the whole catechism by heart yet without hardly knowing left from right. With a whole people in that state—anxious for liberty, but full of old, deep-rooted prejudices—it was inevitable that the various political factions should try to impose a system which would guarantee them control. We would never have needed it, but they did. We had to compromise, and militarization went ahead.''

But wasn't this useful in any way?

Miguel Garcia: "Certainly it was. It was extremely useful for the Communists in their struggle for power. They accept imposed discipline as a basic principle, whilst we believe only in self-discipline which the individual must impose on himself.''

Lastly, what do you think the future holds for Spain?

Miguel Garcia: "It is difficult to say, the fear of vengeance is persistent among the members of the government. The regime, built as it is on the bodies of more than a million dead, is terrified of having to account for its crimes. Something would have evolved long before now were it not for this fear, since the regime has hardly ever known harmony in its midst.

There is one right-wing party which is very strong and with a fairly moderate program, more or less on the lines of the Christian Democrats. They could have taken over if the extreme right-wing Opus Dei had not jumped in ahead of them. The Opus Dei, which is still in power, is like a revival of the Inquisition, as if Torquemada had risen from the grave to reimpose his law.

"The workers are becoming more politically orientated, but are still kept silenced by the law. If only they could organize independent unions outside state control, it wouldn't take long for them to be a big factor in what happens next, and the government will eventually be forced to concede them more rights. This will give them the freedom essential to plan their destiny and the future will be in their hands. Otherwise only prolonged guerrilla warfare such as the one started by us is going to bring us nearer our vision of the future.''

DIEGO CAMACHO:
"Everyone was trusted."

It was through Miguel Garcia Garcia that I met Diego Camacho (whose pen name is Abel Paz). During the summer of 1972 I read Paz's book on the anarchist militant Buenaventura Durruti, and was so impressed that I wanted to translate it from the French into English. I asked Miguel if he knew how I could get in touch with the author. Miguel gave me his address and I wrote to Camacho, who agreed to let me translate the book, which was published by Black Rose Press in Canada in 1977. Earlier, Paz wrote a book called *Paradigma de una revolución* (*36 horas de lucha en Barcelona*) and is working on another, *Comité Central des Milices de Catalogne*.

Diego lives in Barcelona, and in October 1985 I asked friends to look him up there. He came to see them at the Hotel Ritz, where they were staying. He told them that the last time he was there, during the Civil War, he was fourteen, carried a rifle, and came to take over the hotel as a hospital. He also told my friends that in the fifties he had asked SRA for a sewing machine for his wife, and we had given him one.

Where do you come from in Spain?

Camacho: "I was born on August 12, 1921 in Almeria in the province of Andalusia. My parents were peasants and I lived with them until I was fourteen. I started to go to school at the age of eleven, and I went to a school subsidized by the CNT unions for 2 years. It was a rationalist school modeled on those started by Francisco Ferrer in 1909. The school was in Barcelona and the Union which supported it was the Textile Workers Union which had 70,000 members. It was called *La Escuela Natura* and the Director was Puig Elias, who died in exile 2 years ago in Brazil. The school was rather well known and had 400 students.

"As I couldn't go to school in my province, my mother arranged with her mother to take care of me in Barcelona. I was at this school from 1933 to 1935. Then I went to work as an apprentice mechanic in a small shop and was there until the war started in Spain in 1936."

When did you become an anarchist?

Camacho: "I think in that period one became an anarchist quite naturally. The conditions of life led workers to become anarchists. For example, my father was a peasant and he worked 3 months during the year; the other 9 months he was unemployed because there was no work. He had to feed his family of five. So he was forced to go out at night and steal things in the fields to feed us. In reality, almost all the peasant population did that. They stole to eat. So in such a situation and without having any theoretical knowledge about anarchism, I was an anarchist instinctively.

"Then the war came and I was already a member of the Libertarian Youth and I was active with them until the month of November 1936. At that time I was given the opportunity of working in a peasant collective in the Province of Lerida in a village called Cervia. I stayed there until March 1937."

What was this experience like?

Camacho: "Life in a collective was something very interesting. Because in Barcelona, although all the industries were collectivized or socialized, one couldn't see how things had changed since there was no community life in the factories. One works, and then each individual goes home. While in a commune everything was completely different. We all lived together and one could see better how things were changing."

Were you sent by the CNT?

Camacho: "We had been sent by the Libertarian Youth because in this village of 3,500 inhabitants a Libertarian Youth group had also been organized. They wanted to have direct contact with city workers because during a revolution there are always differences between the farmers and the industrial workers. And no revolution has succeeded in establishing a bond between the country and the city. But in Spain this bond was established immediately.

"If you go back to the beginnings of the workers' movement in Spain, in 1870 when the Spanish section of the International was organized, no difference was made between the peasants and the industrial workers. They were all workers. And when people went to the country to work, they didn't live there, they went back to the towns. The peasants in Spain are very different from those in other countries. They have always been very active in their villages and are not just country people, so that liaison was quickly established between the city and the country.

"But there is a question of a certain mentality. The fellows who live in the country are reserved and they think they are always being fooled by those who know more than they do. So there was some distrust of the people from the city. But we were in the process of getting rid of this type of thinking. That is why the libertarians in the village wanted us city dwellers to come and live with the peasants so that they could see that there was no reason to mistrust us. And so we lived there for 6 or 7 months.

"At first the old peasants had a certain pride and said of the city people, 'You don't know how to work—you are not used to work.' But we showed them we were capable of working when necessary and that we were also capable of amusing ourselves. We showed them that we were capable of doing everything that they did with the same courage, perhaps not always with the same skill since we weren't peasants, but we did our very best to do the hardest work. And so we were accepted right away and we were very much loved by everyone there."

Did you work in the fields, or as a mechanic?

Camacho: "No, no, this collective was completely agricultural. It had many olive trees and was rich in oil. There were almond trees too, and vegetables, but the main wealth came from the oil. So there was a mill. But we had to pick the olives in the month of November. It was very cold there and you had to have pluck to pick the olives. You had to get up early.

"But the really interesting thing was how the life had changed. Formerly, people in the country lived rather closed in on themselves. Now they were beginning to live with each other; life became more open. At least twice a week there were general assemblies and all the village attended—including the women, the children, the old people, everybody. Communications were completely different. For example, before the war, young girls didn't walk alone with boys. Now that was no longer true; life had changed 100 percent."

And when they met, is that when decisions for the collective were made?

Camacho: "Work was organized in brigades of 10, 15, or 20, and each brigade had a delegate who was responsible for the work done. In the assemblies all the problems of the community were discussed, such as administration, schools, organizing a theater group, sanitation, all the questions to be resolved. You might think that these assemblies might be boring for the people but not at all—it was more like a festivity. They went to have a family discussion. Before, the family was limited to three or four people. Now there were collective problems of 3,500. Of course not everyone spoke. But everyone came, and if they wanted to give their opinion, they did. In the summer the assemblies took place outdoors. In winter, when it was cold, they were in the theater.

"There are a lot of interesting details about the daily life in a collective. For example, the church had been taken over and it had become the collective's food store. That was where each family obtained their foodstuffs for the week or the day. There were no tickets. Everyone knew each other and there were no problems. For example, if you went to get some meat and you came back a half hour later, the fellow would know you and he couldn't be fooled. But we didn't have such problems. Everyone was trusted. Sometimes you couldn't have a lot of a product because there wasn't enough produced. But the rest you had in abundance.''

Was it the same for clothes?

Camacho: ''No, we didn't make them, so they had to be bought. Or we made an exchange with the things we had, like oil. There was some control. For example, there were two pairs of shoes per year, but then there was the type who needed three pairs because he hadn't taken care of them. He received three, but usually there was a certain control and normally people didn't behave like that.''

Did you return from the collective before the May Days?

Camacho: ''I returned to Barcelona a few days before. I started to work again as an apprentice in my trade, as I was only fifteen. And I worked there during the tragic events of May and the counterrevolution. But I'm not going into all the question of the Spanish revolution here. We, the young libertarians, began to be persecuted by the Communist Party on the one hand and on the other we were in opposition to the CNT and the FAI for their political position in relation to the government.[1] And this is how we lived during the war, until Barcelona was taken by Franco, and we went into exile in France.

''In France I was put into concentration camps [See chapter 6]. First I was in St. Cyprien, then Argeles-sur-Mer, and finally Bram. From there I was sent out in a work company and I remained until the Germans cut France in half. After June 1940 I went to Bordeaux. There we made a little propaganda and sabotage until we were forced to flee to the free zone. The situation then became such in France that either we had to fight the Germans or join them. A few friends studied the situation and decided, not out of patriotism, that we would prefer to return to Spain to fight against the Spanish Fascists directly.''

When was this?

Camacho: "It was in June 1942 in Barcelona that we tried to rebuild a Spanish resistance movement and we managed to carry out quite a few little jobs. We organized several groups of young people, people we knew already. But in December 1942 I was caught by the police. I was imprisoned and condemned to 30 years by a war council for clandestine activities and for having helped rebuild an organization which the Fascists thought they had destroyed.

"In 1947 I escaped by falsifying my identity papers. It's not worth giving you the details. Many comrades got out this way and it wasn't the first time. Three months later I was back in another underground organization with young libertarians from Madrid. Three months after that I was back in prison again under another name, because I always used fake names. I had been picked up in Madrid but they made a new dossier for me, not knowing about the first one. This is complicated to explain, but is due in part to the disorientation and confusion in the Fascist administration. I was in prison until July 1953 when I left again by devious means and went back to Barcelona.

"At that time a National Plenum of the CNT was taking place and they were discussing the problems of the Congress that the International, the AIT, was holding in Paris. The CNT wanted to send delegates to the Congress. So I and another comrade were chosen. I came to France to attend a Congress and to stay for 8 days, and now it's 1974 and I'm still here. Well, that is a little resumé of my life.''

PEDRO AND PEPITA DURAN

Pedro and Josefina (Pepita) Duran had been married for 5 months when the Civil War broke out in Spain. They were separated for 10 years. He was in Franco's prisons at the beginning of the war and then in work companies. Being thirty-two, he was freed in 1939 as no longer of military age. He was able to escape to France over the Pyrenees in June 1939 and was taken in by an uncle in Toulouse. In December 1946 Josefina came to France via Andorra, where they had friends.

My first contact with Pedro was in March 1946, when he was living with the Llachs and their five children at rue Paradoux. *Politics Packages Abroad* had sent him a CARE package which

33. Pepita and Pedro Duran, Toulouse 1965. Their friendship and affection is "inalterable."

he shared with the Llachs. And immediately he sent us the names of other friends who needed help.

As was described, I met the Durans in 1952 in Toulouse, and they were endlessly cordial and helpful. They gave me lunch every day and often dinner, and even offered an extra room where I could live. After seeing their bathroom facilities, a little black closet in the central courtyard with a hole in the floor, I decided to stay in my grim hotel, the Capoul. Pepita and Pedro lived in three very dark little rooms on the ground floor, with two small children: nine-month-old Rose Marie, diminutive, looking like a little old lady, was very oral about what she wanted (no language, but little shrieks): Girard, four years old, was visiting his grandmother in Spain.

Rose Marie was well integrated into all parts of the Durans' life. With one hand Josefina cooked, with the baby on her arm. Rose Marie moved from one member of the family to another. Pedro came home from work for lunch every day, and stayed for several hours. The first day I saw the baby eat she was offered gruel, fish, brioche, tomatoes, a peach in its skin, and mother's milk (whenever she wanted it). After a long lunch, Pepita packed up a bag of wet laundry to be dried in the factory, put the baby in her carriage, and the family went off to work.

Pedro, a member of the POUM, was a mattress maker in Spain, and so was Pepita. They received a loan of 900,000 francs from the IRO to start their mattress co-op in Toulouse. When IRO closed down, the loan was taken over by the Caisse de Prets aux Refugies. A French friend acted as director, since Spanish refugees were not allowed to run such enterprises. Pedro and Pepita taught their trade to some of the comrades of the POUM. Since these friends were amateurs the returns at first were minimal. But when I first met the Durans in 1952 the co-op was going well and they were making mattresses and inner springs for 25 percent of the stores in Toulouse which carried them. Watching the Durans and friends at work, I noticed that they all did the work interchangeably and even the baby, Rose Marie, cooperated.

From 1952 to 1985 I visited Toulouse regularly and I always went to see the Durans. Pedro once wrote me that their friendship and affection was "inalterable," but that he communicated rarely because "when I pick up my pen it is an "*evenement*". Pedro and Pepita have retired. The mattress co-op is no more. They baby-sit for Girard's two children, visit Rose Marie and her husband in Tarragona, see and entertain their friends. Girard has an important position in the Toulouse Conservatory of Music and owns a remodeled house. In 1985 he brought me to dinner at rue Belfort in his car during a hailstorm.

The Durans are still in the old building, but one flight up above the courtyard. They have their own phone, bathroom, and kitchen—but *they* are just the same. Pepita presents the food, one course after another, including "bullets," especially for me, her grandchildren's favorite dish (tiny meatballs with parsley, mushrooms, and peas). Pedro cuts the bread and pours the wine and brings out the French champagne ("we used to have it every Sunday but now only for special occasions"). We talk about family, mutual friends, work, and, finally, politics. Pedro disappears into the back room and comes back with a book for me. This time it is Volume I of the *Complete Works* of Pierre Mendès France, whom we both admire. The first book was *La Croisade Contre les Albigeois,* which Pedro gave me on our trip to Albi, long ago in 1952.

I think back to the first time I knocked on their door at 9 rue Belfort; how Pepita went to the nearest telephone to call Pedro at work to say that I had come; and how Pedro returned home, and our friendship began.

NOTE

1. He is referring to the fact that there were Anarchists in the Central Government, contrary to Anarchist principals.

14

Return to Spain?

For almost 50 years, returning to Spain has been the leitmotiv of the "legion of the forgotten." The first return occurred when the Basque region fell to France in 1937. Many of the defeated soldiers returned from France, where they had fled, to Catalonia to fight again. In 1939 after the exodus of 500,000 Spaniards to France, many returned willingly and others by force. During the Nazi occupation of France, some of the Republican political leaders, rounded up by the Gestapo, assisted by the Vichy government, were delivered to Franco. This return to Spain meant death by the Fascist firing squads to Luis Companys, Julian Zugazagoitia, and others.

When World War II ended, many Spanish exiles believed that with the fall of Hitler and Mussolini, Franco, Spain's dictator, would be forced out by the Allies. In 1944 de Gaulle told the Spanish maquisards that the French Government would never forget the services they had rendered to France, but that the frontier was forbidden to them. Nevertheless, during the autumn of 1944, 4,000 Spaniards crossed the border at the Val d'Aran into Spain. Their return to Spain ended in total defeat.

Later, many refugees returned to Spain secretly to fight as

guerrilleros in the Spanish underground. Their lives were short and full of danger. Miguel Garcia Garcia (see Chapter 13) managed to survive and write about his experiences in his book *Franco's Prisoner.*

Many amnesties were declared by Franco from 1945 until his death in November 1975, but very few exiles returned. A final amnesty was proclaimed on March 11, 1977. But even by 1983 many exiles did not return because they had no family in Spain or were too old and sick to go. In 1985 a member of the Spanish Cortes told me that there were still 1,500 Spaniards in the U.S.S.R., who want to return to Spain but cannot until they receive their Russian retirement pensions.

I made 18 trips to France since the founding of Spanish Refugee Aid and I also visited Spain six times. I have described my first return after a 25-year absence, in June 1977.

On my second return to Spain in May 1978, I found Madrid to be a very different city from the one I had visited 26 years before in 1952. Elections were going on and there were posters everywhere—Socialist, Communist, and UCD (Union Centro Democratico, the party of Prime Minister Adolfo Suarez, who had spent most of his life in right-wing Falangist politics). Noisy cars decorated with banners honked their way through the streets and young people of both sexes were in evidence everywhere, free to express themselves volubly and physically. During this visit I was interviewed by the liberal daily, *El Pais,* whose article was entitled *The Spanish People Should Assume the Burden of Caring for the Political Refugees.*

During these early years after the death of Franco, many people were optimistic and hoped that the refugees would be able to return triumphantly to Spain. In an Op-Ed piece in the *New York Times* in January 1976, I wrote that the Spanish Government should give full restitution to the Spanish refugees, similar to the indemnification granted by the West German Federal Government to those Spaniards employed as forced labor by the Nazis during the occupation of France.

But the picture was quite different. As was earlier noted, in 1976 there were still 40,000 political exiles in France, to say nothing of the 530,000 Spanish immigrant workers, who had gone there to find work. In 1977 there were three and a half million individuals over the age of sixty-five in Spain, and a quarter of a million of them received no pension at all. In 1978 when SRA questioned the exiles, only 8 out of 664 said that they planned to return to Spain.

In 1979 the French Government declared that they now considered the refugees to be Spanish Nationals. This announcement was aimed mainly at the Basque terrorists, who had been seeking asylum in France. A friend of SRA visiting Spain the same year wrote us that virtually no one was interested in the exiles and that they are called *sobrevivientos* (survivors), *rojos* (reds) or "French."

In 1980 the Spanish Socialists suggested we advise refugees not to return to Spain since it was almost impossible to get into Old People's Homes. In 1983, the Socialists, then in power, had many problems including over 2 million unemployed, and they preferred not to "reopen or expose publicly the wounds of the Civil War." As late as 1985 I was told by a Socialist Deputy from the Spanish Cortes that local Fascists in Madrid were still sabotaging the granting of invalids' pensions.

These pensions had been granted on 7 April, 1976 by the Spanish Government, to be paid to disabled Republican veterans of the Civil War. By 1981 five decrees had been passed, the first very discriminatory. A Republican who had lost a leg received $144 a month. A *Caballero,* who had fought for Franco, received $500. The fourth decree almost equalized payments and the fifth stated that arrears would only be completely paid by April 1985. Exiles in France had to go to their birthplaces in Spain, with three witnesses to justify their claim. If they were too old to travel, they had to find someone to go for them, and to whom they had to give a percentage of the pension.

While the widow of Franco received a pension of 290,000 pesetas a month (about $1,740), as has been mentioned, the widow of Manuel Azaña, President of the Spanish Republic, received almost as much. Civil servants were still mostly Fascists and were often able to block payments to the "legion of the forgotten." Seven years after the first decree was passed, there were 48,640 people still waiting for their pensions. Of these, 19,640 were invalids, 16,000 civil invalids, 3,000 war widows, and 10,000 widows of war invalids. The deadline for all payments was moved from December 1981, to June 1983, to November 1984; and there are many still waiting.

Because of a French-Spanish Convention adopted before the death of Franco, many of the refugees received small Social Security payments from Spain, if they had worked there prior to the Civil War, and were covered. Also, civil servants and army officers of the Republic could apply for pensions. Teresa Palacios, who had worked for SRA in Montauban, was able to apply, and after working for 6 months in Spain, was granted her pension as a former civil servant.

Eventually, those who were political prisoners in Spain will have the right to Social Security—one year for each year passed in prison. Many of them had worked in prison and their sentences had been shortened by "redemption through work."

My last four visits to Spain were again divided between seeing art and working for the refugees. In 1979 I went with my son, Nick, and his family, from France to spend a few days seeing the Gaudis in Barcelona. We also visited Adelina Ripoll, whom I had known in Montauban. She was in a Catholic Home in Spain and was thrilled by our visit. She showed us off to her friends among the nuns, and seemed happy and well cared for.

In 1980 I visited Carmen Aldecoa again in Madrid and we not only visited the Socialists but also the Republicans, José Maldonado, former President of the Republican Government-in-Exile and Emilio Torres Gallego. They had led Carmen to believe that there was some Republican fund which might be given to SRA for the exiles. But when we talked to them, we were disillusioned about this possibility. Later, Carmen, her sister Pilar, and I went to Malaga and from there visited Grenada, Sevilla, and Cordoba, a visual marvel, which I had never experienced before. We also went to the beautiful small white town of Mijas in the hills above Fuengirola on the coast.

In 1983 I visited Carmen in Madrid and this time we saw many

34. Carmen Aldecoa, my friend and guide to the new Spain.

officials and groups and we tried to urge the speedy payment of the pensions for exiled invalids. We saw Julio Feo, right-hand man of Prime Minister Felipe Gonzalez; Francisco Lopez Real, Socialist Deputy, who had been a refugee himself; John Darnton, *New York Times* correspondent; Amalia Miranza, senator from Cuenca; Julio Busquets, deputy from Barcelona; Carmelo del Valle, who was in charge of the 12,000 pension cases pending at that time. All these people were very friendly; but not sanguine about speeding up the granting of pensions or any kind of special aid.

I also visited CNT headquarters. They had moved from the crowded, chaotic offices I had seen in 1978. Now they had a large, neat suite of rooms and their new secretary, Antonio Perez, voted in by a recent CNT Congress in Barcelona, gave me his undivided attention. He told me proudly about the documentation they had recently received from Amsterdam, including about

4,000 photographs. I looked at the pictures of Durruti's funeral, collectives in Aragon, and armored cars (fascinating and human looking). But the CNT had financial problems and obviously could do nothing for the exiles.

During another trip to Spain in March 1984, I went to Alicante with Carmen, where I started writing this book. On my return trip to New York, I stopped in the airport in Madrid and met Rocio Linz and her cousin, Ritama Fernandez Troyano. They were organizing a committee in Spain to raise money for SRA's exiles. Rocio, a friend of Carmen's, was a fellow exile in New York. The new Amigos de los Antiguos Refugiados Españoles (AARE) was founded in 1984 and its first contribution to SRA was $14,000.

Epilogue

Of the Spanish refugees in 1954, Casals wrote: "The great majority of these people during all those terrible years have given proof of a dignity and nobility which commands respect." Looking back, I hold wonderful memories of those exiles, many of whom have become my friends. Despite the poor conditions in which they lived, their generosity and dignity was striking. They

35. *Eusebia Moreno (right) instructs my friend, Virginia Chamberlain (left), in flamenco lore.*

always thought of ways to give me something in return for what we had done for them. A few memorable encounters:

Bringing me a rose, Pedro Tejero, once a commander in the Republican Army, saying to me: "The clothes I am wearing, the money with which I bought you this flower, and the will to live, have all been given to me by Spanish Refugee Aid."

Luis Garcia de la Fuente offering me his live rabbit in a bag . . . . Juan Gay bringing me a box of peaches at the station . . . Sixto Fernandez finding a bunch of lilacs for me . . . . Francisco Reguera singing for me and showing me his treasured snapshots . . . . the Puentes killing one of their precious chickens to celebrate my visit . . . . Juan Porcel sending me cards of castles, beaches, and cathedrals in his area for my collection . . . . Eusebia Moreno, a flamenco singer, bringing her mantilla to our hotel and showing my friend, Virginia, how to wear it . . . .

And, finally, the picture I received with a note saying "Your letter was a consolation in my sorrow at the death of my wife. As a remembrance I am sending you a small picture of my Dolores, who was a true type of Spanish woman. Our life together for 48 years was a poem."

Sponsors, Directors, New York Staff

SPONSORS OF SPANISH REFUGEE AID

Carmen Aldecoa
Robert J. Alexander
Rudolph Arnheim
Herman Badillo
Roger Baldwin
Katrina M. Barnes
Alfred H. Barr, Jr.
John T. Bernard
Hans Bethe
Bruno Bettelheim
Algernon D. Black
Elinor G. Black
Claude G. Bowers
Fenner Brockway
Albert Camus
Mme. Albert Camus
Hodding Carter
Noam Chomsky
Albert Sprague Coolidge
Dorothy Day

Jesus de Galindez
Mrs. Fernando de los Rios
Mrs. John Dewey
Hugo Ernst
Waldo Frank
Erich Fromm
Francisco Garcia Lorca
Martin Gerber
Harold J. Gibbons
Joseph Glazer
Bernard Greenhouse
Rev. Donald Harrington
Michael Harrington
Lillian Hellman
Julius Hochman
Irving Howe
Faith Hubley
Christopher Isherwood
Mrs. Alfred W. Jones
Alfred Kazin

Paul Krebs
Rocio Linz
James Loeb, Jr.
Robert Lowell
Allard K. Lowenstein
Nicholas Macdonald
Juan Marichal
James Merrill
Jaume Miravitlles
Mrs. R.W. Morgenthau
Robert Motherwell
Lewis Mumford
A.J. Muste
Louis Nelson
Reinhold Niebuhr
Mrs. George Orwell
A. Phillip Randolph
Sir Herbert Read
Rev. Herman F. Reissig
Victor G. Reuther
Lawrence Rogin
Michael Ross
George Rubin
Meyer Schapiro
Arthur Schlesinger, Jr.
Adelaide Schulkind
Ramon Sender
José Luis Sert
George N. Shuster
Ignazio Silone
Robert Snyder
Barbara Probst Solomon
Martin Sostre
Stephen Spender
A.J.P. Taylor
Norman Thomas

Barbara Tuchman
Esteban Vicente
George Wald
Mrs. Charles R. Walker
Rowland Watts
George Woodcock
Leonard Woodcock
José Yglesias
Charles Zimmerman

Honorary Chairpeople

Alexander Calder
Luisa Calder
General Lazaro Cardenas
Pablo Casals
Marta Casals Istomin
Salvador de Madariaga

Chairpeople

Hannah Arendt
James T. Farrell
Dwight Macdonald
Nancy Macdonald
Mary McCarthy

Treasurers

Harrison De Silver
Margaret De Silver

Secretary of the Corporation
Executive Secretary
Director

Nancy Macdonald

MEMBERS OF THE BOARD OF DIRECTORS OF SPANISH REFUGEE AID

Carmen Aldecoa
Hannah Arendt (Chairman)
Bowden Broadwater
Joseph Buttinger
Gene Clemes
Carmen Conchado
Lucy Dames
Harrison De Silver
  (Treasurer)
Margaret De Silver
  (Treasurer)
Anita Altman Du Brul
James T. Farrell (Chairman)
Ernest Fleischman (Counsel)
Sally Genn
Amparo Granell
Bertha Gruner
Jeanne McMahon Hall
Martha Hall
Gabriel Javsicas (Asst.
  Treasurer)
William Kemsley
Jane Kirstein

Allard K. Lowenstein
Ynez Lynch
Dwight Macdonald
  (Chairman)
Michael C.D. Macdonald
Nancy Macdonald (Secretary
  & Chairman)
Christine Magriel
Mary McCarthy (Chairman)
Ruth Katz Muhlen
Frances O'Brien
Rose Pesotta
Mary Pincus
Herbert Robinson (Counsel)
Hilda Rodman
Vera Rony
Daniel Rosenblatt
Maria Elena Schiffrin
Marvin Schlaff
Adelaide Schulkind
Barbara Probst Solomon
Betty Thompson

NEW YORK STAFF

Betty Aridjis
Margaret Childers
Selma Davis
Olaf Domnauer (Translator)
Marie Englert (Translator)
Sally Goodman

Carmen Guillen de Pardo
Joan Herbst
Margot Karp
Sonja Leobold
Ruth Leopold
Ynez Lynch

Nancy Macdonald
Nick Macdonald
Jeanne McMahon
Frances O'Brien
Lee O'Brien
Elizabeth Pollet
Jane Potter

Meg Randall
Hilda Rodman (Volunteer)
Evalyn Steinbock
Judith Steinhoff
Rhoda Waller
Madeleine Weidlinger

Bibliography

Agirre, J.   *Operation Ogro: The Execution of Admiral Luis Carrero Blanco*. (B. P. Solomon, trans.) New York: Quadrangle/New York Times Book Company, 1974.

Barea, A.   *The forging of a rebel*. New York: Reynal & Hitchcock, 1946.

Bartoli, José, & Molins   *Campos de concentración 1939–194 ...* Mexico: no publisher, 1944.

Bates, R.   *The olive field*. New York: Washington Square Press, 1966.

Bénédite, D.   *La filière Marseillaise—Un chemin vers la liberté sous l'occupation*. Préface de David Rousset. Paris: Editions Clancier Guénaud, 1984.

Benson, F.R.   *Writers in arms: The literary impact of the Spanish Civil War*. Foreword by S. de Madariaga. New York: NYU Press, 1967.

Bernanos, G.   *Les grands cimetières sous la lune*. Paris: Plon, 1938.

Bolloten, B.   *The grand camouflage: the Communist conspiracy in the Spanish Civil War*. New York: Praeger, 1961.

Bookchin, M.   *The Spanish Anarchists—The heroic years: 1868–1936*. New York: Free Life Editions, 1977.

Borkenau, F.   *The Spanish cockpit*. London: Faber & Faber, 1937.

Bowers, C.G.   *My mission to Spain: Watching the Rehearsal for World War II*. New York: Simon & Schuster, 1954.

Brenan, G.   *The Spanish labyrinth*. New York: Macmillan, 1943.

Brenner, A.   *Class war in Republican Spain*. New York: Modern Monthly, September 1937.

345

Brome, V. — *The international brigades: Spain 1936–1939.* New York: William Morrow & Co., 1966.

Broué, P. & Témime, E. — *La Révolution et la guerre d'Espagne.* Paris: Les Éditions de Minuit, 1961.

Calder, A. — *Calder, An autobiography with pictures.* London: Allen Lane/Penguin Press, 1967.

Camus, A. — *España libre.* South America: Editores Mexicanos Unidos, 1966.

Carr, V.S. — *John Dos Passos—A biography.* New York: Doubleday, 1984.

Carrasco, J. — *La odisea de los Republicanos Españoles en Francia, 1939–1945: Album souvenir de l'exil Republicain Espagnol en France.* Barcelona: Edicions Nova Letra, 1980 (?).

Casado, Col. S. — *The last days of Madrid: The end of the Second Spanish Republic.* (R. Croft-Cooke, trans.) London: Peter Davies, 1939.

Casals, P. — *Joys & sorrows: His own story as told to Albert E. Kahn.* New York: Touchstone Books/Simon & Schuster, 1970.

Castillo, M. del — *Child of our time.* P. Green, trans. New York: Alfred A. Knopf, 1959.

Cattell, D.T. — *Communism and the Spanish Civil War.* Berkeley & Los Angeles: University of California Press, 1956.

Chiaromonte, N. — *The worm of consciousness and other essays.* (M. Chiaromonte, ed.) Preface by Mary McCarthy. New York: Harcourt Brace Jovanovich, 1976.

Chomsky, N. — *American power and the new mandarins.* (Chapter 1: Objectivity and Liberal Scholarship). New York: Vintage Books/Random House, 1967.

Choumoff, P.S. — *Les chambres a Gaz de Mauthausen, camp de concentration Nazi.* Paris: Amicale des Deportes Mauthausen, 1972.

Clavel, B. — *The Spaniard.* Chicago: Henry Regnery, 1971.

Commission Internationale contre le Régime Concentrationnaire. — *Livre blanc sur le système pénitentiare Espagnol.* Paris: Les Editions du Pavois, 1953

Corredor, J. M.   *Conversations with Casals.* New York: E. P. Dutton & Co., 1957.

Dolgoff, S. (Ed.)   *The Anarchist collectives.* New York: Free Life Editions, 1974.

Escobal, P. P.   *Death row: Spain 1936.* (T. de Gamez, trans.) New York: Bobbs Merrill, 1968.

Etchebehere, M.   *Ma guerre d'Espagne a moi.* Paris: Denoel, 1976.

Fraser, R.   *Blood of Spain: An oral history of the Spanish Civil War.* New York: Pantheon, 1979.

Garcia Garcia, M.   *Franco's prisoner.* London: Rupert Hart Davis, 1972.

Guttmann, A.   *The wound in the heart: America and the Spanish Civil War.* New York: The Free Press of Glencoe (Macmillan), 1962.

Hemingway, E.   *For whom the bell tolls.* Philadelphia: The Blakiston Company, 1940.

Hernandez, J.   *La grande trahison.* Paris: Fasquelle, 1953.

Jackson, G.   *The Spanish Republic and the Civil War, 1931–1939.* Princeton: the Princeton University Press, 1965.

Kirk, H.L.   *Pablo Casals: A biography.* New York: Holt, Rinehart & Winston, 1974.

Koestler, A.   *Scum of the earth.* New York: Macmillan, 1948.

———   *Spanish testament.* (Includes Dialogue with Death; with an Introduction by the Duchess of Atholl). London: Left Book Club, Victor Gollancz Ltd., 1937.

Krivitsky, W.G.   *In Stalin's secret service.* New York: Harper & Brothers, 1939.

Laroche, G.   *On les nommait des etrangers: Les immigrés dans la Resistance.* Paris: Les Editeurs Francais Reunis, 1965.

Leval, G.   *Collectives in the Spanish Revolution.* (V. Richards, trans.), London: Freedom Press, 1975.

Lorenzo, C.M.   *Les Anarchistes Espagnols et le pouvoir: 1868–1969.* Paris: Éditions du Seuil, 1969.

Macdonald, D.   *Memoirs of a revolutionist: Essays in political criticism.* Cleveland: Meridian, 1958.

Madariaga, S. de   *Spain: A modern history.* New York: Praeger, 1958.

Malraux, A.	*Man's hope.* New York: Random House, 1938.
Medina Sidonia, Duchess	*My prison.* New York: Harper & Row Publishers, Inc., 1972.
Mera, C.	*Guerra exilio y carcel de un Anarco Sindicalista.* Paris: Ruedo Iberico, 1976.
Montseny, F.	*Pasion y muerte de los Españoles en Francia.* Toulouse, France: Édiciones 'Espoir', 1969.
Morrow, F.	*Revolution and counter-revolution in Spain.* New York: Pioneer Publishers, 1938.
Nelson, S.	*The volunteers.* New York: Masses & Mainstream, Inc., 1953.
Orwell, G.	*Homage to Catalonia.* London: Secker & Warburg, 1938.
Paz, A.	*Durruti: The people armed.* (Nancy Macdonald, trans.), Montreal: Black Rose Books, 1977.
Peirats, J.	*La CNT en la Revolución Española* (3 vol.). Paris: Ruedo Iberico, 1971.
Pétrement, S.	*La vie de Simone Weil—1909–1934* (2 vols.). Paris: Fayard, 1973.
Pike, D.W.	*Vae victis: Los Republicanos Españoles refugiados en Francia, 1939–1944.* Paris: Ruedo Iberico, 1969.
Pons Prades, E.	*Republicanos Españoles en la 2a guerra mundial.* Barcelona: Editorial Planeta, 1975.
Prunier, A.	*Temoins—Fidelité a L'Espagne.* Paris: Printemps-Été, 1956.
Puzzo, D.A.	*Spain and the great powers, 1936–1941.* New York: Columbia University Press, 1962.
Razoli, M. & Constante, M.	*Triangle bleu: Les Républicains Espagnols a Mauthausen.* Paris: Gallimard, 1969.
Regler, G.	*The owl of Minerva.* New York: Farrar, Straus & Cudahy, 1959.
Richards, V.	*Lessons of the Spanish Revolution.* London: Freedom Press, 1953.
Rolfe, E.	*The Lincoln battalion.* New York: Random House, 1939.
Salabert, M.	*L'Exil intérieur.* Traduit de l'espagnol et préfacé par Claude Couffon. Paris: Les Lettres Nouvelles-Jullard, 1961.
Sedwick, F.	*The tragedy of Manuel Azaña and the fate of the Spanish Republic.* Foreword by Salvador de

Madariaga. Ohio: Ohio State University Press, 1963.

Semprun-Maura, C. *Révolution et contre-révolution en Catalogne.* Tours: Maison MAME, 1974.

Sender, R.J. *Seven red Sundays.* (Sir P. Mitchell, trans.), New York: Collier Books, 1936.

Serge, V. *Memoirs of a revolutionary: 1901–1941.* (P. Sedgwick, trans.), New York: Oxford University Press, 1963.

Sola, P. *Las escuelas Racionalistas en Cataluna: 1909–1939.* Barcelona: Tusquets Editor, 1976.

Solomon, B.P. *Arriving where we started, an autobiography.* New York: Harper & Row, 1972.

Sommerfield, J. *Volunteer in Spain.* New York: Alfred A. Knopf, 1937.

Souchy B.A. *Entre los campesinos de Aragon: El comunismo libertario en las comarcas liberadas.* Barcelona: Ediciones Tierra y Libertad, no publication date.

———— *The tragic week in May.* Barcelona: Edición de la Oficina de Información Exterior de la CNT y FAI, 1937.

Sperber, M.A., (ed.). *And I remember Spain: A Spanish Civil War anthology.* New York: Macmillan Publishing Co., 1974.

Stansky, P. & *George Orwell: The transformation.* New York: Abrahams, W. Alfred A. Knopf, 1980.

———— *Journey to the frontier: Two roads to the Spanish Civil War.* Boston: Little Brown & Co., 1966.

Stein, L. *Beyond death & exile: The Spanish Republicans in France, 1939–1955.* Boston: Harvard University Press, 1979.

Suarez, A. *El proceso contra el POUM—Un episodio de la Revolución Española.* Paris: Ruedo Iberico, 1974.

Szajkowski, Z. *Analytical Franco-Jewish Gazetteer: 1939–1945.* New York: American Academy for Jewish Research, 1966.

Taper, B. *Cellist in exile: A portrait of Pablo Casals.* New York: McGraw Hill, 1962.

Tellez, A. *Sabate: Guerrilla extraordinary.* (S. Christie, trans.), London: Cienfuegos Book Club, 1974.

Thalmann, P. & C. *Combats pour la liberté: Moscow, Madrid, Paris.* (Caroline Darbon, trans.), Préfacé de Max Gallo. Quimperlé, France: La Digitale, 1983.

Thomas, H. *The Spanish Civil War.* New York: Harpers, 1961.

Trotsky, L. *The Spanish Revolution: 1931–1939.* New York: Pathfinder Press, 1973.

Vernant, J. *The Refugee in the post-war world.* Preliminary report of a survey under the direction of Vernant. Geneva: no specific publisher, 1951.

Vilanova, A. *Los olvidados: Los exilados Españoles en la segunda guerra mundial.* Paris: Ruedo Iberico, 1969.

Weintraub, S. *The last great cause: The intellectuals and the Spanish Civil War.* New York: Weybright & Talley, 1968.

Wyden, P. *The passionate war: The narrative history of the Spanish Civil War.* New York: Simon & Schuster, 1983.

Zugazagoitia, J. *Historia de la Guerra en España.* Buenos Aires: Editorial La Vanguardia, 1940.

Index